T0358414

# Complex Policy Planning
## The Government strategic management of the social care market

**PHILIP HAYNES**
*Health and Social Policy Research Centre,*
*University of Brighton*

**Routledge**
Taylor & Francis Group

LONDON AND NEW YORK

First published 1999 by Ashgate Publishing

Reissued 2018 by Routledge
2 Park Square, Milton Park, Abingdon, Oxon, OX14 4RN
711 Third Avenue, New York, NY 10017

*Routledge is an imprint of the Taylor & Francis Group, an informa business*

Copyright © Philip Haynes 1999

All rights reserved. No part of this book may be reprinted or reproduced or utilised in any form or by any electronic, mechanical, or other means, now known or hereafter invented, including photocopying and recording, or in any information storage or retrieval system, without permission in writing from the publishers.

Notice:
Product or corporate names may be trademarks or registered trademarks, and are used only for identification and explanation without intent to infringe.

Publisher's Note
The publisher has gone to great lengths to ensure the quality of this reprint but points out that some imperfections in the original copies may be apparent.

Disclaimer
The publisher has made every effort to trace copyright holders and welcomes correspondence from those they have been unable to contact.

A Library of Congress record exists under LC control number: 99072606

ISBN 13: 978-1-138-61756-8 (hbk)
ISBN 13: 978-0-429-46161-3 (ebk)

# Contents

# List of Figures

# List of Tables

# Preface

This book seeks to investigate the development of planning in community care policy, that is, the provision of social care to adults in the community, and community based institutions, who suffer a long term illness.

> 'Community care was never clearly and consistently defined and the political will, in the form of policy-making and planning machinery and especially resource allocation and reallocation were never mobilised to achieve it.' (Walker, 1989, p. 205).

The movement of health and social care services from institutions into the community has lead to attempt to differentiate between health and social care where health care is the domain of the NHS (National Health Service) and social care the jurisdiction of local authority social services. Bebbington (1996, p. 10) has proposed that:

> 'health care interventions have the objective of ameliorating disability: for example, drugs or physiotherapy to improve mobility; while social care interventions are concerned with compensation or assistance to cope with the effect of the disability on daily life: for example, assistance with the problems caused by mobility difficulties such as shopping.'

But in practice the rigid separation of health and social care is difficult to achieve and arguably a total professional separation is unhelpful to service users. Those placed in the community still have important health needs that can be provided for by the universal domiciliary nursing care of the NHS. The onset of long term illness often has disabling affects, with the result that social care is required. Social care includes a broad range of services that must be offered if a necessary quality of living is be maintained following the diagnosis of a long term illness. Social care can include such items as housing adaptations, maintenance and up-keep of the home, assistance with meals and personal hygiene, and assistance with social activities such as shopping and interacting with peers in the community. Social care is not only about prescribing for such material and psychological needs, it also requires a subjective definition of quality of life from the recipient (Clark, 1996, p. 162). What is defined by the individual as necessary to maintain a quality of social existence may be rather different to what another person requires. It is in part a recognition of the individuality of those suffering from long term illness that social care services have increasingly had to grabble with concepts like diversity and choice. The emphasise on these aspects of individuality is also the result of the pervading social ethos of the last two decades with the growth of individual expression, privatism, consumerism and market forms of social organisation.

When social care is provided in an institutional or residential setting it is easier for the material elements of health and social care to be fully integrated and for the inter-relationship of the two aspects to be monitored. The move towards community care and the policy aim to support people living independently as long as is possible (House of Commons, 1990) creates some important challenges for the planning and management of social and health care if a fully integrated and a user defined quality of social care is to be provided. Professionals are concerned that a limited provision of social care that does not embrace health care needs will lead to increased occurrences of health care emergencies and missed opportunities to prevent the escalation and increased severity of disabling illness (House of Commons Health Committee 1995, Vol II).

With the attempt to remove social care responsibilities from the long stay NHS institutions, as increased demands and expectations were placed on health care expenditure, the state has tried to reinforce the universal perception that social care services are not free at the point of delivery. Since the 1948 National Assistance Act the involvement of local authority personal social services in assisting adults suffering long term ill health was based on a selective model of welfarism, where applicants were subject to assessment and means testing. The process of deinstitutionalisation and community care evident in the 1980s with its associated drift of social care provision from the NHS to local social services departments has increased the prominence of selective means tested social care rather than the universalist tradition of the NHS. Given the parallel growth in the older population and a higher incidence of disability this switch from universal provision to means tested provision has not gone unnoticed by the public and has been perceived as unpopular (Parker and Clarke, 1997). Policy options to include social care in a universal taxation based welfare system have not been seriously considered recently by either of the two major political parties in Britain. Before losing the General

Election of 1997 the Conservative Party was moving towards encouraging private long term illness insurance by tax subsidy (Secretary of State for Health, 1996), this despite commentaries that argued such a scheme would leave many people unprotected (House of Commons Health Committee, 1996; Wistow, 1997). Other policy proposals that attempt to keep the organisation of funding outside of the state domain and look to release capital and property value late in life, such as equity release schemes, have similar problems of social exclusion (Oldman, 1991). More imaginative recommendations have come from the Joseph Rowntree Foundation (1996) who argue for a partnership approach where the state is willing to take substantial responsibilities. Such an increased element of planned state involvement is seen as inevitable if policy is to offer a diversity of care to all social groups and minorities.

Planning in social policy has been traditional linked with corporate ideas of monolithic provision, with essentially large bureaucratic processes delivering welfare to the public (Walker, 1984, p. 1). The accountability of such planning in western democracies was intended to be political and sustained via central and local government representative elections. But in the 1970s the weaknesses of such simple political lines of accountability became apparent with the process of monopolistic state bureaucracy and professionalism itself dominating much of the decision making over service delivery (Niskanen, 1973; Tullock,1976; Dunleavy, 1991). This led to policy scientists and politicians seeking alternative models of service delivery that gave more resources to private and voluntary organisations.

Of influential in the 1980s were the political projects of Conservative governments with their belief that the market place should generate accountability explicitly through customers and services users. Market methods were prompted to deliver both choice and accountability (Self, 1993; Le Grand, 1991; Walsh, 1995). The dysfunctional attributes of the free market were to be constraint in the public interest and public demand for welfare managed in a system where demand was replicated by managers and professionals rather than users themselves. The local authority was to enable the provision of services from outside bodies in the private and independent sector (HM Treasury, 1991).

If state managers and professionals are to replicate market demand they need a good quality of information on which to base their judgements. Information must exceed summation of individual need and assess the prevalence of a community's general needs, and the supply realities of meeting such need within a geographical area and from a limited tax base (Bebbington, Turvey and Janzon, 1996).

The managerialist control of markets helped to ensure that some equity remained in service provision without a sudden unleashing of market inequalities that could prove political unacceptable. In effect some compromise via political brokerage limits the radical impact of reforms (Saltman and Von Otter, 1992, p. 36). Marketisation represents the evolving welfare ideology in Britain in recent decades. Although choice, supply diversity and economic efficiency were the primary aims of the marketisation of social care a secondary commitment to equity was also evident (Hamnet and Mullings, 1992).

Since the 1970s there has been a growing belief that market disciplines are able to deliver better value for money in the provision of public services, but also able to bring an economic method that allows choice and more direct involvement from the service customer, and thereby reductions in some of the dependency, stigma and alienation previously linked to a monopoly of public provision. The new state economic planning has become synonymous with the creation and use of market forces, rather than limiting and constraining market forms of organisation. It is often referred to as 'market enabling' (Leach, Stewart and Walsh, 1994; Clarke and Newman, 1997, p.133). The logic of marketisation has also been associated with attempts to reduce the proportion of GDP (Gross Domestic Product) absorbed by public expenditure. Public expenditure has proved difficult to reduce as a total proportion of GDP, despite large privatisation projects to sell off nationalised industry. The challenge of rising unemployment and increased numbers dependent on state benefits and pensions as they grow older run counter to the moving of the ownership of production from state to private sector (Hogwood, 1992, Ch. 11). Governments in the last two decades of the twentieth century have been determined to resist any large scale increases in state intervention and expenditure and have encourage personal and family responsibility as the key determinants of social care. As a result, social care not provided by the family has become increasingly means tested. For the middle income groups of society, housing equity has become the method by which social care is financed this halting cross generation dispersal of property wealth at the point of death (Hutton, 1991, p.13).

The focus on assessing priorities, means testing and providing for a diversity of social care needs has lead to a new type of planning within the personal social services. It is the task of this book to explore the process of central and local government planning that now determines the allocation and provision of social care for adults.

The initial phase of the book constructs a descriptive theory of the recent developments in social care planning. Documentary evidence is used to validate this emerging theory. The later part of the book is more prescriptive. Having developed a theory that defines and describes the structures and processes of current planning, some themes are explored about how government social care planning might progress in the new policy environment.

The underlying theoretical argument is that public sector planning is complex and entangled in numerous systems, structures and contingencies. Historical models of social service planning that depended on simple linear projections of trends are seen as inadequate (Ministry of Health, 1963; Department of Health and Social Security, 1972).

Chapter one examines the defining characteristics of public sector planning. The chapter examines the two main historical types of planning activity in the public sector; first the administrative planning rationalities apparent before 1976, such as rational-comprehensive and corporate planning, as compared to the subsequent managerial and market rationality of the 1980s and 1990s often referred to as 'strategic planning.' This chapter discusses the evolution of planning activity away from the rationality of administrative-managerial planning - where priorities were related to analysing information on need - to a more strategic method whereby the emphasis moved to understanding public sector limitations and externalities and managing a market place and implementing a market structure to meet public demands. The dominance of the logic of 'marketisation' over this evolving process is critical (Walsh, 1995) . A theoretical model of social care planning is proposed whereby government planning activity is situated on a constantly changing social system composed of three major sub-systems: politics, state management and markets.

Chapter two discusses the underlying theory of the book. The aim of the book is to explore recent developments in the application of chaos and complexity theory to the social sciences and to attempt to apply these to an examination of planning in social care. This chapter describes chaos and complexity theory and its relevance to social science and social planning. It also outlines the main methodological concepts and language of the book.

Both chapter three and chapter four focus on the definition of planning proposed in the NHS and Community Care Act, 1990, and related policy guidance. An attempt is made to conceptualise current local community care planning. Using government policy documents and local authority plans a theory is constructed of how community care plans (CCPs) emerge from the social systems of politics, state managerialism and markets , and what 'logic' associated with these systems dominates the current practice of planning. In chapter 4, a document analysis of local plans is used to validate a proposed theoretical model.

Chapter five examines the relationship between planning and the market. The relationship between planning and markets is argued to be pivotal in the satisfactory definition of the new planning task for the public sector in the late 1990s policy environment. David Blunket (The Guardian, 23rd June, 1994, page 1), whilst opposition spokesperson on health, said of the market in health care: 'that you can't have plans for the future and the operation of the internal market.' Similarly on arrival at the Dept of Health in 1997 the new Labour Secretary for State for Health, Frank Dobson was quick to question the workings of the NHS internal market place.

New Labour's embracing of the 'Third Way' (The Economist, May 2nd, 1998, page 26) and the development of a public sector partnerships with markets across the developed world contests these statements and suggests that there does not have to be a dichotomy of market versus planning - instead a juxtaposition exists. The Labour Government's recent consultation paper on 'Best Value' uses language that proposes a long-term partnership between public planning and private markets (Department of the Environment, Regions and Transport, 1998a).

Chapter five explores how state planning can be conceptualised to best fit with a market system of service supply. It is observed that government social care planning has a number of key economic tasks: improving the organisation and definition of social care transactions; explicit planning for vertical equity in relation to the complexities of need and demand; the facilitation of equal opportunities for market entry; the achievement of a satisfactory degree of horizontal equity between spatially defined areas; and the monitoring of, and intervention in, the supply side. Initial planning activities after the implementation of the NHS and Community Care Act 1990 concentrated on increasing activity on the supply side of the social care market. Although there was some discussion of demand side planning, this remains an under-developed aspect, especially at a national level. Chapter six begins to focus on the difficulties of reconciling needs based planning with the facilitation of economic demand in the market. The research develops a local quantitative model to explore the relationship between theoretical demand and the actual demand expressed for social care. The associated difficulties for planners in creating opportunities of market entry for all users are discussed.

In chapter seven the quantitative research examines the limitations of the central government Standard Spending Assessment (SSA) calculation and the Revenue Support Grant (RSG) allocation as instruments of central government planning and demand facilitation.

The last chapter concludes with a description of the complex typology of social care planning that is needed if the full potential of the new policy environment is to be realised.

# Acknowledgements

I am grateful to Dr Michael Cahill, Dr Sandra Winn, Professor Marilyn Taylor and Dr Lynda Measor of the Health and Social Policy Research Centre (HSPRC) at the University of Brighton, and Professor Bleddyn Davies, Director of the Personal Social Services Research Centre at the University of Kent, who provided valuable comments on draft material. Additional helpful comments were also received from Professor Robin Means, University of West of England and Dr David Bryne, University of Durham.

Some of the data used in this study was provided by the Department of Health, Government Statistics Service, who made available their PC KIGS (Key Indicators Graphical System) computer programme. This data is Crown copyright and is reproduced with permission of the Statistics Division 3C.

Census data is supplied by The Census Data Unit at the University of Manchester and is Crown copyright. The Census Unit taught me the basic skills of how to analyse census data at an ESRC funded course in 1994, soon after the 1991 census data was first made available. Map boundaries are supplied by the UK borders project at University of Edinburgh and are Crown and ED-LINE copyright. Both these academic data facilities are supported by the ESRC and JISC/HEFC. My thanks to Ronan Foley, of the University of Brighton Digital Mapping Unit for his assistance. Other data from the Office for National Statistics (formerly the Central Statistical Office and Office of Population Censuses and Surveys) is used with their permission and is also Crown copyright.

Standard Spending Assessment (SSA) data is reproduced with the permission of the Society of County Treasurers. Some of the Local authority budget statistics are reproduced with the permission of the Chartered Institute of Public Finance and Accountancy (CIPFA).

My thanks to the large number of people employed in social services departments and the independent sector who have discussed with me their views on a variety of planning matters. In particular I am grateful to Mike Monk, Judith Brodie, Madeline Iddison and Andrew Voyce. I am grateful to the Association of Directors of Social Services who agreed to support this research when it started in 1994.

I would like to thank my other colleagues at the University of Brighton for their support and encouragement during the last five years and in particular, my recently retired Head of Department, Tony Hadley. Thanks also to Will Medd at the University of Lancaster for his occasional papers and e-mails on the subject of chaos and complexity theory. Odd Lindberg, my friend and colleague at University of Orebro, Sweden, taught me how to use the software NUD@IST to analysis the text of local government community care plans.

Finally I am grateful to Jan, and Jonathan, Mary and Elizabeth who have shown me tolerance while I have persisted with working anti-social hours.

# List of Abbreviations

| | |
|---|---|
| CCP | Community Care Plans |
| CIPFA | Chartered Institute of Public Finance and Accountancy |
| DETR | Department of Environment, Transport and Regions |
| DHSS | Department of Health and Social Security |
| DSS | Department of Social Security |
| ILF | Independent Living Fund |
| KIGS | Key Indicators Graphical System (Government Statistical Service) |
| LB | Local Base (1991 census) |
| LGIU | Local Government Information Unit |
| LTI | Long Term Ill |
| NHS | National Health Service |
| NPM | New Public Management |
| OPCS | Office of Population Censuses and Surveys (now the NS0 - National Statistics Office) |
| PESC | Public Expenditure Survey Committee |
| PPBS | Planning, Programme Budgeting Systems |
| PSS | Personal Social Services |
| PSSRU | Personal Social Services Research Unit (University of Kent) |
| PSS SSA | Personal Social Services Standard Spending Assessment |
| RSG | Revenue Support Grant |
| SARs | Sample of Anonymised Records (1991 census) |
| SAS | Small Area Statistics (1991 census) |
| SMR | Standard Mortality Ratio |
| SSA | Standard Spending Assessment |
| SSD | Social Services Department |
| STG | Special Transitional Grant |
| TSG | Transitional Support Grant |
| WHO | World Health Organisation |

# List of Abbreviations

| | |
|---|---|
| CCP | Community Care Plans |
| CIPFA | Chartered Institute of Public Finance and Accountancy |
| DETR | Department of Environment, Transport and Regions |
| DHSS | Department of Health and Social Security |
| DSS | Department of Social Security |
| ILF | Independent Living Fund |
| KIDS | Key Indicators Graphical System (Government Statistical Service) |
| LA | Local Authority |
| LEDU | Local... Education Information Unit |
| LH | Long term... |
| NHS | National Health Service |
| NPM | New Public Management |
| OPCS | Office of Population Censuses and Surveys (now the National Statistics Office) |
| PESC | Public Expenditure Survey Committee |
| PPBS | Planning Programming Budgeting Systems |
| PSS | Personal Social Services |
| PSSRU | Personal Social Services Research Unit (University of Kent) |
| PSS SSA | Personal Social Services Standard Spending Assessment |
| RSG | Revenue Support Grant |
| SAR | Sample of Anonymised Records (1991 census) |
| SAS | Small Area Statistics (1991 census) |
| SMR | Standard Mortality Ratio |
| SSA | Standard Spending Assessment |
| SSD | Social Services Department |
| STG | Special Transitional Grant |
| TSG | Transitional Support Grant |
| WHO | World Health Organization |

# 1 Planning in the Public Sector

## Introduction

This chapter discusses theoretical planning issues in the British public policy process. It starts by examining definitions of rational planning and the previous attempts to understand planning in organisational literature. This leads to an examination of strategic planning and the recent seminal critique by Mintzberg (1994a) of the strategic planning models developed in the 1970s and 1980s. It is argued that in the public sector there is a particular need to see strategy making in its political context. The chapter concludes by proposing a framework of public sector planning activity.

## Definitions of Rational Planning

It is necessary to attempt to define planning as part of an organisational and inter-organisational process, to define its bureaucratic location and purpose. Rational ideas lead to a prescriptive top-down focus where planning is clearly identified at the beginning of things and the means to acquire organisational ends. This type of rational approach has been referred to as traditional, comprehensive, or corporate planning, although its practice includes a considerable range of diversity, it having been applied to both the public and private sector (Clapham, 1984; Bryson and Einsweiler 1988). The use of these rational planning types in the public sector is closely related to the rational-central model of the policy process. This model is summarised by Kickert, Kiljn and Koppenjan (1997) as a paradigm that seeks to explain the policy process as a managerialist exercise, characterised by scientific and logical activity. Success is measured on the basis of formal goals being achieved at a later date. A centralised policy system is encouraged. This centralism is seen as necessary to divide clearly the values and ambitions of politicians (who make the outline strategy) from the details of scientific and rational policy management. The key criticism of such a theory is its denial of the political and power realities that permeate all levels of public policy.

**Scientific Rationalism**

Several writers have discussed planning in relation to the debate in policy analysis about rational versus incremental models of decision taking (Smit and Rade,1980; Walker, 1984, chapter 4; Hambleton, 1986). The best known historical proponent of scientific rationalism as a methodology for organisation planning was Herbert Simon (1957). He proposed an ideal model of policy decision making that focused on logically considering all possible alternatives, strategies and outcomes. Simon was aware of the prescriptive and idealised limitations of his hypothesis and his perspective later adjusted to be more pragmatic.

The rational approach to administrative behaviour was based on the premise that policy can discern 'means' from 'ends' and 'process' from 'output'. While it might be argued that such dimensions are discernible in all policy circumstances - to some extent - it should also be recognised that policy implementation can become distracted by unintended consequences and political agendas that distort earlier rational intentions (Hogwood and Gunn, 1984). Herein lies a traditional conflict of approaches in policy analysis; on the one hand a propensity to analyse policy solely in political and ideological terms, contrasted with the alternative application of rational scientific management and organisational processes. This is a dichotomy refuted by Minogue (1983, p. 83) who concludes on the rational managerial model: 'in short, social systems are simply not predictable enough to be described as manageable; rational management and control in such circumstances are impossible.'

In the immediate post war period British policy planning sought to measure human need on the basis of social justice and equity and under the assumption that the growth of the economy and rising public expenditure would allow for an increase in public services. Such planning attempted to be 'comprehensive' and was founded on the belief that it was possible to predict and control the future, hence the terms 'rational-comprehensive' and 'comprehensive long-term planning' (Smit and Rade, 1980).

The incremental school in policy analysis starts from the premise that policy decisions are never complete in their rationality and will always be compromised, fragmented and distorted by political systems. This is in one sense a repeat of the revision of rationality already undergone by Simon, but incrementalism represents an alternative perspective if only because it starts from a different premise and seeks to build from a 'descriptive' stance rather than an 'ideal' one (Smith and May, 1980).

Lindblom (1959) expounds incrementalism as 'successive limited comparisons', but acknowledges that there is some element of rationality within such an approach. A key difference is the starting point of his model, termed the 'branch method'. It is necessary to focus on the basic issue in question, rather than the theoretical root of the problem. In incremental analysis practical difficulties prevent the pursuing of all policy alternatives, for example the cost of research and inadequacy of available information. These strategic difficulties ensure that policy decisions proceed 'piecemeal' on the basis of what information is available rather than what is not. The number of alternative strategies is severely limited and the possible consequences of all likely available strategies cannot be adequately analysed.

This pragmatic approach is descriptive of how policy decisions are made in the real world and moves significantly away from the prescriptive idealism of rationalism. A review of the rational-incrementalist debate by Gregory (1989) renounces the definition of 'incrementalism' applied dogmatically to Lindblom's work, noting that the term is used infrequently in the author's later literature. For Gregory (1989, p.151), Lindblom's later revisions focus on 'political rationality' as the best theoretical interpretation of policy decision making: 'Charles E. Lindblom's enduring message is that public policy making needs to be seen as an essentially political process, driven by a distinctive form of collective rationality.'

**Combining the Rational and Incremental Models**

Despite the differences discussed, observers are unclear about whether to focus on the similarities of rationalism and incrementalism, or to stress theoretical divergence. Smith and May (1980, p. 156) comment: 'The two models are about different social phenomena and as such should seek to perform different functions. We should not expect them to agree.'

Some work has been undertaken to try and unite the two schools, taking the best applications from each perspective. An example is Etzioni's (1967) 'mixed scanning' with its belief that major decisions should be influenced by rational ideals and everyday decisions left to the incremental adjustment . But for Smith and May (1980, p.153) this compromise fails to rectify the fundamental problem that rationalism and incrementalism start from different theoretical points. Smit and Rade (1980) argue for the practical element of what works in different planning circumstances, rather than focusing on the different theoretical starting points.

Three types of decisions are involved in the government planning process (Webb and Wistow, 1986, p. 109). These are chronological: policy making, programming and implementation. This defines planning as operating in parallel to the policy process. Politics starts the strategic policy making process - as the rational central model asserts. But too greater emphasis on the separation of politics and management science is unsatisfactory even when trying to explain the initial conception of a strategy. Political convictions alone are not enough to create a strategy and political ideas have to be refined by scientific logic and policy science disciplines. Although the political system may have more relative influence on strategy formulation than managerial analysis, it is likely that managerial analysis will have influence also.

The instability of the future illustrated by chaos theory has been argued by Cartwright (1991, pp. 45-54) to strengthen the preference for incremental models of planning, but this is because his interpretation of rationalism is based on Simon's earliest and more prescriptive idealism. A modern approach to planning stresses the juxtaposition of the rational-incremental literatures (Gilbert and May, 1985) and the potential for using diverse methods.

> 'The sole alternative to synoptical (rational) planning is certainly not muddling through. There are many different methods of managing the future which are invented both from the top-down and from the bottom-up.'(Schneider,1991, p. 264)

Kiel (1994, p. 14) states that incrementalism is close to much analysis and activity based on complex explanations, but that a more rational approach might be needed in certain situations where change is chaotic and government systems need to transform quickly to radically new situations.

> 'Incrementalism represents only a variation on a theme. With incrementalism we get more of the same. When total transformation and qualitative change in public organisations is needed, tinkering around the edges is unlikely to produce dramatic improvements in organisational performance and service to the public.'

Incrementalism assists descriptive analysis of the immediate past and present, while rationality inspires an attempt at holistic synthesis of the future, albeit visionary rather than predictive.

The difficulties that rational managerialist planning methods encountered led to a managerialist desire to find the perfect rational organisational system that could deliver the management and planning processes required. Post 1970 government planning in Britain became concerned with developing a structure to achieve optimal organisation control. There was a much experimentation with the implementation of new organisational structures and systems, designed to make government management and bureaucracy more efficient.

Government rational planning methods were evolving alongside a new form of organisational managerialism. In a book reviewing the tendency to re-organise government in this period Pollitt (1984, p. 161) remarks:

> 'Organisational designers were infected with managerialism...Briefly a managerialist approach does not adequately explain where organisational objectives come from, nor why some objectives should be preferred to others. It tends to over simplify, underplay or assume away the subjective and inter-subjective aspects of organisational life - the dynamic patterns of reasons, motives, expectations and intentions which explain action.'

This managerial and organisational movement was best typified in central government by the Public Expenditure Survey Committee (PESC) and in local government by the corporate planning method. The theoretical underpinning of local corporate planning was procedural planning theory (Hambleton, 1986) and a structural approach to organisations (Sibeon, 1991). This method was based on a logic that if the optimum organisational structure and system could be designed and implemented, planning would be functional. The tendency to see organisational structure as a solution to the social complexities experienced by the 1970s Social Services Departments (SSDs) was reflected in the influential work of the Social Services Organisation Research Unit (SSORU, 1974) at the University of Brunel (see also Challis, 1990).

By the late 1970s there was some disillusionment with this centralised and structuralist approach. The reasons for this are discussed extensively (Hambleton, 1986; Caulfield and Schultz, 1989; Clapham, 1984; Glennerster, 1980). In summary the failure of local government corporate planning to be effective resulted from: too much emphasise on the mechanics of structure and process; the loss of a strategic view; over bureaucratisation; and a lack of commitment and involvement from councillors and front line staff. Caulfield and Schultz (1989, p.13) comment: 'It is therefore somewhat ironic that the corporate planning process adopted in many local authorities led to the eclipse of such a strategic view.'

The corporate planning of the 1970s focused too much inside the local authority and often failed to consider adequately policy relationships with central government departments like employment, health and social security.

An alternative explanation of the failure of corporate planning was made by political scientists who saw it as a method of managerial scientific decision making that sought to de-politicised issues and alienated local politicians and pressure groups. There is some divergence in the ideological explanation of what caused this alienation. Marxist theory stressed the technical language of rational planning becoming part of the dominant hegemony of advanced capitalist societies, while Neo-Marxist accounts saw the key problem as the dual function of the local state which was left attempting to salvage welfare citizenship from the dominant market economics of the centre (Saunders, 1980; 1986). This led to local conflicts of interest as groups struggled over limited resources. Citing Saunders analysis, Hambleton (1986, p. 24) makes the proposition that: 'Policy planning systems are ways of structuring inter-organisational relationships and conflicts that lead to the advantage of some parties and to the disadvantage of other parties.'

Saunders account of the differences between the central and local state suggests that the structuring of inter-governmental relationships in planning helps to define power relations and that the consumption of services is the key concern of local authorities.

The fundamental tension between using a managerialist logic to define public planning against the political realities of resource distribution was discussed in an article by Howard Glennerster in the Journal of Social Policy (1981). He acknowledged the growth in public sector planning techniques in the 1970s and he placed this in the context of government overload (King, 1975). Glennerster (p. 31) describes: 'the tendency for demands on government for more and better services to outrun its and economy's capacity to respond.'

The technical-scientific approach to rational planning was becoming immersed in political conflict and disputes about resource allocation and priorities.

Immediate post war social planning had placed the provision of universal needs high on its agenda, with less immediate concern given to the prioritisation of need and the allocation of limited resources (Sanderson, 1996). Glennerster (1981, p. 32) defined the subsequent re-defining of government social planning.

'We take social planning to be: the determination of priorities, the allocation of resources and the design of service delivery systems undertaken in implementing social policies...In functional terms social planning can be seen as the interaction between economic and public expenditure planning; the planning of individual social services; the conduct of urban and transport planning; and the allocation of resources within and between local authorities.'

## Strategic Planning

The strategic planning methods adopted in the 1980s tried to come to terms with resource shortfalls by including more assessment of values and externalities before translating the resulting mission and vision into quantitative methods for allocating resources and evaluating outputs. Mission and vision was constraint by a time frame of aims and objectives. Such strategic planning methods reduced complexity to a fairly simple synthesis within an ordered sequence of events. The failure of comprehensive-rational planning was answered by a reductionist approach to strategy. Often strategies were based on a limited pattern of analysis, making them in consequence a limited synthesis.

A variety of strategic planning typologies evolved in the strategic planning literature (for example, Ansoff, 1965; Bryson and Einsweiler 1988; Mintzberg, 1994a), a literature characterised by its acknowledgement of a greater degree of unknowns and 'externalities' in the planning equation and giving recognition of competing values and power bases.

> 'What distinguishes strategic planning from more traditional planning (particularly traditional long range comprehensive or master planning) is its emphasis on: action, consideration of a broad and diverse set of stakeholders; attention to external opportunities and threats and internal strengths and weaknesses; and attention to actual or potential competitors.' (Bryson and Roering, 1988, p. 15)

In a review of three historical types of planning: rational, incremental and strategic, Smit and Rade (1980, p. 89) list six general features of planning:

> '(i) it is concerned with decisions;
> (ii) which are treated in a formal, explicit, systematic process;
> (iii) it is aligned to the future;
> (iv) it concerns itself with both ends and means (both politics and policy);
> (v) decisions are considered in context, from a holistic perspective;
> (vi) planning must lead to changes in behaviour.'

Some years later Mintzberg (1994a) makes similar conclusions about the definition of strategic planning although the power and strategy of planning activity receives greater emphasis. He says that strategic planning is about: future thinking; the control of the future through political and organisational process; the management of decision making; and the formalisation of a procedure to integrate analysis into synthesis and decisions.

The strategic models of the 1980s continued to be expressed as centralised, top-down approaches. This was because many models were first developed in the private sector where managers and shareholders were expected to own the strategy rather than customers. This creates a problem with converting such methods to the public sector where the process should be at least partly bottom-up, so that the public interest and a democratic consensus defines the strategy.

Recently Mintzberg (1994a, p. 43) has tried to extend the theoretical boundaries of strategic planning by undertaking a fundamental theoretical review of its assumptions. He has said that a: 'characteristic of the planning literature in general was as a position (and, of course plan) but not perspective.'

A continuing preoccupation with structure, via organisational diagrams and hierarchy was exposed in what Mintzberg (1994a, p. 78) termed the 'Great Divide' in planning , that is, the inability of 'performance control' to be integrated with 'action planning'. Performance control is summarised as:

> 'Each period, every unit in the organisation finds itself receiving or negotiating a budget and set of objectives intended to evoke a certain level of performance, against which its results can be measured.'

While action planning is summarised as:

> 'The hierarchies of strategies and programs. Together these are labelled action planning because the intention is before-the-fact specification of behaviour: strategics are supposed to evoke programs that are supposed to prescribe tangible actions.'

The need for planning activity to look forward in time and space shows itself here. Planning is more than organisational decision making in the 'here and now', it is linked intrinsically to subjective analysis of lessons from the past, and creating a synthesis of the future.

The method that Mintzberg (1994a, chapter 6) uses to better understand the dilemma of time and space is to separate the characteristics of fixed 'plans' (documents which have to remain static in time) from the ongoing more dynamic activities of 'planning' a strategy.

Mintzberg's seminal evaluation of strategic planning concluded that the loss of faith in strategic planning was largely because it was an oxymoron and a false combination of two activities, an attempt to combine the synthesis of strategy formulation with the analysis activities of management planning.

This, he said (1994a, p. 321), had resulted in the 'planning schools grand fallacy'.

> 'Analysis may precede and support synthesis, by defining the parts that can be combined into wholes. Analysis may follow and elaborate synthesis by decomposing and formalising its consequences. But analysis cannot substitute for synthesis.'

While pursuing Mintzberg's analysis, Brock and Barry (1995) suggest that it is the temporal dimension of planning which presents the solution to his grand fallacy. Strategy should come before planning, so that managerial analysis is focused. Brock and Barry's concern is that research analysis for the development of strategies can take up large amounts of resources, especially where the perimeters of a strategy are unclear. Their argument is primarily related to business, rather than local democracy and public services. The strategic-planning relationship in the public sector is argued in this book to be more circular and heterarchical, with the possibility that strategy can be influenced by analysis.

It is erroneous of Brock and Barry's approach to synthesis and analysis to conclude that the separation of the two activities can be achieved by a time frame. Future thinking can be both an analysis and a synthesis, in terms of understanding what might happen to both parts and wholes. Likewise it can be as difficult to create a synthesis of the past as it is to create a synthesis of the future, although both can be important to planners.

The linkage of strategy and planning over time is complex. Both strategic (synthesis) and planning (analysis) are likely to be interacting with each other at various points of time, rather than being conducted separately. The second part of Mintzberg's (1994c, p. 23) critique of strategic planning proposes that the strategy making process of organisations should be surrounded by a variety of managerial information analysis activities. This includes: providing information inputs that inform the initiation of strategy, analysis that assists while strategy is being formed, and thereafter research and evaluation of the outputs of the strategic process.

Again the definition of what are the boundaries of 'parts' (analysis) and 'wholes' (strategies) is subjective and therefore it is impossible to say with any precision where analysis ends and synthesis starts.

Both synthesis and analysis are important to public sector planning, and one cannot be separated completely from the other. They are not opposites as Mintzberg's 'oxymoron thesis' suggests. Rather these are two activities under the umbrella of public sector planning that tend to follow different kinds of actor and organisational processes. Planning analysis is more likely to be based in a managerial system, while strategic synthesis is likely to be attached to political activity.

To conclude on the definition of government planning it can be said that it is concerned with bringing synthesis and order to complex social phenomena, and as a process of analysis and subsequent decision making the actors involved have to come from both the political and managerial systems. Managerial actors may place more emphasise on the value of detailed analysis, while political actors are more likely to synthesise and seek value based strategies. But these two aspects of the planning process cannot be understood as a dualism, instead they are overlapping and entangled activities.

Mintzberg's (1994b) explanation puts the emphasise on the failure of academic business-school language, with the term strategic-planning resulting in managerial systems trying to combine formally (inside organisational structures) the activities of analysis and synthesis in a single method that is inappropriate and impossible to achieve. The failure of strategic-planning in the public sector is better understood by the historical difficulties of developing a long term rational-scientific planning process alongside the short term political environment. Managerial strategic-planning is entangled fundamentally with the strategies of politicians.

It is argued by Ansoff (1994, p. 31) that the deconstruction of strategic planning into a diversity of types and methods as required by Mintzberg (1994a) started to occur many years before Mintzberg's critique. Mintzberg's contribution has been to highlight the important differences between the managerial processing and interpreting of information and its application to future strategic thinking and decision making.

## Planning Theory and the New Public Sector

Part of the difficulty in applying the incremental, rational and strategic planning models to the public sector relates to their development within the study of organisational sociology and business studies to explain decision making. As a result there are methodological difficulties with applying these models to social and public policy planning scenarios where additional complexities of policy science and politics are embraced. Walker (1984, p. 82) says that models based on managerial and organisation science are 'based on restricted conceptions of power'. Public sector planning, implies some overall context of political strategy and ideological priorities. A public planning process is by definition more than a series of decisions within one organisation. A number of institutional and inter-organisational systems are likely to be involved. It is, therefore, by nature of its definition, a quasi-rational process, but it is also more complex socially than a system of decision making within a single organisation.

The observation by Walker (1984) and Hambleton (1996) that social planning is a large system of inter-organisational behaviour is important. Social planning involves linked decisions across systems, time and space and is necessarily both a managerial-rationalist and an incremental-political process.

Walker (1984, p. 86) proposed a solution to make the power conflicts in planning systems more explicit, particularly at the local level. 'What is required instead are more radical models of planning, which move beyond the discussion of bureaucratic decision making towards structural planning.'

The solution to the weakness of the rational and incremental models is according to Walker the development of a prescriptive political planning strategy. His 'structural' model is linked explicitly to socialist control of production. Such a model determines planning on the basis of social needs, but seeks democratic local support for the definition and acceptance of these needs (rather than central prescription). The management and resolution of social conflict becomes a key component of social planning (1984, p. 91). The ultimate problem with such a politicised model is explained by Mulgan (1994, p. 129):

'Because most people limit the time they devote to participating in democratic structures, control always threatens to fall on to self-appointed cliques who effectively disenfranchise those unable or unwilling to participate. As a result, democratic structures that demand intensive participation often prove unstable.'

Much strategic planning literature is predominantly centralist and top-down. The public sector has an obvious bottom-up requirement, because of its mission to serve the public interest and service user. The traditional rational-centralist policy making model has linked accountability to the top-down authority of elected politicians (Kickert, Kiljn and Koppenjan, 1997). Many policy analysts would now question such a simple model of accountability, seeing parallel and localised systems of public accountability as imperative (Mulgan, 1994).

In a discussion of planning for SSDs, Coulshed (1990) discusses planning as integrated within an agency life and essentially 'bottom-up'. Statements from government of their commitment to bottom-up participative consultation in planning are a central feature of public policy in the 1990s and user participation is pivotal to the current attempts at local social services community care planning (Community Care Support Force, 1993; Bewley and Glendinning, 1994). Discussions continue about what type of public participation is optimal (Jeffrey, 1997).

The paradox of attempting to plan both from the bottom-up and the top-down is described by Waddington (1995) as a key strain within the community care, social care planning process. This is conflict described from the bottom-up perspective in Bewley and Glendinning's (1994) research. Such conflict and tension is political, in that those at the bottom feel that the process is not giving them the access to power over resources they need. They do not always feel that being invited to managerial consultation and planning meetings gives them ownership of the resulting strategy.

*Strategic decisions and central-local government*

Strategic public planning is driven more by political ideas than the practice of scientific managerialism. There is a need to distinguish between central and local politics because of the different economic and power cultures at the two levels of government.

It is proposed by Kontopoulos (1993) that the structure of society is composed of a complex entanglement of logics. The most dominant of these logics he refers to as 'totalizing' and these evolve to pervade all social groups and systems. Significant changes in the balance of totalizing logics underpinning society are more likely to be strategically managed at a central government level even though they are related to changes at the local level. In the last twenty years central political government has restated the total logic of markets. It has done this through long term policy initiatives that reduce state involvement in the supply of services, privatise state resources and encourage market principles to pervade the areas of state activity that remain. Much of this political project can be summarised as the 'logic of marketisation', a logic which has dominated the practice of state managerialism in the last decade.

> 'The development of managerialism has intensified from the mid-1960s onwards, but its is only in the last decade that a systematic practical theory of an alternative approach to the management of the public sector has begun to emerge. It is different from the earlier managerialist movement in that it is based on the development of a new institutional approach founded upon the introduction of market principals.' (Walsh, 1995, pp. 27-28)

The use of market methods of supply has been an increasing feature of the provision of state financed social care in the last twenty years (Wistow, et al, 1993).

After the economic crisis of 1976, governments found that their public policy planning centred increasingly around economic public expenditure targets rather than definitions of social need (Walker, 1984, p. 122). No longer could state planning be based on the assumption that economic growth would lead to increases in public expenditure (Hambleton, 1986, p. 8). This has led to political tactics by central government that force local governments to face financial controls and the marketisation of service supply (Glennerster, 1980, p. 50). Central government has more control over public resources than local government. A central government planning exercise will have more potential to relate its strategies to large scale financial resources. The financial resources available to local government are more limited. Central government has the power to prescribe to local government how to use its resources.

*Space and time in planning*

The division of central and local government planning responsibilities not only effects the definition of planning activities within sub-systems of the political and managerial domains, but also raises important questions about the geography of planning activities. It is argued in the next chapter that complexity theory is concerned with the spatial characteristics of social problems and that geographical features are relevant to the distribution of long term illness in society, the associated demand for social care and the availability of monies to pay for it.

During the 1970s there was an increased focus on mathematical assessments of geographical need and their application to distribute central government block grant to local authorities (Glennerster, 1981; Bebbington and Davies, 1980a). The assessment of local needs based on census and population data relies on statistical 'needs judgements' (Bebbington and Davies, 1980b, pp. 434-436) where it is imperative for statistical judgements to be clearly identifiable in underlying theory if such methods are to be satisfactory (Bebbington and Davies, 1980a). Judgements about need are 'essentially instrumental' and require 'judgements about what ought to be done to achieve ends' (Bebbington, Turvey and Janzon, 1996, p. 8).

Both political and managerial organisational systems have temporal characteristics that define planning activity. Political systems in particular are truncated by time periods that are defined by the occurrence of democratic elections. The timing of these elections will interfere with strategic confidence and the processing and publication of information (Schneider, 1991). Contradictions can occur between central and local elections as a swing towards one political party at the centre is compensated for by a swing in the opposite direction at the locality. Managerial re-organisations can have similar effects in the managerial system, creating uncertainty, low morale and motivational difficulties.

## New managerialism and strategic planning

The 1980s saw an increasing dominance of the logic of marketisation in the public sector. There was a growing desire to establish market principles of competitiveness and a competitive based allocation of resources (Leach, Stewart and Walsh, 1994; Walsh, 1995). The use of managerialism in the public sector to achieve an increase in market mechanisms has been discussed by a number of academics and is often referred to as the 'New Managerialism' (see Pollit, 1990; Pollit, 1993; Clarke and Newman, 1997) or 'New Public Management' (NPM) (Hood, 1991). These writers comment that much of this 'new management' practice can be described as implementing private sector management philosophy in the public sector.

The 1976 public expenditure crisis and attempts by governments to limit the amount of Gross Domestic Product (GDP) spent by government resulted in government planning moving increasingly from the assessment of the need for public services, to a model of planning that was driven by the constraints on public supply and looked to a mix of market and public provision. Public policy was more likely to be funded by a means test and prioritised state subsidy. There was a desire to reduce the expectation that the government could meet demand for services through taxation. The evolving entanglement of the state planning systems with a market system of service provision occurred in the context of increased pressures on government expenditure. The consequences for the Personal Social Services (PSS) were described by Webb and Wistow (1986) as a shift from demand to supply based planning.

## A new complexity paradigm for public sector planning

In the late 1990s a new approach to public sector planning is necessary that is based on the evolving complexities of the public sector policy process. This approach must redress the balance between demand and supply based planning.

Developments in chaos and complexity theory and their application to the social sciences (Byrne, 1997a; Byrne, 1997b; Eve, Horsfall and Lee, 1997; Elliot and Kiel, 1997a) offer some opportunities for a new theoretical approach and these theories are explored extensively in the next chapter.

In this chapter it has been demonstrated that planning activity takes place in the context of a complex interaction of systems. Public sector planning activity results simultaneously in the interaction of the political, state-managerial and market systems, and the communication of actors from these different systems.

The discussion thus far has shown that optimal forms of social planning are likely to have a number of characteristics. Planning will need to include some form of democracy if a strategy is to include public participation, but the planning process must also take account of the distortions in the representative democratic process and cultivate dynamic organisational methods of accountability and consultation.

What is seen as 'rational', 'logical' or 'scientific', will partly depend on how politics and ideology present the boundaries of knowledge and what aspects of social science are seen as of more value and importance than others. Planning is in part about a vision of the future, and planning systems cannot be divorced from the dominant logics and ideas of their time era. The dominance of the logic of marketisation in recent years has been noted. The belief that market forces alone can bring the public increased choice and the efficient supply of service outputs has become a persistent new logic in the planning of the new welfare paradigm.

A picture has emerged of two post war planning processes, one driven by politics and another characterised by state-managerialism. It is proposed that the political system is the more dominant on the strategic direction of public policy while state-managerialism provides the underpinning analysis of information and the operational management of services. But both processes are entangled and have to work together if planning is to be optimal. Sartori (1991, p. 160) is fatalistic about the dichotomy of planning and politics:

> 'The more we lean on the demos, the less we are likely to achieve rational planning; conversely, the more we lean on the expert, the less democratic we are in demo-power terms. This reflection compounds the problems of democratic planning.'

This explanation fails to acknowledge the opportunities that a regulated market system presents for a choice of supply in relation to the diversity of public need. In the more complex world of the 1990s a third system is entangled with the systems of democratic politics and state-managerialism: and this is the market system. The use of the term market here must include the independent, voluntary and charitable sectors. This thesis rejects the polemic of Sartori, preferring instead to see the entanglement of the three social systems of market, politics and state-managerialism as the solution to optimal government planning activity. Similarly there is not a one dimensional logic in government planning, rather what emerges are a number of what Davies (1994, p. 203) calls 'competing logics'.

The three social systems are likely to be dominated by core actor groups and logics at any one point in time, as new logics arise and disperse. But these logics do not rise and disperse in isolation and at times 'totalizing logics' (Kontopoulos, 1993) such as 'marketisation' (Walsh, 1995) dominate all three systems.

Despite the recent influence of market principles on public sector planning there is still a strong influence of scientific management and managerial rational methods. Managerial practice evolves to serve the dominant political logics of the period (Clarke and Newman, 1997). 'New Public Management' (NPM) was the vehicle for achieving the increased marketisation of service supply. Social care planning activities occupy networks and places between the three systems. The analysis of problems and the synthesis of strategies for action, dictates that planning activity often takes places on the edge of system boundaries, or in the 'patches' (Kauffman, 1995) where systems are joined. This suggests that planning activity will highlight tensions between systems and their evolving logics. Because planning is required to understand social change and its effect on systems, those involved in planning become immersed in the requirement that systems and organisations co-ordinate change together and evolve to find optimal inter-organisational partnerships and solutions for the future.

## Conclusions

Both Walker's (1984) critique of organisational planning theory and his proposal for a model that is more explicitly political, and the subsequent general shift in planning practice from long-term comprehensive planning to 'strategic' planning, demonstrate the need for modern public sector planning to be accountable and linked to open political systems. Much of the synthesis of strategy in the public sector has to be explicitly linked to a democratic political system (Healey, 1993).

*Order from chaos*

The dominant political, market and managerial systems and associated logics that influence planning at any one time can be in conflict with each other, although through conflict they can constrain each others excesses. This conflict of ideas and methods - that at times results - may itself be functional. Complexity theorists like Capra (1996), Kauffman (1995) and Waldrop (1993) have restated a belief in the value of a democracy that is 'messy' and at times apparently contradictory in process.

The apparent disorder and conflict between these systems and their dominant logics can create its own paradoxical sense of order (Stacey, 1995). An over structured state managed bureaucracy, which is slow to change and at risk of being unaccountable, can be constrained by experimentation with processes that allow participative interference (Pollitt, 1986). Alternatively dysfunctional bureaucracy can be exposed to a degree of market discipline (Niskanen, 1973). The domination of one system or logic over another might be characterised by some predominating evolutionary weaknesses in policy outcome. For example, the dominance of market systems leads to the creation of inequities: the dominance of political games and compromises results in policy inconsistencies; and the over influence of state-management leads to dysfunctional bureaucracy. In such circumstances, the emergence of conflict between systems and its resolution becomes the imperative for optimal policy solutions. Rhodes (1997, p. 1) refers to this feature of governance as 'self organizing, inter-organisational networks' and emphasises the need for trust and diplomacy in such processes. He says (p. 10): 'no governing structure works for all services in all conditions. The issue, therefore, is not the superiority of markets and hierarchy over networks, but managing networks in the conditions under which they work best.'

Particular places and networks will emerge where planning and planners interact with more than one of the key systems at the same time and these places we can describe as 'patches', using Kauffman's theoretical language (1995). Some planning patches are located at the central government level, others at the local level - some involve both. Some local planning activity can also be devolved to district and neighbourhood geographies. The new 1990s personal social services (PSS), community care planning process and its activities are located primarily at the local government level, as discussed in later chapters. Planning activities also possess important temporal characteristics, especially in terms of how planning networks relate to the periodic cycles of political representative systems and democratic elections.

Public sector planning can be identified as both the activity of information analysis, and the formation of strategy, but the dualist separation of analysis and strategy is not always possible or desirable. Sometimes strategies emerge and then dominate the focus of analysis, on other occasions analysis opens up strategic direction. Although it is possible to locate strategy as taking place predominantly in the political system and analysis as an activity undertaken by state-managers, this is not entirely the case. On some occasions politicians have to analyse and managers synthesise. While it is important to be aware of the differences of analysis and synthesis that Mintzberg (1994a) has outlined, the two activities are partly entangled.

The inter-system patches of planning activity that generate analysis and synthesis do not fit well into formal structures that try to bureaucratise forms of activity. The nature of planning activities (like synthesis and analysis) requires them to be creative and flexible, often allowing ideas to filter across the political, managerial and market systems. The danger with confining synthesis to structures in the political systems, and analysis to managerial structures, is that optimal strategies do not result. Formal structure can reduce creativity and flexibility (Stacey, 1995). This limitation of organisational structure is one of the key concerns of Mintzberg's seminal review of strategic planning (1994b, pp. 12-14).

It is proposed that the activity of public sector planning has four key system tensions. These tensions demonstrate the competing logics of the systems identified.

The first tension is between political activity and management activity. Plans can fail when politicians detach themselves from state managers and an awareness of routine information. Conversely organisations can 'over process' information collection without adequately presenting it to decision makers, so that it is divorced from political strategy and policy usefulness. Users of services may complain about constantly filling in surveys and evaluation sheets if they have little confidence that the information is being passed on to strategic decision makers. A related matter is the ability of politicians, organisations and the public to communicate and plan together, so that the public interest takes the strategic lead. This leads to the next point.

Secondly, should public participation in planning be built on citizen representative democracy, managerial consultation, or market consumerism - or a combination of all three types? How can the public be best included in the formation of a strategy? Should this be done through the traditional voting mechanism, or by individual consumer reactions and group consultation mechanisms - or a combination of these models (Jeffrey, 1997)? How can the strategic element of planning be generated by the public and service users and can this be achieved by a new form of democratic process, as suggested by Pollit (1986) and Mulgan (1994)?

Next is the tension between how much of policy to organise at the central or local state level. What elements of strategy should be formulated at the centre and local? What should the definitions of centre and local geographies be? Where should analysis and strategy making take place and what are the best spatial definitions to use in the allocation of resources?

Fourth is the tension between how much of the supply of public services to manage through strategic intervention and how much to leave to market forces. How and where can market forces best be managed so as to achieve a diversity of service provision? Is strategic thinking based on an analysis that understands an increased market activity? For example, in the area of social care it makes little sense for an information analysis to focus solely on social needs indicators alone, if a price mechanism is used to allocate supply. An analysis of economic and financial indicators and their effect on consumer behaviour and service take-up is also important.

It is possible to locate these activity tensions between the three key social systems (Figure 1.1). It is the emergence of these tensions, the direction and process that they take, that defines where and how planning activity takes place. Public planning tensions are resolved in the patches that develop between organisational systems.

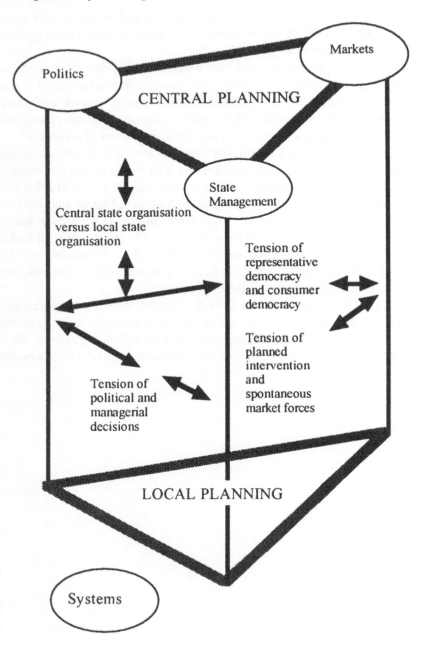

**Figure 1.1   System tensions in the state planning of social care**

# 2 Complexity Theory, Social Science and Social Planning

## A Theoretical Perspective

This book seeks to apply current developments in chaos and complexity theory to an explanation of social care planning and its practice. Chaos is a philosophy of science that sees order as unpredictable and prone to sudden exponential change produced by an accumulation of complex events. As Cartwright (1991, p. 44), writing in the *Journal of American Planning* states: 'the basic idea of chaos theory is unsettling. In simple terms, chaos is order without predictability.'

This interest in chaos can include the study of chaos in the context of a wider field of phenomena. This second approach is often referred to as complexity theory. Complexity theory attempts to understand a social world where chaos is one possible state of change. When social or physical systems are in chaos they are unstable and difficult to predict. At other times systems are relatively stable and subject to some partial prediction of their futures.

The literature on social science and chaos and complexity theory can be divided into two main groups, those text that are meta-theoretical and those more applied volumes that seek to utilise complexity theory with regard to a specific empirical application. The theoretical work includes volumes than give, or start with, a general account of complexity and its application to both physical and social systems (Waldrop, 1993; Kauffman, 1995; Capra, 1996).

Other books have been published where chaos and complexity is related specifically to social systems. Kontopoulos (1993) has undertaken an examination of the nature of social structure. Elliott and Kiel (1997a) have edited a book that includes both, theoretical discussion of the challenges that chaos poses for social scientists, and empirical attempts to measure the phenomena of chaos. Similarly, Eve, Horsfall and Lee (1997), have edited a discussion of the theoretical issues for sociology raised by chaos and complexity theory. Much of the present application of complexity to social science was written by American social scientists. A major British work on complexity and social science is forth coming , with a useful summary of the theoretical issues made available (Byrne, 1997a). Chaos and complexity is an under developed theoretical approach to the applied social sciences in Britain.

Other applied works include empirical attempts to validate complexity and its consequences. Byrne and Rogers (1996) have examined complexity in the provision of education policy and Byrne (1997b) has analysed spatial clusters of deprivation in urban geographies. Kiel (1994) argues that complexity exists in the time management of government administration.

In addition to the studies above, a small selection of articles examine the relationship of complexity and chaos theory with government planning. Parker and Stacey (1994) argue that complexity exists in macro economic trends leading to negative consequences for government's attempts to predict them. Cartwright (1991) discusses the presence of periodic chaos and its implications for government planning practice. He concludes that governments ability to plan are limited. Phelan (1995) acknowledges that chaos and complexity present planners with formidable problems, but argues that an appropriate type of planning is still necessary. Allen, Clark and Perez-Trejo (1992) take a similar viewpoint, and advocate the positive role of government in acknowledging complexity and ensuring that it's economic planning systems do not over rely on traditional indicators.

## Kontopoulos: Logics, Heterarchy and Emergent Structure

Kontopoulos (1993, p. 12) defines a complex theoretical approach to social structure as 'the strategy of heterarchy or heterarchical emergence'. Macro structures are under determined by micro parts and the link between higher level and lower level phenomena is semi-autonomous. This is in contrast to the methods of reductionism, or methodological individualism - where knowledge is strictly micro determined. Kontopoulos (1993, p. 226) argues for a heterarchical theory of social structure:

> 'Any theory that speaks of levels of phenomena that are semi-independent from each other and entangled with each other in other than totally ordered, asymmetrical ways, that is levels that are partially ordered or nonlinearly ordered, is a heterarchical theory.'

Similarly the heterarchical method opposes holist and dualist claims that all micro parts are strongly determined by a hierarchical, macro systems (Figure 2.1). Kontopoulos has developed a complex account of competing micro, meso and macro (total) logics that he suggests account for a complex

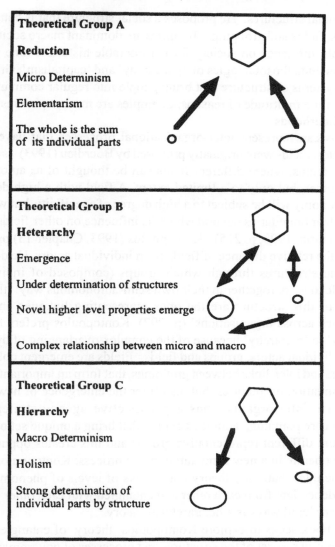

**Theoretical Group A**

**Reduction**

Micro Determinism

Elementarism

The whole is the sum
of its individual parts

**Theoretical Group B**

**Heterarchy**

Emergence

Under determination of structures

Novel higher level properties emerge

Complex relationship between micro and macro

**Theoretical Group C**

**Hierarchy**

Macro Determinism

Holism

Strong determination of
individual parts by structure

**Figure 2.1     Chaos, complexity and social science theory**

*Source*: Based on Kontopolous, 1993.

matrix of social structures. He proposes a social structure that is constructed of totalities, fields and groupings. Totalities are dominant macro social logics that can hold influence on society for considerable historical time periods. Examples include the total logics of 'patriarchy' and 'capitalism'. Groupings are micro systems of structure that bring people into regular communication and action, for a multitude of reasons. Examples are markets, interest groups and neighbourhoods.

Fields can represent inter-organisational processes that have spatial characteristics. Fields were originally proposed by Bourdieu (1993) as patterns of social relations, where different fields can be thought of as autonomous from each other, but only to a limited extent. A field with a high degree of relative autonomy will be subject to a high degree of specificity, but will have relatively clear boundaries beyond which its influence on other fields will be minimal (Peillon, 1998, p. 215). Kontopoulos (1993, Chapter 13) prefers to emphasise the relative distance of fields from individual actors. He describes fields as the structures through which groups (composed of individuals) become able to work together in their own semi-autonomous way: 'the novel properties of this structure are the ones representing linkages and inter-dependencies across organisations' (p. 297). Kontopoulos prefers the term 'heterarchy' to 'hierarchy' because of the complex overlapping of dynamics between individual actors, groups and fields. Fields are emergent collections of groupings and inter-links between groupings, that form an important process in the continuation of totalities, but also filter the emergence of new logics: examples are inter-organisations and collective agency strategies. In community care planning, activities evolve that bring a unique set of actors together from different representative groups and this creates opportunities for them to operate in a new semi autonomous process. Kontopoulos (1993, p. 226) concludes that: 'any theory that speaks of levels of phenomena that are semi independent from each other and entangled with each other in other than totally ordered ways is a heterarchical theory.'

This book seeks to explore Kontopoulos' theory of entangled logics and structures in respect of the structures and processes of government social care planning. It is proposed that social care planning is a complex process that includes a number of social systems and numerous actors. In this book a number of different social logics like choice, supply diversity, marketisation and equity are observed in their influence on social care planning.

Kontopoulos (1993, p. 384) has defined social logics as:

'overarching logics of structuration starting from the semi local level of structures and moving towards the global level: especially emerging as projects of collective agencies (capitalist class, bureaucratic state) referred to sometimes as the logic of capital, the logic of bureaucratisation, they emerge as conscious or opaque collective "projects" (Foucault) with particular modeal orientations; they become totalizing, tending (without complete success) toward the formation of a strong hierarchy of material and or mental control.'

Given the complexity of logics underpinning social structures it is necessary to understand how simplified notions of logic can endure for long periods. Kontopoulos (1993, p. 224) proposes that the high degree of contradiction and fragmentation within society between different competing logics is not faced regularly because certain logics are permitted to dominate over others for social convenience.

'Bourdieu arrives at the conclusion that there is a special "economy of logic"...no more logic is mobilised than is required by the needs of the practice...this economy of logic...allows symbolic objects and practices to enter without contradiction into successive relationships set up from different points of view, making them subject to over determination. This way the "fuzzy logic of practice works wonders" enabling the group to achieve as much social and logical integration as is compatible with the diversity imposed.'

Bourdieu (1977, p. 110) summarises the paradox of economy of logic. 'The fact that symbolic objects and practices can enter without contradiction into successive relationships set from different points of view means that they are subject to over determination through indetermination.' It exists because systems owe their pragmatic coherence and regularity as much to their irregularities and incoherencies as to their own internal coherence. Structures are only utilised and manageable in a complex society because of a poor and economic use of logic (op cit, p. 109). Total logics survive for long periods partly because if they were permanently contested in society an intolerable degree of social instability would result. Total logics are simplified accounts of social reality that are permitted to over determine social processes, giving them an influence beyond the degree of explanation that they possess.

Kontopoulos' theoretical method has included consideration of spatial characteristics in the emergence of social structure. Kauffman (1995) has also described the spatial aspects of structure.

## Kauffman and Landscapes

Kauffman's (1995) theoretical language talks of landscapes rather than logics. While geographical landscapes are of relevance in the study of social science they represent only one dimension of a system. Landscapes are Kauffman's metaphorical definition of social systems. The importance of his work is in its emphasis on the partial determination of social structures and processes through spatial definition. For example, both market and political systems have physical landscape characteristics. In these systems spatial definitions are also associated with the dominant logics and culture of the actors who inhabit them.

The importance of place in a market or political system is explained by a logic associated with the local geographical landscape. For example, a social care day centre is located in a particular physical space, it opens for certain temporal periods each year, but the reasons for this are linked intrinsically with actors beliefs about the value of social care received there. Alternatively, a parliament building is a place on the political landscape, it has a central physical place in the geographical landscape of a nation and capital city, but this is also linked to the logic and culture within that political system. It is because of logic and culture that physical places are given a particular social significance. The same is true of temporal spaces. Day centres only open at certain times of the day and year. Residential care homes are normally able to provide a service 24 hours a day. Strategic political debate is often confined to a limited number of meetings in parliament building, or a council chamber.

All landscapes must be 'local' in some sense, in that they can be examined in terms of the actor behaviour in a relatively restricted physical location. Even within a global computer system like the internet where physical space appears unimportant, the system has millions of subscribes whose contribution is still in part dominated by the geographical location of their computer equipment. It is possible for the actor to easily move his computer, but nevertheless at any one point in time that he logs on, some physical space must be occupied. Even a social system like the internet has some spatial and temporal characteristics. These might be viewed as unstable and highly individualised, because they are not dependent on institutional buildings and the permanence of bricks and mortar.

When considering social systems as landscapes, and assessing the relationship of logical and cultural beliefs to their physical and temporal location, it is important to appreciate that systems often have attributes that are both macro and micro.

Many systems have features that are both global and local. The market system has characteristics that are both international and local. Rich and poor homes can be observed all over the world, although the extremes of definition are more obvious in some countries and localities than others. Similarly political parties with broadly similar ideologies operate on the global, continental, national and local political landscapes. Physical and temporal location explains part of the story about how and why social structures exist. Sheppard (1996, p. 1339) confirms the 'currently prevailing view that, despite the socially constructed nature of space, it is valid to treat space as constitutive of social processes.'

It can be concluded that different types of social systems have different levels of spatial and temporal dependency. The social care system can be said to possess high degrees of spatial and temporal dependency because social care is dependent on people being with each other for lengthy periods of time. It involves personal relationships of an intimate quality and the temporal occurrence of care can be vital. Care is often needed at specific points in the temporal cycle of the day. In contrast a social system like the internet demonstrates only limited spatial and temporal dependency. The internet is available across all time zones and operates 24 hours a day. People who use its services only find limited attachments to time and space, such as the location of their computer equipment and phone line.

Government planning activity has to take account of temporal and spatial dimensions. Planning is often tied to an annual budgeting cycle and strategies will be influenced by periodic elections. Since the establishment of Social Service Departments (SSDs) in the early 1970s there has been a growing awareness of the importance of local geography as a key social feature that defines people's experience of disablement and care (Davies, 1968). Laws and Warnes (1982) have identified national movements of older, retired peoples to specific local retirement geographies and this raises important questions about the targeting and provision of care at a local level. These population movements are more likely amongst relatively wealthy older persons, suggesting that areas with large proportions of older people in their populations do not necessarily have the highest need for state financed services (Corden and Wright, 1993).

In a complex and unstable social world, the dimensions of time and space offer social planners two tangible dimensions on which to base their analysis and synthesis.

*Central places in landscapes*

It is noted that as a consequence of this interaction between physical, temporal and logical realities, some physical and temporal places become 'central' as result. Because of the collective logics of actors - one city in a nation becomes a capital. While there are numerous local councils, one place becomes the central parliament. These central points also continue to exhibit some local characteristics, London is a locality to those that live there, but actors 'local' social experience is changed by the 'central' importance of the physical place. Aspects of the social care market are influenced by this sense of being in a locality that is central to the nation. In London there are less older people as a proportion of the population than in shire counties. More extremes of wealth and poverty are evident. Private residential social care services are not well established due to high operating costs (Bebbington and Darton, 1996a). A central place in a landscape can also be a local place, but a local place with a difference.

*Landscape as a linkage between social structures and systems*

The complexity paradigm suggests that human organisations can be thought of as open systems that are capable of demonstrating characteristics of both stability and instability. Such open systems do not attain to a natural state of equilibrium in order to be optimal in their functioning. A form of stable homeostatis is one possible state that open systems can possess, but an equilibrium does not necessarily correlate with being optimal in performance. This is different to the explanation of closed systems theory. A closed system is a system that settles into an optimal feedback process that creates an equilibrium (Capra, 1996, p. 48). Open systems are dynamic and always evolving. They do not return to a fixed point of equilibrium.

A global landscape has numerous local systems and landscapes. The boundaries between these systems are arbitrary and entangled. Actors are observed in their interaction with both systems and landscapes. Actors whose lives are often dominated by one social system, constantly have to travel through landscapes and other social systems in order to get to their destinations.

Actors will take part in relationships that are defined partly by local geographical landscapes, neighbourhoods and communities of interest. Each social system inevitably has some physical and temporal characteristics, and these spatial and temporal characteristics define part of the way in which social systems interact. Actors have to interact with time and space, and have to decide when to go to work, where to go, and in doing so this effects who else they will meet in the 'time and space corridors' they move in. This in turn effects the future characteristics of the other social systems they experience. Not even the most powerful person can be everywhere all of the time, although technology such as surveillance and the mass media, can be used to help some actor groups dominate the time and space corridors that they cannot occupy physically.

People suffering from a long term illness may have limited access to the time and space corridors in society. This can be both because of the government's management of these time and space corridors (Oliver, 1990) and also because an illness prevents easy mobility. When planners are analysing long term illness and its relationship with service supply, consideration should be given to both the structural and individual causes of social exclusion.

Landscapes are descriptive places in time and space where logics, agency and structure merge and evolve. Social systems have landscape characteristics. While the physical landscape of geography changes fairly slowly in a human time frame, social landscape systems can be much more unstable.

## *Local landscapes and fitness peaks*

The metaphor of landscapes used by Kauffman (1995) to describe systems helps us to understand evolutionary spatial characteristics of actor systems. Each local system has evolving peaks and valleys, where the peaks represent localised actor excellence and fitness.

The health of British adults is known to possess spatial characteristics that relate to both local geographical wards and the social characteristics of wards (Macintyre, 1997; Gould and Jones, 1995; Senior, 1995). Spatial health factors can be demonstrated at a county and regional geographical level. Areas of the country that have larger proportions of people with long term illness relative to age distribution are also the spatial areas where relatively poorer people live. This is similar to the association between poverty and Standard Mortality Ratios (SMRs) (Whitehead, 1992; Wilkinson, 1996; Dorling, 1997). Within defined geographical landscapes it is possible to identify geographical areas where there is a 'fitness peak' of those in better health.

## Chaos and its Relationship with Complexity

Chaos is a component of complexity theory. Chaos is the idea that small changes over time in a locality produce exponential effects later on in other landscapes and systems.

Actors and sub-cultures try to evolve in logical ways to the fitness peak of their local landscape or system Fitness peaks are sub-systems, sub-cultures, or species that have evolved to the 'peak' of their landscape and seek to dominate it, or get the maximum from it. Chaos theory argues that by rising to a local peak a species can put itself and its sub system 'on the edge of chaos'.

When a local sub-group reaches its local fitness peak, it is said by Kauffman (1995) to be on 'the edge of chaos', because through its fitness it has changed its relationship with adjacent landscapes and systems. At this moment in time and space it is highly influential on other localities, distorting and disforming the adjoining systems.

> 'The edge of chaos theme also arises as a potential general law. In scaling the top of fitness peaks, adapting populations that are too methodical and timid in their explorations are likely to get stuck in the foothills, thinking they have reached as high as they can go....the best exploration of an evolutionary space occurs at a kind of phase transition between order and disorder, when populations begin to melt off the local peaks they have become fixated on and flow along ridges toward distant regions of higher fitness.' (Kauffman,1995 p. 27)

It has been proposed that after a fitness peak is reached 'bifurcation' results, whereby species and sub cultures either move into a place of complexity, establishing themselves on a number of new and related landscapes, or alternatively remain on the deforming peak. Because the underlying systems are moving and not stable over time, remaining on a peak does not guarantee that a species or sub culture continues at a high local point, or in an influential position. Decreases in fitness might also evolve (Figure 2.2).

Byrne (1997b) has provided evidence from cluster analysis of 1991 census data that there is a bifurcation of cities into areas inhabited by the poor and excluded and other areas inhabited by those with more income who are social included. Byrne and Rogers (1996) suggest that there is a rising fitness peak of schools selectively recruiting middle class children and they show that this is related to two systems, one is geographical, the other based on

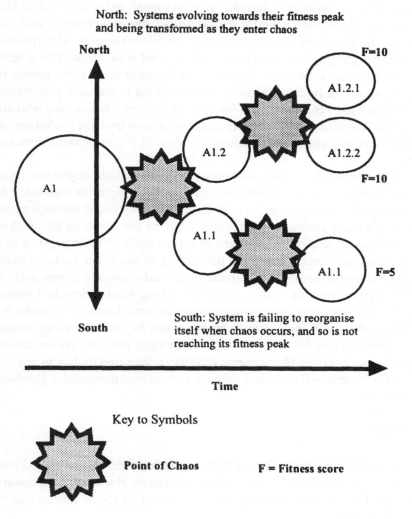

North: Systems evolving towards their fitness peak
and being transformed as they enter chaos

North

F=10

A1.2.1

A1.2

A1.2.2

F=10

A1

A1.1

A1.1

F=5

South: System is failing to reorganise
itself when chaos occurs, and so is not
reaching its fitness peak

South

Time

Key to Symbols

Point of Chaos     F = Fitness score

**Figure 2.2  Chaos and complexity theory: bifurcation**

'cultural capital'. The authors describe 'cultural capital' as the ability of middle class parents to use their superior market knowledge and power in order to maximise the advantages for their children. Similar examples exist in social care where a geographical landscape is associated with rates of long term illness and certain areas have fitness peaks (literally more older people in better physical and financial health) who are living in the local population. Similarly in a market system it is likely to be the same individuals who are developing 'consumer culture' faster and benefit most from the marketisation of social services when they eventually become ill (Baldock and Ungerson, 1994).

This leaves other poorer people and neighbourhoods, dependent upon families, relatives and neighbours for their care. Over time this separation of social groups between geographical localities has other social consequences. For example those caring for poorer sick relatives are unable to take part in the labour market leading to shortages of certain skills. The emergence of a local fitness peak contributes to the disforming of the wider social system. Figure 2.3 shows an example of a spatially defined economic fitness peak. It shows the percentage of retired people with long term illness in London boroughs who own their own home outright. In some London boroughs the population of retired long term ill have a much higher level of economic fitness, than in other boroughs. This has important planning repercussions because Social Services Departments (SSDs) are required by law to pay for services for those who do not have the capital or income resources to purchase their own care.

*Global peaks*

The fusion of local fitness peaks and systems and their inter-dependency drives the potential for what Kauffman calls global peaks, places of evolutionary efficiency, for example, a society that can sustain its social care in equity, quantity and quality.

Kauffman (1995, p. 180) proposes that there is such a place amongst landscapes, a kind of metaphorical heaven. 'If only an adapting population could take a God's eye view and behold the large scale landscape features - see where to evolve rather than just climbing blindly uphill from its current positions, only to become trapped on poor local peaks.'

The shifting of peaks and valleys produces 'substantive evolutionary transformations' (Kauffman, 1995), where certain themes, ideas, groups and trends emerge as more dominant. What is contested is the extent to which

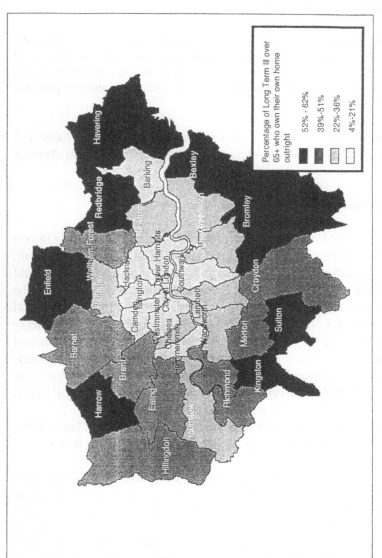

**Figure 2.3  Economic fitness peaks in London boroughs of retired people with long  term illness**

*Source:* 1991 census, Crown copyright. Map boundaries copyright © EDLINE

governments can understand and plan this complex process. For some writers the reality of chaos and complexity implies that governments should do the minimum of planning (Parker and Stacey, 1994) These writers erroneously assume that a market can adjust to chaos and complexity more easily than governments and democratic systems. Byrne (1997b, pp. 66-67) has challenged this view, instead proposing that:

> 'The last potential form of complex based policy is creative - it is neither the fine tuning of stability maintenance nor the acceptance of a divided social world...What this means is agency. It is precisely the human capacity to imagine and seek to construct a future which is so crucial to understanding the potential of trajectories within a complex world.'

This book attempts to use an explanation of system chaos and complexity as a model for understanding government community care planning activity.

*Patches, the places where systems meet*

In complexity theory system boundaries are open and temporary. On one dimension, social care policy logics are transformed in the political system, but there are also other juxtaposed systems with their own evolving logical frameworks. One such system is concerned with state organisation and the management, planning and purchasing of social care, another is the social care market place itself. Networks and frameworks of planning activity emerge from within these systems and merge across to form adjoining patches and places. For example political and managerial systems join when politicians meet state managers at meetings, or in committees. Often there are cultures, roles and procedures that govern these patches. A key patch is the Social Services Committee of the local authority.

It is the detection and definition of these 'patches' that Kauffman (1995, pp. 252-253) sees as the opportunity to explain social processes better.

> 'Have we evolved some other procedure that works well ? I suspect we have, and call it by a variety of names, from federalism to profit centres to restructuring to checks and balances to political action committees. Here I'll call it patches...We are about to see that if the entire conflict laden task is broken into the properly chosen patches the co-evolving system lies at a phase transition between order and chaos and rapidly finds very good solutions. Patches, in short, may be a fundamental process we have evolved in our social systems...to solve very hard problems.'

Patches are the combination of parts of systems, and their physical landscapes, that allow part of the global picture to be better understood and managed. Kauffman argues at the end of his book that complexity naturally breeds diversity and that diversity in general produces orderly outcomes with less chaos. He uses an illustration from economics that analyses the growth and diversity of technology. In his analysis patches are characterised by diversity and cooperation. Sub groups, sub cultures and regimes tend to work best when they cooperate. This means climbing off their individual fitness peaks. 'The evolution of co-evolution tends to favour strategies that lie in this regime, near the edge of chaos' (Kauffman, 1995, p. 221). The challenge to planners is to understand the complexity of systems and landscapes in which they work and to search out the global peaks:

> 'The problems confronted by an organisation is preeminently how to evolve on this deforming landscape, to track moving peaks. Tracking peaks on deforming landscape is central to survival . Landscapes, in short, are part of the search for excellence - the best compromises we can attain.' (op cit, p. 246)

Complexity theory proposes some tentative linking of local patterns to an understanding of changes in the macro landscapes. For example Allen, Clark and Perez-Trejo (1992) developed a model for the development of the Senegalese economy that incorporates traditional notions of macro inputs and outputs, but also includes complex local interactions such as local environmental concerns and population migrations .

A complex planning approach requires a sophisticated political accountability, a correct assessment and utilisation of market forces, and efficient market regulation from managerial systems. This delicate dynamic will shift for disparate social activities and change over time. Kauffman (1995, p. 28) says that disorderly democratic decision making is functional and 'fit' because it is flexible enough to cope with the nature of chaos and complexity: 'democracy may be far and away the best process to solve the complex problems of a complex evolving society, to find the peaks on the co-evolutionary landscape where, on average, all have a chance to prosper.'

Government social care planning is likely to include activity across a number of systems if it is to be optimal. Not only is it a managerial exercise concerned with the analysis of information, but it is also a political exercise concerned with including different logical perspectives and marginalised groups, so as to find the best compromises and strategic possibilities.

## Complexity and Human Organisations

Human organisations are predominantly open systems, where individual actors bring to organisations a number of external contingencies based on their socialisation experience outside of the organisation. Similarly at the macro level, human organisations are constantly being influenced by outside contingencies such as socio-economic change, political change and changes in legal regulation. Public sector organisations appear be to particularly exposed to such outside factors when compared with private sector businesses.

Attempts have been made to model three states of organisational behaviour in a complex society. These are: instability, stability and 'bounded stability' (Stacey, 1995). It is argued that organisations fluctuate between these three states of existence, sometimes changing in a manner that is not intended by their actors, and not predictable.

The theory of bifurcation already discussed can be applied to organisational systems (Figure 2.2). If a system does not transform itself in relation to the evolutions of systems around it then it may become sub optimal. Systems that do transform themselves successfully achieve this by placing themselves on the 'edge of chaos'. Stacey (1995) argues that systems that are transforming themselves find an optimal level of bounded stability, that allows them to migrate towards complexity. By allowing elements of instability, organisations are paradoxically able to transform their conception of order so that they become more flexible. This permits the organisation to change its partnership with environmental contingencies. Thus disorder leads to a new and functional form of order.

Stacey (1995) proposes that in reality this entails organisations having internal sub-systems that are performing in diverse ways and thereby appearing in conflict with each other. The critical point becomes achieving 'bounded instability', rather than the extremes of instability and stability.

Kauffman (1995) has proposed that patches are the place where bounded instability within systems and between sub systems can be managed. Stacey sees patches as essentially similar to informal network behaviour. Recently Stacey (1995, p. 489) has proposed that the critical point about networks, as a form of patch, is that bounded instability requires the correct number, blend and distribution of networks - if the system is to continue successfully on the edge of chaos.

'The science of complexity leads to another proposition about changeable organisations: changeability becomes an internal property of an organisation when its informal network system, consisting of self-organising patterns of connections between people within and across its boundaries , is richly connected enough to operate on the edge of instability, where it produces ever-changing emergent patterns of behaviour.'

Stacey's application of complexity theory to the study of organisations demonstrates that the future of organisations cannot be easily predicted, similar to the fact that public sector organisations cannot simply predict the movement and evolution of society. These findings make Stacey skeptical about the value of planning both in business and the macro economy (Parker and Stacey, 1994). In this book, however, the 'edge of chaos' paradigm is used to argue for a realistic model of government planning, rather than to argue for an end to public sector planning. Stacey's skepticism is largely based on the historic use of simple planning methodologies by government and administrative planners that are unable to take account of the need for organisations to adapt rapidly to sudden change. Such methods can contribute to an organisation erroneously believing that it is more stable and more in control of its environment that it really is.

Past planning failures should not lead to governments rejecting outright the usefulness of planning. Government actors are still required to understand the past, the here and now, and future contexts of their environment. There is a need for a new realism in government planning, and a willingness to embrace complexity.

## Time and Space in Complexity Theory

Time and Space offer important empirical foundations to the complexity theorist. Compared to the complex and largely unpredictable inter-relationships of social science variables, time and space offer background dimensions on which there is some physical stability. It is for this reason that social science methodologists with an interest in complex methods assert the importance of time and space. Sayer (1992, p. 146) has talked of the need to reawaken the spatial dimension in social science analysis: 'while it is common to argue that social phenomena are historically specific and that method should take account of this, little interest has been shown outside geography in their geographically variable character; indeed most social scientists ignore space.'

Similarly quantitative methodologists argue that time is an important underpinning variable in the analysis of social change:

'A recurrent theme throughout the social sciences is that behaviour is characterised by strong temporal dependencies...It will be evident that longitudinal data are essential if the temporal dependencies in micro-level behaviour are to be investigated in any analysis.' (Dale and Davies, 1994, p. 3)

Over time and space the whole mass of systems is believed to be shifting, so that one peak may be undermined by a wider movement of the shifting global system (hence the idea of global peaks): 'life unrolls in an unending procession of change.' (Kauffman, 1995, p.15)

The stable foundations of time and space are not entirely firm when applying a complex analysis. Physical science applications of chaos and complexity theory note the relativity of time and space. For example Boyarsky and Gora (1996, p. 611) note that spacetime is a 'complex, foamy, cheese like object governed by the gravitational field of the experiment'.

Whilst gravity for social scientists may appear to be reasonably predictable, some theorists have discussed how cultural experiences lead to significant changes in how space and time are perceived. This can be as fundamental to social structures as gravity is to physical ones. Giddens (1990) for example discusses how improvements in transport and electronic technology have altered people's perception of time and space and that this will vary between sub-cultures. Measurements of time and space may appear to be reliable operationally in social science research until one takes into account actor definitions of time and space. Cultural definitions of time and space will be diverse.

In a book to examine the relationship between temporality and macro government planning, Schneider (1991) proposed five temporal dimensions: the degree of planning intensity; the variance of time horizons; the average time horizon; a reliance on a means of timing, and a timed order of initiation. Schneider's (1991, p. 263) key finding was that timing and time management was an important element of policy planning, programme implementation and its success or failure, but that no predictable pattern of how best to manage time was apparent:

'There is finally no adequate temporal order for any kind of initiation. It is the context which seem to matter in judging the suitability of timing the initiation of a measure and in subsequently choosing a sequencing strategy. Gradualism, accordingly, is not the most suitable method for solving problems in every situation, as some proponents of pragmatism proclaim.'

## Complexity and Quantitative Analysis

Social planning is linked intrinsically with quantitative research and attempts to use statistical models to explain social reality. In particular, quantitative social planning has become associated with the rational determination of social priorities and the distribution of central government grant (Bebbington and Davies, 1980a; Glennerster, 1981). Planners have tried to analyse mathematically historical trends in an effort to act in the future. Such statistical models and their usefulness are discussed later in this book. What are the implications for quantitative causal analysis given the theory of science proposed by chaos and complexity theory? The evolution of chaos into complexity was explored using Kauffman's theoretical metaphors. But it is also possible to examine this change mathematically.

### *The mathematical modelling of chaos and complexity*

Cartwright (1991) has sought to apply mathematical chaos theory to planning methodology and reached the conclusion that the non linear and undetermined nature of chaos theory leads to a situation where planners should not seek to plan for one linear future, but instead offer a number of possible mathematical scenarios. He also says that planning systems should be focused on the short term, rather than long term.

The development of chaos theory into complexity theory and the substantive implications for planning theory is discussed by Phelan (1995). His hypothesis is that four different types of change can be demonstrated by mathematics and that only one of these states represents the mathematical phenomena of chaos. By implication governments are often confronted with non chaotic phenomena where more predictive and stable social variables are present. Chaos is not always present. The task becomes to judge when it is. A number of American researchers have tried to operationalise a mathematical, non linear account of when chaos occurs in social science data (Dooley, 1997; Brown, 1997; Jaditz, 1997; Berry and Kim, 1997). This empirical work is not without its methodological problems. Sokal and Bricmont (1998, pp. 135-136) comment: 'one constantly hears claims of chaos theory being "applied" to history or society. But human societies are complicated systems involving a vast number of variables, for which one is unable (at least at present) to write down any sensible equations.'

It is often difficult to find social science data of sufficient periodic detail and longevity that can be subject to tests (Jaditz, 1997, p. 87). The complex non linear modelling of one or two variables over time also suffers from the traditional arbitrary limits imposed on quantitative analysis in the social sciences: the relationships between the limited selection of data may be of interest, but what other relevant influential factors have been omitted from the calculations and analysis?

Cross-sectional linear research can still be of methodological value in demonstrating a local fitness peak. This might be the point in a system's existence prior to chaos occurring. For example, Byrne and Rogers (1996) have demonstrated the existence of fitness peak in the state education schools market where schools in middle class areas acquire the most able and successful children. Similarly, a spatial model of economic fitness amongst the retired long term ill in London was proposed earlier in this chapter (Figure 2.3). Byrne (1997b) has demonstrated the occurrence of a socio-economic fitness peaks in urban geography. But the identification of fitness peaks cannot prove that chaos or complexity is about to result on a larger scale as a consequence.

A local evolutionary fitness peak is likely to be undermined at sometime in the future by the movement of the larger environment around it, hence the idea that a fitness peak can put a nearby landscape on the 'edge of chaos' (Kauffman, 1995). In effect the inter-relationship of many variables becomes difficult to understand. Local environments and systems can be observed and partially understood, but causality across a larger horizon becomes impossible to predict (Sokal and Bricmont, 1988). Descriptive quantitative modelling takes place in the hope that it will increase the chances of some prediction, but exact prediction is unlikely. Cartwright's (1991, p. 54) account of chaos theory and planning reaches the conclusion: 'finally, and perhaps most important of all for planners, is the fact that chaotic systems are predictable on only an incremental or local basis.'

A number of authors (Cartwright, 1991; Kiel, 1994; Parker and Stacey, 1994; Stroup, 1997; Elliot and Kiel, 1997a) provide similar basic accounts of the mathematical non-linear thinking behind chaos and complexity theory. Single dependent variables are shown to change over time at an unpredictable rate. Graphical presentations demonstrate three possible outcomes:

    (i) incremental and linear growth;
    (ii) stable, cyclic fluctuations; and
    (iii) chaotic fluctuations.

These three phases can be demonstrated with a computer spreadsheet using the equation $t = (X \times A1) \times (1 - A1)$, where A1 is the first data point in the time series (equal in this example to 0.1); t = the value for the next time period; and X equals the increment of rate of change in the variable between each time period (see Figure 2.4). By changing small values in X (the rate of change) the long term effects are shown to be great. The first linear phase can be sub-divided into two predictable phases (Phelan, 1995, p. 2), but with different results, the first is where a species or sub culture decreases and dies, the second is where it retains perfect stability.

The third and most unpredictable pattern of change over time is when the values of a variable demonstrate quite wild fluctuations, although still within some boundaries (this is the fourth phase in Phelan's model). The presence of these fluctuations within boundaries, leads to the conclusion that chaos is not totally disordered, but represents some element of order within disorder. This chaotic and unpredictable nature of change in the variable is shown to be caused by earlier small rates of change over time. These small changes have an exponential effect on a system in the later time phases. Put simply, small adjustments create large results.

Kiel (1994) cites three stages of change over time in a complex paradigm: equilibrium, rhythms and chaos. Equilibriums may have some linear characteristics. Rhythms show cyclic fluctuations that are predictable within ranges. Chaos is the point at which the prediction of a cyclic pattern breaks down.

The conclusion of Phelan (1995) is that systems can produce predictable states other than chaos. Chaos does not have to be the dominant feature of time series analysis. It is only one possible feature. Such mathematical models of change over time are in themselves 'ideal types' because they only show the mathematical outcome for a single variable, the reality in the real world is that a single variable will be influenced by numerous other independent variables, making the patterns infinitely more problematic to capture in a meaningful way. This results in two possible conclusions, firstly that the entanglement of numerous variables will certainly lead to the dominance of chaos on the dependent variable in the overall mathematical system, or secondly that a complex multi-variable pattern will emerge where dependent variables still possess periods of stability, but these are periodically disrupted by chaos. The second statement is taken as a better logical description of social complexity because the social world is not observed to be in disorder all of the time.

Phelan (1995, p. 4) also concludes that social systems do exhibit prolonged periods of stability and as a result planning activity can be relevant, but it cannot be over deterministic:

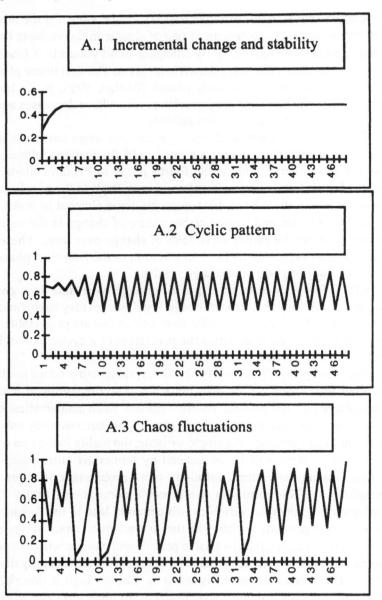

**Figure 2.4 Chaos and complexity theory:**
**three stages of change**

'although it can be assumed that extended transients will follow a fixed trajectory, it should be recognised that at any time an unforeseen interaction with a chaotic element or other transient in the system has the potential to divert or destroy the elements of the extended transient.'

The disruption to dependent variables said to occur over time because of highly complex changes in associated independent variables, is impossible to capture with the use of traditional linear statistical methods. As a result, much application of chaos and complexity theory to social phenomena tends to be theoretically abstract or dependent upon quantitative simulation of the complex interaction of social variables. Chaos and complexity becomes a metaphor rather than a mathematical certainty. Bryne (1997a, p. 2) describes this as: 'to see the quantitative as itself inherently qualitative.'

Capra (1996, pp. 40-41) also states that:

'This new approach to science immediately raises an important question. If everything is connected to everything else, how can we ever hope to understand anything....in the new paradigm it is recognised that all scientific concepts and theories are limited and approximate. Science can never provide any complete and definitive understanding.'

Sokal and Bricmont (1998) have cautioned against taking this uncertainty to a theoretical extreme, and in an indictment of French post-modern philosophy they argue for a clear link between empirical research and theoretical abstraction. This implies that the use of chaos and complexity theory in social science should not rely on metaphors alone, but must be grounded in the mathematical foundation of the theory wherever possible.

Where mathematical cross-sectional linear modelling is used to understand the relationship between variables in personal social service planning, attempts also need to be made to compare this with an alternative time frame so that some sense of a time series trend is available (Dale and Davies, 1994). There is also a need to consider cross-sectional analysis from a number of different meta-theoretical starting points and for complex quantitative models to be clear of their meta-theoretical assumptions (Bebbington and Davies, 1980a).

The importance of using quantitative time series data when seeking to manage organisational behaviour in government organisations is argued by Kiel (1994) and he also explores the importance of 'spontaneous organisational types' (similar to Kauffman's evolutionary transformations) as a method for dealing with chaotic phenomena. For example, there will be a need for organisations to adapt swiftly when clear peaks and troughs can be shown to exist in referrals rates to social care services.

There are a number of challenges when applying chaos and complexity theory to social science applications and the planning of public services. The connectivity of social phenomena is highly complex and unpredictable, but there is still some underlying order within this complexity. The social world is not constantly in chaos. Chaos can be understood as one aspect of social change, when social systems change rapidly and rather unexpectedly. There are no conclusive methods for predicting chaos, but by perceiving the complexity of the world, it may be possible to come closer to understanding the emergence of elements of chaos and to suggest scenarios of the possible outcome. Quantitative research analysis can still be used to create hypothetical planning models, confirming that statistics is as much an art form as a pure science. Time series considerations are important. Cohen and Stewart (1994, p. 442) defend the realistic use of reductionist quantitative research.

> 'Reductionism is great for quantitative aspects of internal details. In contrast, our current understanding of external large-scale effects is mostly descriptive and qualitative, geometric rather than numerical. We can recognise a hurricane from a satellite photo, but we can't tell what it is going to do.'

The interaction of the micro and macro quantitative elements within social systems are partially determined by the physical landscape environment in which they co-exist. The study of spatial and temporal aspects of social life can provide some important evidence about what possibilities the future possesses.

## Conclusion: Complexity and Planning

The science of complexity does not offer a simple planning method based on a reductionist logic, but it can create a new theoretical perspective and resulting change in practice where complexity is acknowledge and idealised methods and solutions treated with caution. Understanding the social, historical and geographical context of policies becomes critical. Quantitative methods of analysis are still appropriate where they are used to provide qualitative examples of reality (Byrne, 1997a). Quantitative modelling still has some value, but the prescriptive use of intricate mathematical algorithms like the

Standard Spending Assessment (SSA) to underpin government planning needs to be treated with caution.

Cartwright (1991, p. 49-51) says that chaos theory implies that planners must spend more time trying to analyse the complexity of present circumstances. He (p. 50) argues that chaos mathematics demonstrates, that if research can accurately describe where one is in a time and order sequence short term predictions are possible, but not long term ones.

'It is impossible to predict the long run evolution of his model at a particular growth rate; that is, you cannot exactly predict the sequence or placement of points along any particular parabola. On the other hand: one can have a pretty good idea of where the model will go next, even in the chaotic regime, if one knows where it is now.'

He (p. 53) also concludes from his mathematical work that planning strategies based on a rational-comprehensive system of perfect foresight are an impossibility and misleading and for this reason planning should be concerned with numerous alternative forecasts that are approximations based on parallel understandings of the surrounding events. Much of this is because (he says) we do not know the present well enough and need different versions of it and different starting points to our models .

The paradigm of complexity theory removes some elements of the uncertainty proposed by Cartwright's application of chaos to planning. In a complex social world the chaos of the present is unlikely to lead to a chaos of the future. In complexity theory, order results from chaos. Complexity theory can be thought of as implying that certain outcomes can be almost guaranteed to take place (for example, economic recession), but that the time periods and forms of social organisation that will relate to such outcomes are extremely difficult to predict. Byrne (1997b) prefers to place emphasis on the possibilities of human actors creating order and improvement through social planning, rather than social planning failing to determine and predict with great accuracy.

A guiding principle from complexity theory is that groups of parts will take a partially deterministic path of their own, regardless of their micro composition. It is this emergence of order from constituent groups of parts than results in writers like Capra (1996, p. 29) concluding: 'the great shock of twentieth century science has been that systems cannot be understood by analysis. The properties of the parts are not intrinsic properties, but can be understood only within the context of the larger whole.'

This confirms the importance of considering structural variables such as spatial area, ethnic group and social class when planning the effects of social policy and public policy on individuals. Quantitative analysis becomes focused on simulating approximations of social reality and used to articulate discourse and argument.

The next chapter examines the development of a planning process in the personal social services and continues to develop the conceptual forms of systems and logics defined thus far. In chapter three the historical analysis is based on literature and government documents. In chapter four, the development of theory is validated using a sample of local authority community care plans.

# 3　The Evolution of Personal Social Services Planning

This chapter examines the evolution of personal social service (PSS) planning since 1960. After a summary of the history of PSS planning the chapter explores the introduction of Community Care Plans (CCP) as implemented by the NHS and Community Care Act 1990. The influence of political, managerial and market logics and systems on this process is examined.

## Post War Community Care, A Planning Disaster?

Although the current community care policy is committed to a planned process prescribed in the NHS and Community Care Act 1990, the incremental development of care in the community since world war two is characterised by a single lack of national planning and overall strategy (Walker, 1989). This was an indictment made by the Griffiths report in 1988 (p. iv, para. 9): 'At the centre, community care has been talked of for thirty years and in few areas can the gap between political rhetoric and policy on the one hand, or between policy and reality in the field on the other hand have been so great.' Before considering the details of the present CCP process it is necessary to review the evolution of PSS planning since 1960.

## PSS Planning, 1962-1975

In 1962 a ten year plan for health and welfare was introduced by central government. In 1963 local welfare plans were produced by local authorities independently of the Ministry of Health. They required the joint publication of social service and health data and this necessitated attempts at the coordination of the two care providers. These plans were essentially based on quantitative estimates of outputs, such as the number of staff to be employed, building programmes, and estimated capital and revenue expenditure. A plan was to be produced for each financial year up until 1967-1968 and thereafter to indicate growth over a five year period until 1971-1972 (Ministry of Health,

1963, p. 46).

As a result of the plans the Ministry of Health projected that total staffing levels in community care would grow by 39% in 9 years with a revenue expenditure rise of 47% at 1961 prices with no allowance for inflation (op cit, p. 47). Hambleton (1986, p. 66) lists three reasons for Enoch Powell's (Minister of Health, 1963) implementation of the plans, these being: to keep a check on local authority expenditure under the requirements of the Public Expenditure Survey Committee (PESC); to promote community care policies; and to coordinate with the hospital plans of 1962 .

These early plans were important in that they promoted community care resources and shifted attention from the central Ministry of Health to the local authority social and welfare services, but they used an unsophisticated methodology being based on a number of simple volume indicators. Elements of tension existed between central and local government because of the amount of data that had to be collected and the key driving force was central governments planning of expenditure. Nevertheless central government was not autocratic in supervising the collection of indicators and their use (Davies, 1968, p. 206). The hope was that local authorities would revise their plans in accordance with data available from neighbouring local areas and comparable authorities. There was no consideration of resources provided in the private and charitable sectors.

In 1972 the Department of Health and Social Security (DHSS) introduced another attempt at ten year planning. In England and Wales, local social welfare services had changed significantly after the report of the Seebohm Committee (1968) and the subsequent passing of the Local Authority Social Services Act. Seebohm argued for an increase in  social services planning activity and a need for a growth in resources. In response, general local Social Services Departments (SSDs) were created.  Personal social care work was now consolidated from numerous small local specialist departments to one larger municipal organisation.

The DHSS had a mandate to review the use of long term hospital beds and supplement them with alternative provision and this was to increase the role of local authority SSD. At the beginning of the 1970s the Department again projected that PSS would be a growth area, likely to require increased public expenditure funding in the approximate range of 10% real growth per year. Similar to ten years earlier, the collection of statistical information was seen as necessary to continue the facilitation of PESC and the general management of public expenditure. The planning process envisaged was supposed to be more than merely projecting future trends on the basis of current behaviour and Webb and Wistow (1986, p. 100) state that the plans were more analytical and comprehensive in their methodology than the methods used previously.

The post 1972 plans were based on similar quantitative indicators to the earlier plans, but an added emphasis was placed on centre-local dialogue as a process of collaboration. Local authorities' comments and reflection on how capital and revenue targets were to be achieved were welcomed, but by linking the quantitative information required with future block grant negotiations a new centralism and rationing of resources was implied. The central-local tension increased given the oil price rise of 1973 and public expenditure crisis of the mid decade.

The end products of the 1972 planning process were largely quantitative trend projections despite the more analytical typologies the DHSS had sought. For example the Government stated some quite specific trend projections which the DHSS had forecast for the end of the decade and asked authorities to either confirm or deny these. Such figures rested on the assumption that public expenditure for local authority social services would continue to grow at approximately 10% per annum (Hallet, 1982, p. 87). The 1972 plans anticipated the new rational strategic planning of the NHS implemented in the mid 1970s and implied a more centrally directed agenda (Hambleton, 1986, p. 67). This planning for growth was undermine by the restraint on public resources that followed the public expenditure crisis of 1976.

The period 1963 - 1975 is summarised by Webb and Wistow (1986, p. 120) as one of 'demand based planning', a time span when the awareness of demand for care was the primarily drive in service planning. This in effect was need based planning, seeking to find the expenditure to allow services to meet increased social need. The measures of need used were not complex and based on increases in the older age population groups and the supply of standardised service outputs as a method of meeting need (Wistow and Hardy, 1994). The state's planning method was at times restrained by political concerns about public expenditure and even in this more interventionalist period, it was not possible to find all the expenditure requested or required. The emphasis on social need and the context of growth changed fundamentally in the mid 1970s with the Treasury needing to control public expenditure so as to provide the stability required by the market economy.

*Towards the short term planning of the personal social services*

The instability of the economy in the 1970s and the resulting public expenditure crisis led to a revision of planning activity and a new system of three year planning. In June 1977 the DHSS requested that local authorities submit Local Authority Planning Statements (LAPS). These were to specify an authority's likely arrangement of services for the next three year period (Walker, 1984, p 171). The NHS had moved to state publicly its priorities, given criticism of its own internal planning structures. LAPS required that statistical returns based on the 1976 DHSS priorities document were accompanied by a narrative through which the social services department discussed the broader qualitative purpose of it hopes and aspirations (Webb and Wistow, 1986, p. 107).

The creation of the DHSS in 1972 was designed to encourage the development of strategies that could span health and social service boundaries (Hunter and Wistow, 1987, p. 22). This proved difficult to achieve and could not be assured by the structural reorganisation of central government administration (Pollit, 1984). One of the key criticisms of the DHSS structure was that it permitted the innovation of new ideas without the responsibility to implement them (Hunter and Wistow, 1987). Similarly, the policy units within the DHSS continued to operate in isolation, leading to a fragmentation of broad policy. Income maintenance policy failed to be integrated with health and social services policy. As a result of such criticisms a Policy Strategy Unit was established in the early 1980s with the brief to take a departmental overview of policy. But this coincided with a degree of political ambivalence about quantitative national planning for social services.

A more concerted attempt to make progress on the shift of resources from hospitals to community based social care was attempted by Joint Finance in 1976. The Joint Finance scheme encouraged local planning by matching planning agreements with a transfer of money from the National Health Service (NHS) to local authorities, although there were some difficulties with the long term revenue funding of improvements established by such transfers. As indicated below, Joint Finance was important because it gave local joint planning forums a clear financial incentive to produce collaborative planning statements.

## Joint Planning and Finance

Joint Finance was, in effect, a proportion of central government expenditure on the health service which had to be spent on local authority social care services. The use of this money had to be agreed jointly, involving collaboration between Area Health Authorities (AHAs) and local authority social services departments. It was anticipated that services delivered by personal social services as a result would be of relevance to NHS patients and support the movement of such individuals out of long stay hospital beds into local authority care and accommodation. As a social policy mechanism the introduction of joint finance thereby sought to redirect resources rather than increase them.

The 1974 reorganisation of the NHS had, with the exception of London, resulted in co-terminus local authority and Area Health Authority boundaries. Joint Consultative Committees (JCCs) were set up as a result of the new structures. This was beneficial in the non metropolitan counties, but conversely destructive of the informal networks previously established in metropolitan areas of London (Edwards, 1978, p. 21). In 1976, Advisory Joint Care Planning Teams were established to swell the integration of NHS and local authority activity.

Joint Finance was an important policy development in the evolution of community care. It was characterised by an enthusiastic launch from Barbara Castle as Secretary for State for Social Services. It remained as a long term policy that transferred hundreds of millions of pounds of NHS expenditure into the personal social services and relocated resources from hospitals into the community. Although there was a lack of rational planning at its inception it has been consistently reviewed and problems monitored (see for example, House of Commons Social Services Committee, 1982, para. 53-57; House of Commons Social Services Committee, 1985, para. 36-37). One of the main criticisms of Joint Finance is that it distorted general personal social services expenditure because of the government's failure to link joint finance with subsequent rate support grant payments (House of Commons Social Services Committee, 1982, op cit).

The political and incremental launch of the Joint Finance initiative was in contrast to the population needs assessment based rationalism of the early 1970s and the 1963 ten year plan initiative. It represented the beginning of a drift towards supply side planning, implemented by the Labour Government of 1974-1979 because of severe international economic difficulties. Supply side planning is preoccupied with allocating and rationing service provision, as opposed to measuring total need and attempting to increased provision to meet it.

From the mid 1970s forward Webb and Wistow (1986, p. 121-123) define social services planning as based on 'needs-scarcity' rather than demand led. This was a period characterised by very low or nil rates of growth, leading to an emphasis on the internal organisation and administration of social services departments, utilising the voluntary sector, and focusing social work on the most chronic of social circumstances rather than seeking to be universal and preventative.

Central government fears about rising public expenditure diluted the demand led planning typology. Demand for health and social care began to increase rapidly in the 1970s as the proportion of older people in the population grew. Planning became characterised by 'a radical approach to resource reallocation' (op cit, p. 121) whereby efficiency criteria and the identification of priorities began to predominate (Glennerster, 1981).

At the local authority level, corporate planning was used increasingly . This involved the centralised planning of the local authority services through a local authority policy and resources committee and officer based planning unit. Attempts were made to use rational techniques of need analysis. In some areas, more comprehensive methods of analysis were used, such as cost-benefit analysis and the Planning, Programming, Budgeting System (PPBS). These centralised local initiatives meant that social service expenditure had to be rationalised alongside demands for other services in the local community. The increased use of managerial logics of analysis needs to be set in context. The dominant mode of strategic decision making was still political.

> 'The ability of local authorities to allocate resources across departments using methods akin to rational analysis was higher in 1977 than it was in 1974. In other words, one consequence of financial restraint has been to make local authorities somewhat more rational in their approach to budgetary choice. The share of services that go to the social services is a little less the result of political skill than was the case...The dominant mode of analysis remained political.' (Greenwood, 1979, pp. 95-96)

Webb and Wistow (1986, p.184) identified the national political initiative of Joint Finance as a more pragmatic approach to planning when compared to the local government and NHS administrative reorganisations which were based erroneously in their view on 'pure rationality'.

Formal attempts to plan nationally the development of local social services using quantitative measures of growth in client group size and available service outputs, ended with the general election of 1979. The only national planning that remained was the formulation and scrutiny of annual public expenditure documents. A House of Commons Social Services Committee report in 1981 noted the effect of public expenditure based planning on the personal social services and expressed concerns about the narrowness of a public expenditure planning typology. The authors noticed that such a typology gave a lack of attention to the strategic direction and purpose of policy and that the financial indicators used were at times unreliable and invalid (p. xx-xxii). One year later, when commenting on the 1982 Public Expenditure White Paper the committee made broadly similar recommendations (p. xlix-lii). Again in 1985, the Social Services Committee reported: 'we are not entirely happy with the degree of policy guidance from the DHSS to social services authorities' (p. xv). This lack of national policy guidance was contrast with a large scale restructuring within the DHSS of NHS policy management. But the Public Expenditure White Paper methodology for dealing with personal social services had not significantly changed leaving the committee of the view that the figures were 'as misleading as in past years' (op cit). Despite the central responsibility of the financing of the block grant to local government, central government ministers could hide from their planning responsibility by blaming difficulties for local services on the discretion that local government still had to cross subsidise its other local budgets from its social services budget.

In recent years the managing of public expenditure as the central form of social planning has evolved further. Supply planning reached its optimum with the introduction of the Revenue Support Grant (RSG) and Standard Spending Assessment (SSA) in 1991, reducing the flexibility of local taxation and budget subsidy more than any other time in post war history. Local planning had to start with a relatively fixed view of what monetary resources were available for the supply of services and then sought to decide what proportion of demand could be met with this sum. The methodology of the SSA as an instrument of national planning are discussed in detail in chapter 7.

## The Conservative Government of 1979 and Community Care

On its arrival in power in 1979 the Conservative Government removed the national LAPs planning cycle. Some academics saw an opportunity for a fundamental review of the Social Services Act and the difficulties inherited by the new general SSDs. Brewer and Lait (1980) criticised the bureaucratic hierarchy and ambitious expenditure patterns of the new general social services departments. Such allegations of misused resources ignored the inflation of the 1970s decade and the reality of cuts in real funding that had been inflicted on some authorities given changing demographic profiles.

Personal Social Services growth needed to keep pace with the programme of deinstitutionalisation and important democratic changes (Webb and Wistow, 1986, p. 34-37). Deinstitutionalisation was supposed to extract savings from the NHS, but in reality demand for health facilitated by technology and health specific inflation were in themselves major challenges for ministers and the DHSS.

In contrast to a lack of attention being given to population need assessment, demand for services and public expenditure inputs, the Conservative Government of 1979 quickly made some important decisions about the nature of personal social services supply outputs. Growth in the use of the voluntary sector had been a key development in the late 1970s and in the early 1980s service provision was to be encouraged by the private sector. The Government also suggested that the supply of care was sometimes appropriately provided by families and relatives and that it was erroneous to assume that a constant and standardised provision of care by the state was optimal. This introduced the notion of 'care by the community', rather than 'care in the community' and debate followed about whether or not communities and family ties still existed that could take on such responsibilities (Derricot, 1983; Bulmer, 1987).

The DHSS moved to increasingly meet the full costs of care in private homes for those dependent upon state benefits. This incentive for private residential care became the focus of community care for several years, even though it was contested whether or not residential care really was 'community care' or merely an alternative institutional existence (Sharkey and Barna, 1990).

This focusing on institutions rather than community support was maintained by the 1983 Care in the Community initiative (DHSS, 1983) that sought to encourage the run down of large psychiatric hospitals by reassessing Joint Finance and its possible extension. The problem was that local authority planning was dependent on policy decisions taken in hospitals and the health service before personal social service community care developments could take place. Social services policy was still reactive rather than proactive indicating a weakness in the planning of cross-department finance.

The decision by the Department of Health in 1983 to fund and develop a broad range of action research services, including respite and day care, was a small but innovative development (Knapp, et al, 1992). It showed that community care could work if given an adequate profile and resources. However there were some concerns that these new innovative projects were not typical of general developments because they had attracted special focus and status and did not involve those suffering from the most chronic of conditions.

## The Audit Commission

The Audit Commission was part of Mrs Thatcher's strategy to make local government more accountable to central government and the Treasury (Mather, 1989, p. 216; Thatcher, 1983). The Commission was instructed to evaluate current policies and analyse their difficulties, making published reports to government. Its methodology is one of rational managerialism that focuses on the structure and administration of government. It's weakness includes not entering into an interactive peer based dialogue with local government and thereby not helping to facilitate cultural awareness and development from within (Parton,1994).

The Audit Commission evolved from the political concerns of national politicians.

> 'He [Michael Heseltine] brought in the block grant system and grant related expenditure assessments (GREAs), targets, hold back, limits on local authority capital expenditure and the Audit Commission, as well as beginning a general squeeze on the central government grant - all designed to give ratepayers an incentive to think twice before reelecting high-spending councils.' (Margaret Thatcher, 1993, p.643)

Having stated the weakness with the type of evaluative process used by the Audit Commission, its is also necessary to acknowledge that its work has a degree of professional regard from academic researchers and local authorities, it being seen as competent and efficient in its use of quantitative and classical managerial methods (Davies, 1994, pp. 202-203).

In 1986 the Audit Commission published a major evaluation of community care entitled 'Making a Reality of Community Care'. It was critical in approach attacking both the local government corporate centralism and rigid bureaucracy found by the team of enquiry: 'Successful local schemes have only been possible because local people have in effect ignored the existing rules and taken radical action', (p. 65) and: 'centralised planning arrangements in a range of different agencies do not allow the necessary degree of flexibility and local delegation required for schemes to operate effectively' (p.73).

The report commented that bureaucracy had become dysfunctional because the services needed by users were not provided and instead inappropriate outputs were over produced. This implied a lack of ability to develop new innovative services and a tendency to provide standardised outputs. 'It will be unkind even to discuss the concept that the existing bureaucracies within the public service should focus on action. They usually exist to ensure fairness, to prevent mistakes and to see that rules are followed' (Audit Commission, 1986, p. 73).

In difficult policy environments, bureaucrats can seek 'personal convenience' rather than status and ambition (Self, 1993, p. 32). This is particularly likely where policy is fragmented and poorly planned, and the responsibilities between central and local government unclear. The Commission was also critical of the committee based political structure of PSS in local government, suggesting that the traditional method of local government political accountability was not resulting in service users getting a diversity and quality of service provision.

> 'The public service is generally suspicious of personal leadership by officers. Members often feel threatened by it; committee-based consensus is the norm, particularly in local authority social services departments. In most cases, champions of change are likely to be regarded as "difficult" mavericks, to be controlled rather than encouraged.' (op cit, p. 80)

Evident in the Audit Commission's 1986 report is a manifestation of distrust with the traditional political-administrative hierarchy in local government. The analysis ignores the possible disadvantages of removing political accountability from service supply. It prefers an explanation that is sympathetic to the ideas of new public managerialism (NPM) and the increased use of market logics in the operation of public policy. The report's strongest allegiance is to strategic management solutions, via planning, this reflected in three of its seven main recommendations (1986, p. 3 and 4).

The report was less resolute in its language towards the market. The movement of government monies into direct cash transfers for the user are not mentioned, but in perpetuating the argument for an economic clarity and a more individualised consumer rationality the report embodies elements of a market logic: 'a more rational way of arranging services would be for one agency to take lead responsibility and to buy in services as necessary' (1986, p. 74).

The report suggests that monetary incentive systems are a key means of improving service delivery and accountability, these methods being preferred to readjusting the processes of large hierarchical and monopolistic organisations.

This language of market incentives predated the Audit Commission and had already become part of the post 1979 public sector culture. Early in its term of office, the Conservative Government of 1979 had loosened DHSS controls on welfare benefits that could be paid to private residential homes, a policy action to encourage the marketisation of social care. This resulted in an inefficient national policy criticised by the 1986 report. The fact that community care benefits such as attendance allowance were less generous and more rigorously rationed became known as the 'perverse incentive' (Audit Commission, 1986, p. 44).

This 'perverse incentive' resulted in commentators arguing for an adequate competing funding arrangement that subsidised informal domiciliary community care. Frank Field, MP, has argued for a carer's pension, Jordan (1990) for a basic income that recognises looking after dependents and Davies (1993a) for a means tested, but locally administered, flexible transfer payment. The 1996 Community Care Direct Payments Act goes some way to recognising Davies' recommendation, but it will not be payable to resident family carers, or available to those over 65.

After 15 years of the private residential care subsidy social security expenditure on residential care had grown exponentially from almost nil to over £1 billion (Department of Health, 1989, p. 3). It was the highlighting of this 'perverse incentive' for which the Audit Commission's 1986 report is best known, but it was the later Griffiths review (1988) that was to succeed in fully illuminating the degree of policy fragmentation. This subsequent review was proposed by the 1986 report, the text having shown the distortion and mismanagement that health, social service department, national and local administrations were presiding over.

The Audit Commission's diagnosis as to why policy had failed was to highlight the dysfunction of local politics, bureaucracy and administration, rather than to focus on the possible distortions of restricted welfare markets. This was despite the discovery of a 'perverse incentive' for private residential homes. The 'perverse incentive' was not strictly speaking a market distortion, rather a political one. It resulted when DHSS social security policy worked independently of local authority expenditure. Davies (1993b, p. 13), quoting Hansard, suggests that the policy was politically driven, resulting from the government's ideological determination to spend on services in the private sector rather than the public. This failure of ministers to consider the implications of this conviction was not evaluated by the Audit Commission because the inspectorate had to focus predominantly on local government activity.

A political analyst would see the situation rather differently. Politicians come under brokerage pressure from relatives who feel unable to look after their kin and also from business interests in residential homes. For public choice theorists, these political distortions are as equally significant to policy failures as bureaucratic deviations (Self, 1993; McLean, 1987). This illustrates one of the key tensions in public sector planning. How can policy strategy be linked with public accountability? At what point does consumer choice have to be checked by local political voting, or managerial consultation with consumers? This tension has been described as the point at which 'exit' gives way to 'voice', to quote Hirschman (1970). How can the behaviours of consuming, consultation and voting interact to manage the distortions of political, managerial and market systems?

*Political-strategic developments*

By the mid 1980s some of the previous political ambivalence towards community care was changing. 'Over the 1980s, in part a consequence of the emphasis at the start of the decade, community care moved from a loosely-formulated professional concern to an ever-present item on the political, public policy and administrative agenda' (Knapp, et al, 1992, p. 4).

Davies (1993b, p. 34) discusses the important political motivation that was evident in the 1980s, he makes the distinction between 'breakthrough politics' and 'technical politics'. For Davies the technical politics of policy revision and evolution are as important for long term development once that break through politics have made their initial impact.

*The Griffiths Report*

It was Norman Fowler, who in 1986 as Secretary of State for Social Services commissioned the review recommended by the Audit Commission (1986). The late Sir Roy Griffiths formerly with Sainsburys PLC was requested to undertake the review. He appointed eight advisors and did not take formal evidence. Means and Smith (1994, p. 53) have summarised four main themes of the resulting report published in 1988.

Firstly it found no link between community care policy objectives and resource allocation. Secondly it confirmed there was no coordination of policy between agencies at a local level (to which could also be added Griffiths was critical of coordination at the central-local level). Thirdly, a mixed market of public, voluntary and private supply was encouraged. And finally, financial means testing for private rest homes was considered inefficient if actual need for residential care was not also measured. On this last point the report continued to pursue the Audit Commissions' concern with the 'perverse incentive' (1994, p. 53).

Given this confirmation of policy fragmentation and a lack of planned direction Griffiths set some key recommendations about how a policy strategy could develop, he proposing a structure that he believed would deliver political enthusiasm, managerial efficiency and market logic.

His concern with the national inefficiencies of process is demonstrated by a comment early in the report.

'The problem is compounded by the responsibilities for inputs to community care at the centre being divided between the two arms of the DHSS, the Social Security and the Health and Personal Social Services sides, and the Department for the Environment - a feeling that community care is a poor relation; everybody's distant relative but nobody's baby.' (Griffiths, 1988, p. iv)

To maintain more political interest and ensure an enduring central strategy he proposed the introduction of a Minister for Community Care with a designated team of civil servants dedicated to a policy overview (op cit, p. 16). In the event, since the publication of the report, the large DHSS was split, and although a notional undersecretary of State in the new Department of Health was appointed for community care they did not have the kind of policy overview, extending into other government departments that was needed. In effect the separation of the Department of Social Security (DSS), although perhaps necessary through growth in public expenditure on welfare benefits, has further undermined government attempts to deliver a coordinated fiscal policy towards community based social care.

It is one of the disappointments of community care implementation that political-strategic planning at the centre has not followed-up the opportunities presented by Griffiths. This is partly because of political resistance to his suggestion of an enhanced role of local authorities and fear in the Treasury about any restructuring of central government ministries into a system that might make the hierarchical control of public expenditure more difficult. In any event the opportunity to establish a heterarchical planning process that could combine political and bureaucratic energies across central and local government was partly lost. Central government had failed to develop a system of policy management that worked across a matrix of departments and created new activity patches between traditional systems.

*Political logic prevails*

The compromise that followed was symptomatic of a central political ambivalence. In accordance with Griffiths' suggestion, local authority SSDs were given the lead role in organising and coordinating local care planning and enabling market provision. This recommendation was politically difficult for the Government given its policy of reducing local government power and expenditure in the 1980s. There were political problems with the local poll tax at the time of Griffiths' publication and a continuing desire to keep local authority expenditure to a minimum so as to control total public expenditure levels (Stoker,1991; Thatcher, 1993).

By increasing local government discretion over community care services, central government could distance itself from any future problems that might emerge during implementation (Fimister and Hill, 1993). Here lay some political safety as community care was going to be a difficult programme by which to win votes given increasing demographic pressure and growing demands for services.

By proceeding with the localisation of community care policy the government was partly disassociating itself from future responsibilities, especially at a time when its own public finances were in difficulty due to an economic recession. The resulting legislation put much emphasise on the development of a local planning process rather than a national process.

*Griffiths and market logics*

Sir Roy Griffiths background was in the private sector and the language of the report is unsympathetic to any notion of singular, monopolistic provision of services by the state. The report proposed expanding the already existent 'mixed economy of care' (1988, p. 5). In this sense the report is broadly market orientated and it specifies that a market machinery is needed to check the inefficiencies of political and public sector bureaucracy. His suspicion of large forms of political- bureaucratic hierarchy is similar to public choice theorists and is confirmed by a number of quotations in the report.

> 'In general Social Services Authority activities tend to be dominated by the direct management of services which take insufficient account of the varying needs of individuals.' (p. 8)

> 'Some things are fundamental, and in particular the creation of a budgetary

approach, centrally and locally, which aligns responsibility for achieving objectives with control over the resources needed to achieve them, so that there is a built in incentive and the facility to make the best use of resources available.' (p. 11)

His mention of objectives in the context of 'means' and 'ends' is synonymous with rational theories of management, planning and decision making.

## From political vision to devolved management

In the mid 1990s, planning in PSS was built on a local model as suggested by Griffiths. But Griffiths' discussion of planning also related to national government activity. He had as much to say about national planning as he did about local plans. In paragraph 5.7 he lists in some detail the organisational process that he recommends for both local and national planning and management. He concludes (p. 11): 'the absence of such a process at national level is inconsistent with any claim that there are serious national policy objectives to be achieved. Such a system should be an integral part of the central decision making and management process.'

The report criticised the financial instability of local authority social services departments due to the methodology of central government grant allocation (p. 12-13). Some clear guidance was made about how central government should plan and allocate financial resources through a specific community care grant (p. 17). This guidance came at a time when the central-local block grant was being reviewed, later to be replaced by the SSA (Standard Spending Assessment) and RSG (Revenue Support Grant). The SSA local authority expenditure system, with the focus on the composite block grant and a combined services local authority TSA (Total Spending Assessment) is incompatible with specific grants for individual service areas. Although individual SSAs are calculated for specific service areas like PSS, these individual service SSAs are for policy guidance and not singularly enforceable.

The Government delivered a budgetary compromise. The NHS and Community Care Act 1990, was implemented with a time limited Special Transitional Grant (STG), although the SSA assessment and RSG allocation constituted the majority of local authority expenditure on social care. In later years the calculation of STG has also been tied to the PSS SSA, and the grant has remained in use longer than was intended originally.

Griffiths was more independent than the Audit Commission and this allowed him the scope to be critical of the lack of political strategic will to drive a national policy strategy forward (Davies, 1994, pp. 197-198). His approach reflects the reality of the three overlapping planning systems defined in chapter one, with his arguing for devolved market and managerial logics under a clearer central political umbrella. His exact vision of the planning role for local politicians is unclear.

*The local needs based planning typology*

For Griffiths, local and central planning was to be co-terminus, but if still alive today he would be disappointed with the disproportionate focus now placed on planning at a local level. Authorities produce highly presentable glossy products having spent thousands of pounds consulting and designing them. What remains unclear and a central issue for this book is what kind of planning results and how effective it is.

On local plans Griffiths (p. 18) made the following observations.

'As a condition for the payment of specific grant I recommend that social services authorities should prepare plans with costed objectives and timetables for implementation which demonstrate their approach to the delivery of community care in their areas, and the adequacy of their management systems. The plans should show that local activity has been well thought through in relation to local needs and that what is planned represents value for money. They should also give evidence of the support given to voluntary groups and their involvement in the preparation of the plan, as well as showing how informal carers are being supported. Importantly plans should also demonstrate that systems for joint planning and action exist and that the other relevant agencies, particularly health and housing authorities are content with the proposals for action. Progress against past objectives should also be reported.'

The reference to the importance of objectives can be linked to rational models of organisational decision making and managerialism. The financial emphasis on value for money and his reference to the involvement of community groups can be seen as introducing consumer and voice accountability, these two methods offering an alternative to the simple traditional political voting accountability mechanism in local government. Overall his planning model is constructed around a state-managerial system, rather than being located in a system that is primarily political or market driven.

What Griffiths failed to articulate, however, was the difficult area of quantifying needs, given that interpretations of need vary and depend to a large extend on conflicting social and cultural perspectives. Need defies easy objective quantification (Bradshaw, 1972; Forder, 1974). In reality the definition of need used by the subsequent NHS and Community Care Act 1990 Guidance was broad, encouraging access to both user base qualitative subjective assessments and quantitative statistical indicators (Department of Health, 1993a). What does remain contentious is not whether user's subjective accounts of their needs are on the national and local planning agenda, but are they listened to and converted into resource decisions (Goss and Miller, 1995)? A method of listening to users that relies on public managerial consultation, rather than local government political representation, still has the problem of identifying a democratic method for synthesising a collection of needs into a corporate policy that articulates budget priorities. The process by which a community seeks to understand its own needs, and debates competing priorities, is activity that has more in common with the culture of a political system rather than a managerial one (Kouzes and Mico, 1979; Kakabadse, 1982). Issues of representation are vital to address (Jeffrey, 1997). For the actors involved, skills of debate, brokerage and leadership become central.

## Caring for People

Once the Government had made its decision to act on the Griffiths report, a White Paper entitled 'Caring for People' was published (Department of Health, 1989). It sought further clarification of the method of planning to be implemented by local authorities. The White Paper stated in paragraph 5.6 (p. 41) that plans should set an agenda by which performance can be monitored. This was similar to Griffiths' suggestion. The practice of using plans to evaluate performance was undermine by the climate of central-local conflict that followed the implementation of SSAs and RSG capping formula. Some local authorities avoided stating clear output objectives, that were measurable at a later date, for fear of repercussions if they failed to deliver.

Plans are supposed to provide evidence that local authorities are implementing policy as required by central government. Plans should enable social services to 'organise their move away from the role of exclusive service provider to that of service arranger and procurer' (p. 42, paragraph 5.6). The logic of marketisation is explicit here. Plans became a managerial tool for implementing increased marketisation.

The White Paper established 1st April, 1991, as the date by which the first local plans would be published. This had to be delayed until April 1992. Some local authorities began experimenting with a proposed planning methodology before this date (Means and Smith, 1994, p. 91). 'Caring for People' prescribed what was expected to be contained in the first annual plans. It was envisaged that each yearly document would focus on a three year strategy (p. 42, para. 5.10). Thirteen detailed points were listed relating to the content of the first plans. These can be summarised as: an initial needs assessment with comment on how it could be developed in the future; local objectives stated and related to national criteria; a demonstration of the workings of the new purchaser provider split with reference to individual assessment, discussion of case management and budgetary strategy; and finally, an indication of how quality would be assured and standards regulated. Output objectives were recommended. The White Paper requested general statements of strategic policy from social services departments rather than specific details of operational intentions.

'Caring for People' was less prescriptive than Griffiths about the extent to which Health Authorities should plan and coordinate their work with SSD, although the theme of collaboration remained high on the agenda. The political-strategic responsibilities of national government were largely ignored by the report, but the managerial and market logics of the text were broadly similar to Griffiths. The divergence from Griffiths was in the blending of logics, with there being more emphasis in the White Paper on the ability of local voluntary organisations and private bodies to achieve efficient policy output.

## The NHS and Community Care Act 1990

The NHS and Community Care Act 1990 made the publication of local plans by local authorities a statutory duty and institutionalised the requirement for plans to be profoundly linked to user feed-back. Section 46, subsection 2, required that user groups and carer groups be consulted during the formulation of plans. Local authorities must consult:

> 'such voluntary organisation as appear to the authority to represent the interests of persons who use or are likely to use any community care services within the area of the authority or the interests of private carers who, within that area, provide care to persons whom, in he exercise of their social services functions, the local authority have a power or a duty to provide a service.' (House of Commons, 1990, p. 55).

The decision to include reference to user groups in the actual legislation can be seen as endorsing two possible lines of accountability and participation within the new policy environment. The move to increase consumer choice and market provision is an example of public choice's belief in market solutions, with it confirming supposedly 'exit' empowerment to users (Hirshman, 1970). The logic implied is that consumers move to another service if the first is not satisfactory. The inclusion of a requirement for verbal consultation with users in the legislation concedes the imperfections of the market's ability to always deliver an exit choice and seeks to facilitate a means by which authorities can make the less competitive areas of service delivery more accountable to actual consumer opinion, especially where a public monopoly is still in existence.

Despite the inclusion of a 'voice' alternative in the writing of the community care legislation, Glendinning and Bewley (1992) reported that only 16% of the first annual plans clearly consulted user groups. These concerns continued when the House of Commons Health Select Committee (1993a) evaluated the success or otherwise of community care implementation. As one witness, representing carers, said to the committee: 'the consultation process is only a means to an end. I think we are quite concerned at the moment that the consultation process is being seen as an end in itself by some people who are organising it' (Ms Pitkeathley, The National Association of Carers, giving evidence to the House of Commons Health Committee, House of Commons Health Committee, 1993b, p. 166, para. 518).

Both the White Paper and the 1990 Act established a planning system for personal social services, based on maximising the utilisation of management systems and stimulating the activity of the local social care market. Similar to the earlier Audit Commission work, there was an avoidance of national political responsibilities and the reality of how political systems create the culture, vision and momentum of strategic policy programmes.

This has resulted in an unrealistic focus on the ability of local authorities to plan and deliver services. What is generally ignored, especially by the 1990 Act and the White Paper, are central political and macro-economic contingencies. National policies on taxation, regulation, means-testing and benefit levels have considerable influence on the demand side of the social care market, as discussed in chapter 5, and these factors need clear national planning if differences between theoretical need and actual demand expressed are to be reconciled. These are national realities managed by Cabinet meetings and Treasury officials and kept out of the jurisdiction of local planners, with the implication that the local planning system might become based on idealism and illusory planning. Also plans might become rather stale documents, produced because of the requirement in law, but produced by local councillors and managers who see them as insignificant in a landscape where local authority expenditure is limited and market allocation of resources difficult to regulate. Griffiths (1988) openly exposed what he called the 'unmentionables' with his comments about the need for ministerial vision (by implication the Cabinet) and adequate central expenditure, but subsequent government texts did not address these substantive points.

A logic for community care planning was emerging in the early 1990s, albeit based on an economy of logic. The new planning process can be described as a modification of earlier rational-strategic planning types, with it being based on a strong commitment to goals and objectives. Hudson has proposed that Community Care Planning is a shift from incrementalism to a new form of rationalism. He (1992, p. 190) emphasises the organisational comprehensiveness of the system developed with numerous requirements being listed by the various statutes, policy guidance and review documentation: 'these requirements constitute a major challenge to all purchasing and providing agencies involved in community care, and seem to foreshadow a shift away from an incrementalist towards a rationalist model of policy making.'

But Hudson is not explicit about what predominate form of rationality or logic he thinks was influential. There is little evidence in the research in the next chapter that this planning rationality was characterised by a new belief in managerial technocratic and managerial scientific applications, such as a rigorous analytical requirement that many details and options should be considered. Rather the driving logic was the central government belief that the organisation of the social care sector, and public and merit goods provided by the local authority, should be exposed increasingly to market principles. The increased use of market criteria and market exposure were promoted as the logic to reconcile needs based planning with a diversity of supply outputs that apparently offered choice, efficiency and quality. The marketisation of service supply was the driving logic behind the policy reforms.

In an early overview of how community care planning might evolve to support the 'Caring for People' vision of an enhanced mixed economy, Wistow (1990, para. 5.6) proposed the following objectives for the planning task. Firstly that values underpinning policy should be clarified; secondly that objectives should then be established on these values; and thirdly that demand for services should be identified by an assessment of need. Fourth, that there should be an audit of current provision. Fifth, planning should stimulate a rolling programme of three year priorities and targets. Sixth, authorities should establish contract specifications. Seven, empirical performance reviews should take place. And finally, values should be reviewed against operational experience and changes in demand. Wistow's analysis is reminiscent of 1970s rational planning and similar to the rational-central process of policy decision making documented in the mid 1980s (Hogwood and Gunn, 1984; Kickert, Kiljn and Koppenjan, 1997). It also draws implicitly on the strategic literature and models developed for business in the 1980s (Bryson and Einsweiler, 1988). Similar to Hudson's evaluation of developments, Wistow's analysis suggests that the new CCP system was presenting an opportunity for a return to more rational managerial methods. Wistow's discussion is somewhat isolated from the politicising of governments, councillors and user groups. It does show some limited awareness of the political system, given that its beginning and end point are essentially linked to a value base and participatory process. These are patches in a planning process where a managerial system can be linked directly with political activity. What is needed is a recognition of system complexity, rather than a drift back to the old rational-central model. In later writing, Wistow and Hardy (1994) appear to give more credence to the political-strategic element of community care planning and the need for political strategy to be more integrated with managerial analysis.

*The Price Waterhouse consultancy*

In an effort to contribute to the quality of the new local plans, the Department of Health commissioned Price Waterhouse to work with them in the writing of a good practice guide on population needs assessment (Department of Health, 1993a). This document defines population needs assessment as the starting point of strategic planning (p. 1). Mintzberg (1994c) has referred to this kind of 'analysis for strategy' as 'strategic programming'.

The document gives comprehensive guidance about ways in which initial planning information can be gathered from secondary sources, such as the 1991 census, prior to a local authority being able to establish its own data base generated by actual processed individual assessments. In any event, secondary information would have to be balanced against population needs, so that some perception of unmet need could be predicted. In recognising the importance of an operational definition of need the report made the following proposal: 'need is defined as the ability of an individual or collection of individuals to benefit from care' (Department of Health, 1993a, p. 6, para. 16).

From this definition population needs assessment is said to be:

'estimating, projecting and categorising the needs of a local population'(op cit). Although the tone of the report is predominately based on a quantitative approach, the consultancy also acknowledges the importance of using calculations in an inclusive and dynamic process that is constantly reviewed and incorporates the local communities views and perspective. The methodology is less clearly linked to market indicators of demand and supply. The consultation document made few suggestions about the inclusion of financial and costing information in the planning process. The work of the consultancy was an early attempt to prevent the new planning systems delivering a fragmented analysis and the planning guidance persisted with a relatively safe form of underpinning quantitative logic. In addition, qualitative discussion with users and carers was seen as imperative, as laid down by the new statute.

## The first plans, April 1992

The first local plans to be published in 1992 followed a simplified structure and purpose. Summarising the Department of Health's guidance on community care plans (Department of Health,1990) Hardy, Wistow and Leedham (1993, pp. 2-3) conclude that there were four central government requirements for the first community care plans, these being: preparation and publication; consultation; joint ownership; and public accessibility. As a result of these priorities initial content research by the authors showed the early plans were weak on forward planning and tended to be descriptive statements of values, general purpose and available services. Returning to Griffith's criteria (1988, p. 18) the plans fell short on proactive strategic planning that discussed costed objectives and timetables.

The first evaluation (Wistow, Leedham and Hardy, 1993) analysed 22 social service department plans. Although half of the sample identified priorities across services only two attached costing. One example was Wandsworth that attached costing to 40 service targets for the financial year in question (op cit, p. 15). Few authorities made reference to the internal resource implications of proposed developments. Most authorities did make crude estimates of need using the 1981 census.

The London borough of Sutton had attempted a qualitative assessment of need based on users and carers accounts in addition to some innovation with quantitative figures (op cit, p. 17). There was a reluctance from authorities to use secondary data for forecasting future need. Three exceptions were Islington, Cambridgeshire and Cornwall. Cambridgeshire demonstrated a degree of sophistication in its forecast, using the census, the 1988 OPCS Disability Study and the General Household Survey alongside local studies (op cit, p. 18).

Whilst some limited work had been done on demand assessment, no work was evident to establish a forecast of future supply. Some listing of present output resources was evident, but this varied greatly between the plans studied. It might be argued that this was an easier task in 1992, given that local authorities were still providing much of the supply themselves, prior to the transfer of DSS monies for residential care. The event of national government transferring social security monies to local authorities for the purchase of independent residential beds raised significant further challenges to understanding the supply side.

As regards the development of a mixed economy little detail was available about what was to be expected for contracting arrangements. Cambridgeshire was an exception, 'detailing the key components of contracting arrangements - both service specifications and service level agreements - and also the criteria by which providers were assessed' (op cit, p. 22). There was no general evidence in plans of an agreed joint policy with health authorities on hospital discharge and the related use of nursing homes.

Wistow et al concluded their review by stating that the priority aims of government were being met in some form, although it was difficult to gauge to what extent this was more than cosmetic. Nevertheless the prioritisation of consultation and making surface information available had distracted from economic market planning in the spirit of the Griffiths and 'Caring for People' reforms (p. 31). In particular explicit costed purchasing strategies were absent and there was no real sense of how local authorities were going to evolve from the previous decade's emphasis on providing the supply of domiciliary and residential care to a more open purchasing policy.

*The second annual round of plans and planning*

Although planning and coordination at a national level were ignored there continued a national monitoring of local attempts to cope. In 1992 the Department of Health (1992a) issued further guidance to local authorities about the content of their community care plans for 1993-1994. Ten specific items of information were requested: details of planned service developments; details of resources to be devoted to community care in 1993-1994; details of arrangements for individual need assessments; details of arrangements for purchasing residential and nursing home care; details of authorities' charging policies; details of arrangements between local authorities and health authorities; indication of how GP fund holding responsibilities have been taken into account; details of agreements with housing associations; explanation of how client choice will be achieved; details of how information will be given to local service users and carers.

In an evaluation of the second cohort of CCPs that followed this guidance, Hardy, Wistow and Leedham (1993, p.66) found that the response to the Department's requirements was variable, especially in terms of the amount of detail given. The evaluation concluded: 'authorities must have a clear view of the changed planning context and, in particular, see the essential planning purpose as being to shape and manage a market. At present...few plans have been prepared with this core task in mind.'

The Audit Commission continue to be involved in monitoring. A report 'The Community Revolution' (1992) focused on the 'information deficit' experienced by local authorities and urged that resources should be devoted to developing financial and population information adequate to the task of achieving strategic planning and market intervention.

The later Commission's document, 'Managing the Cascades of Change' (1993) repeated the need for needs assessment to be a firm foundation for developing good purchasing strategies and solid management practices. The document made conceptual planning links between: needs based assessment, managerial efficiency, and criteria for markets to operate on, namely the requirement for sophisticated costing that informs budgets.

Again the logic of managerialism and scientific quantitative measurement is dominant, but the geographical organisational focus is consistently on local authorities rather than central government. This continued disengaging of responsibility from the centre was an anxiety expressed by one of the first independent evaluations of the process. Reporting on the delays to implementation and lack of central government policy structure, Henwood, Jowell and Wistow (1991, p.4) stated: 'The result is altogether a weaker structure which both reduces the capacity of central government to steer local developments, whilst also distancing its direct responsibilities for such action.'

Much of the monitoring supported by the Audit Commission and the Department of Health failed to note the reality that there was little incentive for local authorities to develop highly sophisticated needs assessment methodologies if they did not have the resources to meet many of the needs that might be identified.

*A return to rational local planning?*

The lack of policy coordination and planning at a national level has reinforced a local managerial model with central government apparently seeking to de-politicise community care planning and expenditure (Fimister and Hill, 1993).

A number of authorities began to develop the needs assessment and strategic financial planning that was intended by the reforms. For this to be possible, clear links between needs and costs had to be made and the problematic area of developing a science of unit costing began. One such development was Gloucestershire's computer system designed in cooperation with the Social Services Research and Development Unit at the University of Bath (Wright and Kerslake, 1994). This programme linked population needs assessment with local costed examples and thereby predicted the total cost of meeting local need. Planners could manipulate and align the supply side of the model to assist with different planning scenarios.

A more recent project on needs based planning by the PSSRU (Personal Social Services Research Unit) at the University of Kent uses a more sophisticated methodology and has some more direct links with supply side actualities (Bebbington, Turvey and Janson, 1996). The research was operationalised in partnership with Surrey SSD and includes reconciling population based secondary data with local surveys of users requirements and supply side trends. Local definitions of service need are then costed. The result is a comprehensive quantitative approach to local needs analysis that is able to indicate high levels of unmet need in the locality, in addition to identifying current demand for different types of care, different sub locality scenarios, and likely rising demand over time.

The linking of population needs based assessment with costing is an important evolution in the new local community care planning typology but it will not represent market planning in its fullest sense until it is linked with clear attempts to change the supply side. An example of such a strategic implication is the closure of homes when there is over supply, instead shifting resources to an area of under supply.

There remain question marks over the ability of the new CCP process to find an integration of demand and supply planning. Hudson (1992, p. 185) says of the local personal social services community care planning process launched in 1992: 'this constitutes both an important policy development and a paradoxical ideological shift, for it seems to herald a degree of state intervention which would not normally be associated with a New Right approach to social policy.'

But it is necessary to distinguish government planning activity that attempts to facilitate and stimulate market provision of supply from planning that questions the ability of the market to provide market access and seeks a long term growth in public expenditure to facilitate demand. As an overall strategy the recent national government activity is incremental and designed to get the best compromise from incremental short term adjustments in public expenditure. This adjustment process works alongside the institution of a new local managerial system that encourages market methods of allocation and supply.

This process raises fundamental questions about the nature of the new PSS planning system. Wistow and Hardy (1994, p.55) state that: 'such questions lead us back to the very issues about the respective roles of central and local agencies...Such issues are inherently political, not technical.'

*Consultation and strategic ownership of the local plans*

One characteristic of the new planning system is a form of user consultation based on Hirschman's (1970) model of 'voice' feed back. This introduces a 'new politics' to local authorities, whereby accountability to specific policy areas and services is seen as preferable to the traditional democratic accountability of pluralist pressures being exerted on local councillors. Community care is not alone in facing this new consumerist brand of local politics. Housing policy, for example, had adapted to it earlier with the introduction of 'Tenants' Choice' and 'Housing Action Trusts'. While the community care planning process has to establish arenas and structures whereby the user's voice is heard, there is still disagreement on whether this translates into the real power for service users to influence decisions about services and resources. The research literature on the use of managerial consultation in community care planning (Glendinning and Bewley, 1992; Ellis, 1993; Martin and Gaster, 1993; Hoyes, et al, 1993; Bewley and Glendinning, 1994; Goss and Miller, 1995) casts doubt on how much participant's do influence policy strategy.

In his discussion of the newly emerging rational planning system in PSS, Hudson (1992) appears to assume that the evolving managerial activity and logic were not necessarily in contradiction with the requirements of a public participation process. But if managers are increasingly taking the strategic decisions about the purchasing of market services in isolation, is Hudson's optimism justified? The problem remains that the culture of managerialism and managerial consultation may not be sufficient to empower, articulate and synthesise the 'political' concerns of user groups and other social care sector interests. These issues have historically been channelled through a representative process which the local political system and culture are more used to dealing with than the management domain (Kouzes and Mico,1979; Kakabadse, 1982).

## Conclusion

This chapter has discussed the emergence of a new typology of planning and plan production in social service departments during the 1990s. The new typology is different from earlier pre 1979 planning models. There is now more focus on the local context. Previous exercises sought to plan the local social care system in a national context and placed national standardisation and area comparability high on the agenda. The implementation of the new typology is driven more by local actors than those at the centre. Nevertheless the actors who brought the typology into existence were predominantly centrally based: elites and officials who reviewed national policy, and national politicians and ministers who established a local planning structure in a national statute and subsequent policy guidance.

The new typology of CCPs and planning is more complex that the relative simplistic social services planning methods of the 1960s and 1970s. This is partly related to a new local policy environment that has had to move increasingly into a market system. This has led to key changes in the system of state management. The focus for state managers has shifted gradually from organisational and administrative logics to ideas based on market managerialism (Hood, 1991; Clarke, Cochrane and McLaughlin, 1993; Walsh, 1995).

Inevitably there is increasing overlap between state managerialism and the market system as patches of activity develop that are influenced by both state and market actors, for example the negotiation of contracts. Similarly, it is impossible to completely dislocate the activities and institutions of political actors from these places. The political system inevitably has overlapping patches with state managerialism and market operations. But in relation to the patch of inter-system activity now called community care planning, national political actors are noted by their absence. Similarly local political actors only have a limited input.

It is argued that the patch of systems activity now known as community care planning is occupied predominantly by state managers and to a lesser extent by market suppliers and users. Politicians, both local and national, are rather remote from the new local planning network. The occupation of planning activity by certain actors over others can be shown to relate to underlying shifts in social logics. Of greatest influence here is the central political project of 'marketisation' that results in a greater diversity of the supply of services. This has increased the importance of new mangerialist, or NPM logics in local authorities.

The chapter finishes with a hypothetical diagram (Figure 3.1) of where community care planning activity is situated and the book validates this model by analysing the content of CCPs in chapter 4. Figure 3.1 shows a configuration of logics that underpin inter-system CCP activity. The dominant system that initiates planning activity is central politics through which the defining legislation has passed. The logic of marketisation and new managerialism emerge as important defining themes. These themes are more loosely related to a belief that the increased role of managers and markets create a more minimal form of direct government and representative democracy. The local state management system becomes the dominant system in the actual process of implementation. This system has to: enable the market, consult with users and allocate subsidy. These logics require an increasing dialogue with the market place about the appropriate use of the price mechanism and the creation of supply competition that ideally gives users opportunities to choose as consumers. This new pattern of interaction begins to supersede the traditional local government administrative system of professional and client based interaction.

Service users negotiate access to CCP activities in three ways. Firstly, as users through the managerial consultation process; secondly, as consumers through the market process, and thirdly, as voters and campaigners in the local political process. It is in the last two of these roles that users have less clear and direct access to the CCP process.

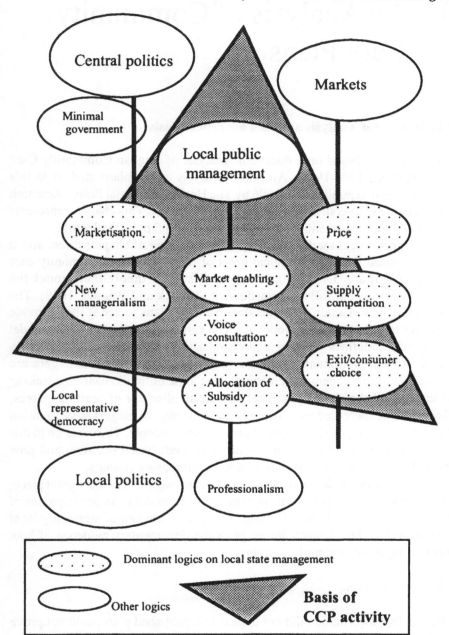

**Figure 3.1    Systems and logics, and the location of community care planning activity**

# 4   An Analysis of Community Care Plans

## The Document Analysis and its Theoretical Basis

This chapter is based on a document analysis of English Community Care Plans (CCPs), 1994-1995. An initial analysis of the plans studied in this chapter was first published in 1996 by The Health and Social Policy Research Centre at the University of Brighton (Haynes, 1996). This chapter represents a later and more substantial analysis than the initial published work.

A theoretical model was proposed at the end of chapter three and it conceptualised the current logical basis of local authority community care planning (Figure 3.1). By starting with such a theoretical model the methodology which follows is deductive (Tullock and Wagner, 1978). The research in this chapter examines documentary plans to see if they provide evidence that the proposed model of social care planning is valid. The model in Figure 3.1 defines social care planning activity as a structure and process carried-out predominantly by state managers. Local state managers are hypothesised to be operating planning to the logic of 'marketisation', seeking to understand the use of price and cost as an allocator of scare resources, alongside the increased use of supply competition. Managers have to ration the state financing of the supply of care to poorer people. The research in this chapter examines the development of local needs based planning and how this is linked to the development of a local purchasing strategy.

Alongside the demand and supply side management of the market place, social services managerialism is engaged in extending the participation of the local community in the planning process with the aim of increasing local accountability. This chapter investigates the documentary evidence of how this participatory process is evolving.

### Plans and planning

The fact that information did not appear in a published plan could not prove conclusively that such information had not been gathered or considered by the Local Authority. There is a danger that an authority might be criticised here for not planning, based on a lack of evidence in the published plan, when it has been carrying out planning activities, but has chosen not to publish certain details. There are clear methodological problems with relying solely on published annual plans as statements of planning activity, but it is proposed that published plans will bear some resemblance to planning activity.

*Methodology*

This research selected a sample of care plans for the third year of operation of the policy (1994-1995) that required local authorities to publish plans (NHS and Community Care Act 1990). All shire counties in the central and south of England were approached as were all inner and outer London boroughs in the southern half of London. In total 29 were approached for a plan and 14 responded. This left a sample of five shire counties, seven outer London boroughs and two inner London boroughs. The social services department CCPs studied were from: Bexley, Bromley, Croydon, East Sussex, Greenwich, Isle of Wright, Kensington and Chelsea, Kent, Kingston, Richmond, Southwark, Surrey, Wiltshire, West Sussex.

Substantial sections of the text, and summaries of text, from these documents were entered into the qualitative data analysis computer software, NUD@IST (Non-numerical Unstructured Data Indexing, Searching and Theorising) so that the text could be scanned systematically for reoccurring words and phrases.

In the methodological literature (Carney, 1973; Krippenddorff, 1980; Robson, 1993; Atkinson and Coffey, 1997; Prior, 1997; Hastings, 1998) five key factors are identified as being important when analysing official documents:

(i) the organisational history and context of the production of the documents in question, the relationship of the document with other documents;
(ii) the linguistic style and format and content of the document;
(iii) the document as a source of statement about its organisation authors, its dominant actors and their cultural values;
(iv) the social theory and version of social reality put forward by the document; and
(v) the relationship of the document with time and space.

These five factors inform the analysis in this chapter. Before outlining the results and discussion, each of the five methodological issues identified above is discussed.

*Organisational history and context*

Much of the organisational history of current CCPs was discussed in the last chapter. Local authority CCPs are local documents that are closely related to other documents of policy guidance and statute and they are much informed by these previous and co-terminus texts. Atkinson and Coffey define this link with the categories and themes of other related documents as 'intertexuality' (1997, p. 55).

The organisational process of how a document is written, evidence collected, what meetings are held, drafts circulated and final copies stored, is useful evidence in understanding the social context and meaning of texts. Atkinson and Coffey (1997, p. 46) say that data collection and analysis: 'must incorporate a clear understanding of how documents are produced, circulated, read, stored and used for a wide variety of purposes.'

Government has said that the process of producing CCPs is an important opportunity for policy consultation with users (Department of Health, 1990). In chapter one, the book explored the tension between plans and planning and the reality that activity associated with producing written plans may not necessarily be future orientated thinking, but rather concerned with achieving organisational control and communication of what an organisations priorities already are (Mintzberg, 1994, p. 351). The activity taking place in the production of local CCPs is only a small part of total government planning activity. In particular it was argued in the last chapter that national planning is eclipsed by the focus on local plans and that this formed an implicit political strategy to avoid difficult public expenditure decisions.

*Linguistic style and format*

The most observable pure data available in a document is its written text, the letters, sentences, paragraphs and tables. It is for this reason that some documentary analysis focuses on the detail of the written text and rigorous quantitative searches are made for the occurrence of certain words and phrases (Robson, 1993, p. 281). The problem with this approach is that the numerical occurrence of some words and phrases does not necessarily guarantee that the social context which the document demonstrates will be correctly understood. The relationship between quantitative content and qualitative context therefore remains critical to the researcher. As Krippenddorff (1980, p.21) says when defining content analysis: 'content analysis is a research technique for making re-applicable and valid inferences from data to their context.' 'Content analysis' of linguistic style and recording can represent a methodological focus on data that is not an inductive exploration of a whole document, but rather a specific technique based on a clear hypothesis (Carney, 1973). In the research in this chapter word searches have been used that follow the deductive reasoning of the theoretical model proposed at the end of the last chapter (Figure 3.1). For example evidence is sought for the existence of political, managerial and market logics in the text of the plans and reference to words like 'choice', 'quality' and 'priorities'.

The textual organisation of a document is often significant to uncovering relevant categories and themes. Therefore contents lists, glossaries, codes, and diagrams may be as important to analyse as the implicit language. Such lists and key headings can give important clues about the choice of categories for analysis (Robson, 1993, p. 277).

Although there was some diversity in the textual organisation of CCPs studied, a general unifying textual organisation could be summarised in all the documents. This included a basic quantitative needs assessment followed by a purchasing intention for the next year for each client group. There was considerable heterogeneity in the method by which plans accounted for these two broad areas of content.

Written documents represent a different form of human communication to speech, they are often a more calculated and formal part of culture, more explicit in their social controls, but nevertheless concealing a more complex social context from that which is explained. Take for example the written legal statute, it will be explicit in places about what people can and cannot do, but elsewhere it may be vague, reinforcing complex professional disputes between lawyers about what it does mean implicitly. Similarly, formal written accounts and budgets pass explicit messages of control through organisations about where money can and cannot be spent, but they disguise implicit and complex judgements about competing priorities. Communication in a documents depends on reading rather than hearing. This presents different threats and opportunities to both author and reader. Some realities may be clearer while others are more hidden.

*Documentary authors and their cultural values*

Documents can function as items of self description, presenting the opportunity to a group of actors to make a calculated statement about themselves. Similarly, in the case of plans and strategies, these documents present a group of actors with an opportunity to make a calculated statement about their field of interest.

Although government plans and documents may not explicitly carry a named author, the reality is that someone, or some group of people has written the document, albeit in submission to a higher group or alongside some other persons. Atkinson and Coffey (1997, p. 58) state: 'it is part of the factiticity of many official and organisational documents that they are not identifiably the work of an individual author.'

Government documents contain both explicit and implicit values and logics, sometimes they are a source of conflict between the groups of actors having power over the production process. What is the relationship of the document and its authors with powerful social systems? Documents only offer indirect methods for answering these questions.

Similarly documents are often read by a particular audience, and may represent a form of communication between one group of 'author' actors and another group of 'reader' actors. Atkinson and Coffey (1997, p. 61) comment: 'it is important to think about documents in relation to their production (authorship) and their consumption (readership).'

A key aim for the researcher of documents is often to discover the logics and discursive forms emerging from the merger of actors and cultural values and the production of a text. The text may represent a particular version of an actor group's logic or discourse. The CCP research in this chapter includes an examination of who the authors are and what their logic and value base is.

*Social theory and the version of social reality presented*

All the above activities of a researcher lead to a theory about the indirect relationship between social reality and the document of interest. The key point when considering the text is what theory and version of social reality the document portrays. As Atkinson and Coffey (1997, pp. 60-61) state:

> 'documentary reality does not consist of descriptions of the social world that can be used directly as evidence about it. One certainly cannot assume that documentary accounts are "accurate" portrayals in that sense. Rather they construct their own kinds of reality.'

Documents will normally contain explicit and implicit subjective social facts and social definitions, often applying official statistics and professional language in this process. Most documents adopt systems of conventional signs and modes of representation which can be attributed to specific sub-cultures and by implication casts a story, or account, about an area of social life.

'A text instructs us how to see the world, how to differentiate the parts within it, and thereby provides the means by which we can engage with the world. One might even argue that in many spheres of human practice one can only know the world through the representational orders contained within text.' (Prior, 1997, p. 67)

The language and construction of a document can contain underlying assumptions about the definition, causes and effects of social problems (Hastings, 1998). Some documents may have a clear rhetoric and an explicit bias, for example political manifestos and advertising brochures, but even these paradoxically seek to codify some aspects of social life so as to substantially reinforce the explicit and simplified version of events given. Atkinson and Coffey (1997, p. 61) remark: 'rhetoric is fundamentally about how texts persuade their readers and hearers.' Documents contribute to the 'economy of logic' principle identified in chapter one. Complex situations are simplified so as to make them manageable and comprehensible, although this does not mean that situations are any less complex as a result.

Other documents are explicitly apolitical, seeking to avoid party politics and a clear identification with one interest group, or product. Many government texts such as policy reviews, consultation documents, statutes and plans seek to offer consensual versions of reality, because their explicit aim is to achieve a social consensus and organisational control rather than to provoke dissent. CCPs fall into this category. A government document that seeks consensus and avoids conflict has to pursue a certain definition of reality in achieving this aim. Such a singular version of events is unlikely to be satisfactory to all minority interests and some logics will dominate over others. As a result powerful groups can control the policy environment at the expense of less powerful groups. Documentary plans are not in themselves full and transparent representations of the conflict of groups in organisations and networks, rather they seek to bring a consensus into a certain version of events, in this sense they are implicitly political, offering a particular type of organisational and political reality.

*The time and space context*

It is proposed in this book that time and space are important aspects of complex accounts of policy and planning systems. Documents can detach themselves from time and space in a unique way. Planning is about the nature of social change over time and so documentary plans easily become dislocated from planning activity. Nevertheless such documentary plans offer an important anchor in culture, a culture that cannot always change at speed, but will have some enduring features, many being preserved for generations. A document, 'has a permanence' (Prior, 1997, p. 76) and can represent stability, especially during rapid social change. In this sense documentary sources: 'suppress time, by lifting events out of the flow of lived experience, and recording them in the decontextualisized language and formats of official reports' (Atkinson and Coffey, 1997, p. 57).

Documents can be clearly located in a time horizon and thereby used as one indicator of subsequent change, this is particularly relevant to the understanding of political change, as political systems in a representative democracy are subject to clear temporal horizons (through the occurrence of representative elections). Documents also relate to a given geographical area, and help define and reinforce the social construction of geo-political boundaries. CCPs can be clearly linked with a particular local political administration by the date of their publication. Similarly CCPs are clearly attributed to a geo-political geography.

## Theoretical Analysis

Chapter one of this book makes a number of theoretical deductions about the nature of state and government planning. Using the metaphor of open systems it was deduced that planning takes place in three systems, politics, managerial and market. Also it was proposed that these systems exist because of underpinning social logics, as proposed by Kontopoulos' (1993) account of social structure. Therefore the main defining features of government planning are the macro (or 'totalizing') logics of: capitalism (in the market system), the technical organisation of state bureaucracy (in the state-managerial system) and representative democracy (in the political system).

Planning activity is a network of activities, decisions and interactions that frequently overlaps the three systems. Meetings of people involved in government planning often take place in a 'patch' (Kauffman, 1995) that is located on the boundaries of the dominant systems and logics.

In this chapter the aim is to explore CCPs for content that is associated with the three systems of politics, markets and state managerialism and the logics that underpin these systems. It is necessary to see the three systems as permeable, so the systems only provide a starting point for the categorisation of textual data, and it is hypothesised that planning activity overlaps these systems and is likely to lead to the integration of parts of systems into what Kauffman has called 'patches'. The micro logics that are imperative to this construction of patches for CCP activity were identified at the end of chapter 3 (Figure 3.1). The logics of CCP were summarised as: new managerialism, marketisation, market enabling, managerial voice consultation, price allocation, allocation of subsidy, supply competition and consumer choice.

An initial checklist (Table 4.1) of textual categories was drawn up by reference to the contents pages of plans and previous studies that have examined the content of plans (Hardy, Wistow and Leedham , 1993; Wistow, Leedham, and Hardy, 1993, and Brodie, 1994). This checklist was consigned to the three theme headings, political, managerial and market, although the content in plans can have links with more than one system. The scrutiny of content was interested in both analysis of details and synthesis of overall strategies, so the definition of planning here includes strategic planning. The research also examines the different methods of managerial information analysis presented in CCPs.

## The Results of the Document Analysis

In this section each of the dominant systems is addressed in turn.

*The political system and evidence of strategic planning activity*

*Political signatures* In order to ascertain some measure of the political interest of councillors in strategic level planning the documents were examined for evidence of named councillors taking responsibility for the document. Only five of the 14 plans were signed in the opening pages by a councillor. These were East Sussex, Greenwich, Isle of Wight, Southwark and Surrey. These CCPs were signed by the chair of the Social Services Committee. This finding does not imply that councillors in those authorities where CCPs were only signed by managers had no interest or involvement, but political signatures my indicate a greater degree of political interest and involvement. Of the remainder, all except Richmond, Chelsea and Croydon were identified in the opening pages with a named senior member of the social services management team. It should be noted that plans signed by councillors were also signed by a named senior manager.

**Table 4.1**      **Planning activities searched for in a sample of 1994-1995 Community Care Plans**

### Political System

Evidence of Strategic Planning
Political Sigs                        Have local political representatives signed the plan?
Mission/values                    Is there a mission and value system underpinning the plan?
General Strategy                  Is there a strategic direction?
Objectives and Priorities      Are clear objectives and priorities established?

### Managerial System

Housing
Health                                 Have SSD worked with other parties and who has
Vol Sector                          contributed to joint planning?
Private Sector
Probation

Evidence of Joint Planning
Users                                  Is there evidence of consultation and joint planning
Carers

Management information analysis
Financial Information         Are background financial statistics given?
Definitions of need            Is need locally defined into priority groups?
Background Data.               Is population needs data discussed?
Assessment and Supply side   Is data provided for supply side assessment?
Explanations about implementation and process
                                          To what extent do the plans discuss the context of
                                          community care policy and the internal re-organisation of
                                          SSDs?

### Market System

Financial Information
Costing examples                Are costed local examples given?
Budget Actual                    Is infomation given on the last budget actual?
Budget Forecast                 Is information given on the budget forecast?
Grants and Loans Stats       Are statistics available on the grants to be
                                          made?
Local Market Research       Is the local supply market researched?
Charges                             Is charging policy discussed?
Evidence of Commissioning
 and Purchasing Joint?       Are services purchased jointly?
Market Strategy                 Is a market development strategy explained?
Sharing economic plans      Is SSD making explicit requests to indep sector?

*Strategic Mission and Values* Seven of the plans, Bromley, Chelsea, Croydon, Greenwich, Isle of Wight, Kingston and Richmond included some reference to a synthesis of philosophy, mission and values in their introductory text, or early chapters. In one case, the underpinning values appeared to be presented as if owned by councillors (Greenwich, p. 1), but in the other plans this was not explicitly the mode of presentation.

Mission was linked predominantly with the values of 'choice' and providing a 'diversity' of service provision for the individual user. For example, Croydon's plan (p. i) states that services should be provided 'with a choice where ever possible.' The Isle of Wight's (chapter 2) short chapter on 'a shared vision' places the emphasis on individual choice in seven separate sentences. Kingston quotes the government policy document, *Community Care in the Next Decade and Beyond* and states that people should be able to remain in the community 'for as long as they are able and wish to do so'. This places choice in the context of some resource limitations, a characteristic also of the Isle of Wight and Croydon documents. Greenwich's (p. i) concise introductory 'principles of community care' record four choices that the long term ill are entitled to expect . Chelsea's introductory statement is the only plan identified from the seven with value and mission statements that does not mention choice.

Chelsea's (p. 2) plan states that: 'services will be provided by statutory and independent sector organisations in a way that ensures high quality and good value for money.' The word 'quality' also occurred regularly in other value and mission statements (for example Greenwich, p. i; Kingston, p. 15).

Equal opportunities for ethnic minority groups was emphasised as a priority in some London boroughs (for example: Croydon, p. i; Greenwich, p. 1; Richmond p. 11). East Sussex (pp. 74-75), Wiltshire (pp. 36-37) and Kent (p. 17) had no clear explanation of mission and values in their opening pages but did include sections on anti-discriminatory work later in the text. A general mission to target social inequity, or the need for social justice, was not mentioned explicitly in any of the plans studied.

Chelsea (p. 2), Croydon (p. i) and the Isle Wight (p. 7) used the context of mission and value statements to make explicit the need to prioritise services to those in most need.

Only Kingston made the direct textual link between their own mission and values and those espoused by national government policy. The Kingston report quotes the Department of Health's (1990) *Community Care in the Next Decade and Beyond* in some detail (p. 15).

*General strategy: objectives and priorities*

All the plans studied contained evidence of a general strategy, but they varied in terms of the clarity with which this was specified. All gave a breakdown of action for each client group, although the language used to describe such statements of intended action was diverse. Terminology used to describe future commitments included: 'strategic objectives', 'priorities', 'purchasing intentions', 'programmes' and 'action.' Bromley's plan was one of the least developed in respect of such statements, referring only to 'work programmes' for the coming year (pp. 13-17). Since this research was undertaken the Department of Health (1995a) has recommended a strategic approach to CCPs more explicitly.

A minority of plans included costing forecasts alongside their key client objectives, or in an appendix, examples being Bexley (Appendix C), Croydon (pp. 22-25), Surrey (pp. 92-93) and West Sussex (pp. 37-49). The others listed service development plans without always clearly estimating costing; examples are East Sussex, Greenwich and the Isle of Wight. The latter tended to present numerous lists of possible service developments with little or no costing attached.

Three plans (Chelsea, p. 2; East Sussex, p. 4; Greenwich, p. 4) did present a very brief summary of their overall direction in the introduction, although this was not identified under a heading 'strategy'. In two plans (Richmond and Wiltshire), there was some integration of content that described mission and values, strategic objectives for the social services internal organisation, and strategic objectives for service purchasing.

Summarising a county strategy is particularly difficult in a large diverse shire county where needs may vary greatly from one locality to the next. For this reason Kent only publishes a limited plan for the whole county and refers to the intention to devolve the responsibility to local areas for the production of separate locality plans. The difficulty with summarising a large shire county strategy is a point made in the initial summary of the East Sussex plan (p. 4) although some common priority areas for service provision are identified, these being respite care, day activities, and transport services. West Sussex (pp. 22 - 26) makes a clear and concise synthesis of its feedback from the voluntary sector, users and carers. It summarises the material as a 'strategic framework'.

Reports that attempted to summarise and synthesise their overall strategy could be grouped into two types: those with discussion that centred on an initial strategic statement directed at the internal organisational system and culture; and text that centred on a strategic statement in respect of service supply. It is important to point out that plans that tended to focus in the earlier chapters on a strategy for organisational system and culture, often had detailed objectives for service provision which were related to a number of specific client groups later in the report.

Wiltshire (1994, p. 8) focused its initial strategic summary on structure and culture.

> 'In the last nine months Social Services has been reviewing its organisational structure to take forward these strategic aims: to promote choice for service users and, where applicable, their immediate carers; to stimulate more responsible and flexible services by placing the money to buy services with the local fieldwork care management teams;  to devolve management responsibility and decision making to be closer to users and carers.'

Greenwich (1994, p. 4) also focused its introductory strategic summary on organisational matters rather than details of service provision.

West Sussex outlines a strategic framework after a descriptive discussion about how community care policy is working in the locality.  The strategic summary relates directly to service provision. Transport, respite care, domiciliary care, occupational therapy services and advocacy are identified as strategic priorities as a result of consultation.  This clear link between strategy and consultation is a valuable feature of the West Sussex plan. It presents the concept of a strategy in a tangible and meaningful manner that creates an impression of public ownership.

Kingston (1994, p. 15) falls between the two types, with a summary that includes both organisational matters and a commitment to improve domiciliary and respite care service provision. The Isle of Wight has a similar content in its summary with a list of organisational principles that lead into a discussion of strategic intentions. The intentions centre on the aim to:

> '...bring care to clients in the setting of their choice, rather than maintain an institutional regime for care. Therefore the development of Home Care Services and Day Care are the strategic objectives.' (Isle of Wight, 1994, p. 7)

The introduction to Croydon's (1994, p. 2) plan indicates that its main strategic priority is service provision and passing information to providers about what might be financed by the borough.

> 'This plan in its final form will seek to specify what key changes we intend to

fund in 1994/95...The Community Care Plan is still open to all who wish to read it. But we hope that this one will send a clearer message to providers as to the key changes we want to see happen and fund as purchasers. Unless providers know what we, the purchasers, want, they will not be able to develop a wider range of services in Croydon that will offer more choice.'

The Surrey (p. 21) plan attempts to define a 'strategic language' for the reader. For this purpose it defines the terminology 'overall aims', 'impact objectives' and 'service objectives'. This helps to contextualise the problem of linking changes in the internal organisational with the strategic provision of outcomes. The overall emphasis in the Surrey plan is towards refining a rational-managerial system that can deliver a choice and quality of services in the mixed economy of social care.

In summary the plans showed many features of the tradition of strategic planning as defined in management literature (Bryson and Einsweiler, 1988; Caulfield and Schultz, 1989; Mintzberg, 1994) with an attempt to synthesise material and state clear output objectives. But the reader is given an impression of political distance from these strategies, in that the national and local political context is rarely explicitly discussed. For example, discussion of the strategic implications of resource short-falls and external factors were the exception. The Isle of Wight discussed a shortfall in its RSG allocation in the opening pages. It appears possible that while local councillors are responsible for the strategic direction of an authority, in many authorities much of the language and construction of the details of a strategy (such as defining objectives and priorities) is performed by managers and then occasionally sanctioned at committee by councillors (Department of the Environment, Transport and Regions, 1998b)

## The Management System

*Consultation and joint planning with other services*

All of the 14 plans made some reference to health authorities and health services. Seven of the plans analysed were signed on the opening pages by both senior social service and health service managerial representatives, these being East Sussex, Greenwich, Kingston, Isle of Wight, Surrey, West Sussex and Wiltshire. Bexley, Croydon and Southwark also gave a high public profile to joint working with health agencies mentioned on the cover of the plan document and in the opening pages. These London boroughs can be contrasted to Richmond and Kensington and Chelsea where joint working with health received a limited profile in the opening pages.

The Royal Borough of Kensington and Chelsea mentions joint planning with health services very briefly in the opening pages, but later in the text makes consultation with health services more explicit in a diagram of the joint planning structures in the borough. 'The local reorganisation of two district health authorities into a single authority - the Kensington, Chelsea and Westminster Health Authority - has resulted in improved coordination and planning of community care services' (p. 10).

Similar references to organisational structures that link SSDs and Health were evident in all the London borough plans read, even where the plans were not jointly signed. In organisational structural diagrams and textual explanations of cooperation, health services tended to be represented at the top of organisational hierarchies where the largest budget decisions are likely to be made (see also Figures 4.2 - 4.7).

When considering the quantitative volume of text used to document these arrangements, health partnerships appeared as the most valued area of joint working to SSDs. This is not unexpected given the guidance from central government to local government exhorting the importance of integrating joint planning and purchasing between health and social services (Department of Health, 1990; Department of Health, 1992; Department of Health, 1995b).

Housing authorities were referred to in all 14 plans. Liaison with Housing bodies is required by the 1990 NHS and Community Care Act (House of Commons, 1990, Section 24,2,e) and Department of Health (1992; 1993b, paragraph 5) directions. In Croydon's plan (p. 13) the reference to housing was minimal (only a few paragraphs), but in the context of a discussion of accommodation issues where housing was seen as significant when assessing and identifying needs. For some London boroughs the joint involvement of housing departments in planning was relatively straight-forward given co-terminous organisational structures and political accountability. The following plans all make references to actual joint decision taking with housing agencies: London Borough of Bexley, 1994, pp. 16-17; London Borough of Southwark, 1994, pp. 36- 38; London Borough of Kensington and Chelsea, 1994, pp. 24-26.

Local authorities mentioned consultation with the voluntary sector less than consultation with users and carers. Often when the voluntary sector was mentioned it was in connection with the sector as a facilitator of user and carer support rather than a service provider. Private providers were rarely mentioned as key partners in joint planning and there was little evidence of consultation with the private sector as providers. One notable exception to this was East Sussex (1994, p. 14) who stated in a chapter on 'working together':

> '...the role of the private sector in the planning and provision of community care is of considerable importance...regular meetings are held by the statutory authorities with the trade associations representing residential and nursing homes...representatives of the private sector have begun to take their place on planning teams across the county.'

Such an explicit acknowledgement of the need for the private sector in the planning process was unusual. Other studies researched in the early 1990s indicated that SSDs were suspicious of forming partnerships with independent providers (Wistow, et al, 1993; Hardy, Young and Wistow, 1996). Surrey Social Services Department included the views of the private sector in its chapter review of consultation and feedback (Surrey County Council, 1994, p. 129). Department of Health (1993b/1994a) circulars issued early in the development of CCPs required local authorities to liaise with independent sector providers. More recently the government has expressed the view that liaison with local businesses is a necessary component of providing 'best value' services to the public (Department of Environment, Regions and Transport, 1998a).

Consultation with the probation service was a low priority. Twelve plans did not mention the probation service, despite its involvement with the homeless, people with mental illness and substance misusers. Richmond upon Thames mentioned joint deployment of resources with the probation service in connection with alcohol misuse and East Sussex included probation staff in its planning and consultation system.

There was evidence of joint consultation with a variety of agencies and groups, but less evidence of actual joint decision making. Joint planning implies a structure and process where the power to make strategic decisions about commissioning services has been significantly shared with outside groups. Evidence in the plans of such partnerships was limited. Social services were most likely to share strategic budget decisions with Health and Housing organisations, as evident from the organisational diagrams in Figures 4.2-4.7.

Many of the new consultative organisational structures on joint planning were imaginative and clearly gave a multitude of groups (in addition to the NHS) the chance to be consulted. But often users, carers and the independent sector felt excluded from the top groups in the hierarchy that made final decisions on purchasing and commissioning (Martin and Gaster 1993; Bewley and Glendinning, 1994). The key decision making bodies responsible for the expenditure of budgets also varied in their political accountability.

Bromley, Greenwich and the Isle of Wight all include political elected councillor representatives in their strategic commissioning groups (see Figures 4.3, 4.4, 4.5), the other authorities did not. Other authorities, like Surrey and East Sussex, had an implicit link between their main commissioning group and a committee with political representation, but the group that appeared to have most control over the strategic use of budgets seemed not to include direct political representation. The Commissioners and Joint Chief Officers group in East Sussex had some indirect links with the Joint Consultative Council that included councillor representation (Figure 4.1). Surrey's consultation structure had a county forum for purchasing at the centre, but this did not include councillor representation. The group is implicitly supervised by a joint Health and Social Services meeting of council chairs, directors and chief executives (Figure 4.6).

Figures 4.1 to 4.6 examine six consultation structures. These were selected from six of fourteen plans where there was felt to be sufficient detail and explanation to construct such diagrams. This does not imply that the other authorities did not have such structures, merely that insufficient detail of the structures was recorded in the CCP for the purposes of this research. The six structures show the diversity of consultation structures constructed by authorities. There are similarities and contrasts. The points of contrast can be summarised by three dimensions:

(i) simple structures as opposed to more complex structures;
(ii) political and managerial functions as opposed to purchasing and providing functions; and
(iii) hierarchical as opposed to heterarchical (matrix) structures.

East Sussex's structure (Figure 4.1) demonstrates a complex structure with five levels of groups identified which are sub-divided into local and client specific sub-groups. The groups tend to be defined by political or managerial functions. For example three of the groups have memberships comprising of only managers, planners and professionals (Locality Joint Planning Teams; Community Care Steering Group; Commissioners Group). The indirect input of the Joint Consultative Council has a more explicitly political membership. Finally the overall structure is described as a periodic cycle, attempting to input users' and carers' views into managerial analysis

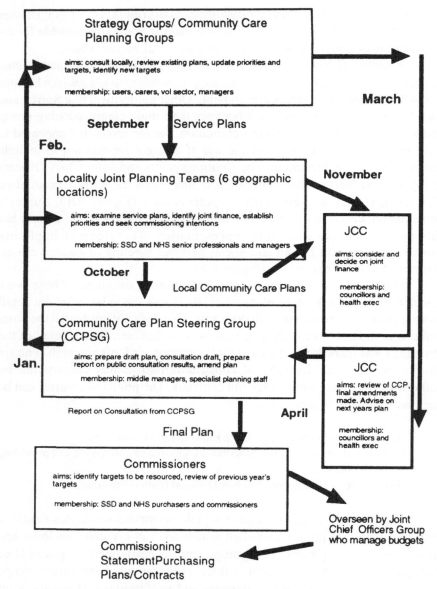

**Figure 4.1  East Sussex Community Care Plan:**
**consultation structure and process, 1994-1995**

*Source*: East Sussex County Council (1994) Community Care Plan.

and refinement. This analysis is later processed into expenditure decisions. A lack of political representation when expenditure decisions are made could undermine the intention of transferring user and carer ideas into actual expenditure decisions, but the periodic cycle appears more as a heterarchy than a hierarchy. In the results of an internal evaluation into part of the planning process by East Sussex County Council an officer concludes: 'some respondents commented that the decision making process at a senior level in all organisations seemed to be divorced from the CCP process.'

Figure 4.2 shows Bromley's consultative structure. The overall structure is complex rather than simple, with some twelve groups feeding into the process at three different levels. The overall structure appears as a hierarchy with the Joint Commissioning Strategy Group at the top. This group includes three councillor political representatives, but there is no political representation lower down the structure. The structure appears to be defined by political and managerial functions. It is an example of a traditional local authority SSD structure as proposed by Kakabadshe (1982) and service users are rather dependent upon the traditional system of representative local democracy and the efficiency of management consultation if policy is to be changed as they want.

One of the most interesting commissioning structures was in the London Borough of Greenwich (Figure 4.4). The Borough structure had five key elements, with two elements, the Advisory Panels and Joint Commissioning Teams, contributing further sub-divisions. The central point is a Joint Commissioning Council made up of social service councillors, health authority directors and elected representatives from the voluntary sector. This group met four times a year to make major commissioning and strategic decisions. These meetings were open to the public (see Greenwich, 1994, p. 20).

Of all the plans sampled this appeared as the most democratic and politically accountable commissioning body and this suggested that the authority had gone some way to integrating political and managerial functions. The process indicates a heterarchical flow of information, but is simpler than some other hierarchical authorities. The structure and process that feeds into the central Joint Commissioning Council is defined by political and managerial attributes. There is a close overall supervision from the Social Services Committee and its councillors.

Greenwich can be contrasted with a number of more hierarchical and organisationally complex consultation systems like the Isle of Wight and Surrey (Figures 4.5, 4.6). The Joint Commissioning Group at the top of the hierarchy in the Isle of Wight includes the chair of the Social Services Committee. The

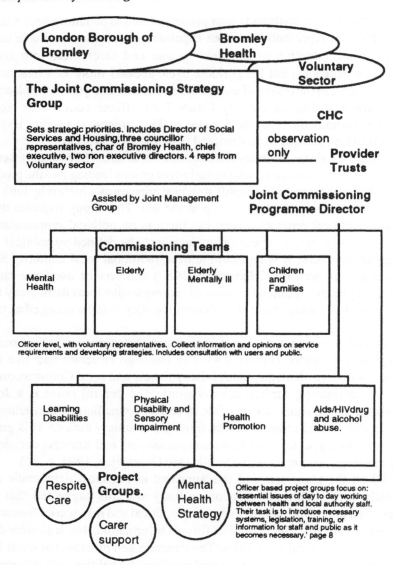

**Figure 4.2  Bromley Community Care Plan:
consultation structure and process,
1994-1995**

*Source*: Bromley Community Care Plan (1994) pp. 8-11.

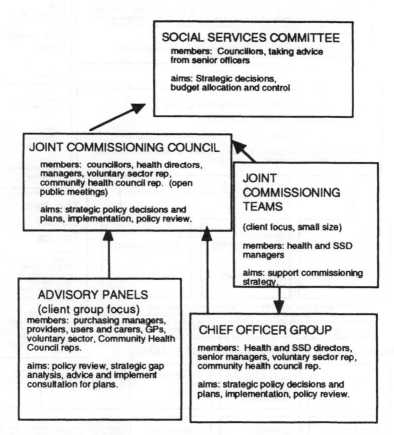

**Figure 4.3  Greenwich Community Care Plan:
consultation structure and process, 1994-1995**

*Source*: London Borough of Greenwich (1994) Community Care Plan.

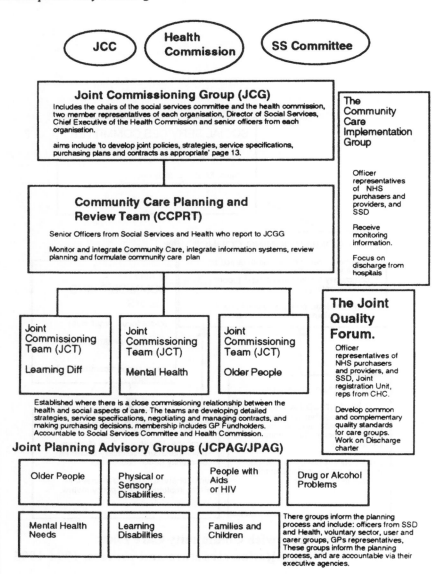

**Figure 4.4  Isle of Wight Community Care Plan:
consultation structure and process, 1994-1995**

*Source*: Isle of Wight (1994) Community Care Plan.

Isle of Wight structure is dominated by its commissioning process, indicating a clear link between planning and commissioning as recommended by the Department of Health (1995b). One part of the process, the Joint Quality Forum, focuses at the provider end of the social care market, seeking to establish some link between provider quality and future commissioning policy.

In Surrey, a hierarchical structure, that allows diverse membership at a local level, filters upwards to a county forum for purchasing and care planning (Figure 4.5). This forum is made up of chief executives and purchasing directors, but with no explicit central involvement of county councillors or service users in the spending of budgets, although the forum is overseen by a Joint Health and Social Services meeting of political chairs and chief officers (Surrey, pp. 18-19).

Finally, the Wiltshire consultative structure is not as well integrated as the Isle of Wight and Surrey structures, and is composed of two small hierarchies side by side (Figure 4.6). One side of the process is concerned with user consultation and planning, the other side with purchasing and commissioning. Both are managerial based at the lower level, but have a simple political identify at the top, being overseen by the traditional Social Services Committee and Joint Consultative Committee. This is likely to allow macro decisions on budget allocation to remain closer to political representatives, but might prevent the integration of the consultation, planning and commissioning of services from the lower levels.

In summary, all the plans studied contained claims that users and carers were involved. Three plans (Richmond, Surrey and Southwark) were more convincing in arguing that consultation was leading to changes in purchasing policy. These plans contained reference to the results of consultation, lists of what users and carers had requested, and tried to link this with future policy action. For example, Surrey devoted chapter 7 of its plan to a summary of comments received on an earlier draft plan. This included how issues raised would be considered in the next planning cycle (op cit, p. 133). Richmond had employed a temporary worker to research users' and carers' needs and this had helped to allocate specific funding for services that would support carers, such as holiday care scheme (Richmond, p. 17). Southwark listed the issues of concern to all client groups and showed how it planned to respond to these issues. Transport, respite care, services for black and ethnic minorities, adapted housing, occupational therapy, home bathing and the assessment process were said to be priorities to users, and carers support was noted as worthy of special prioritisation (Southwark, p. 26-27).

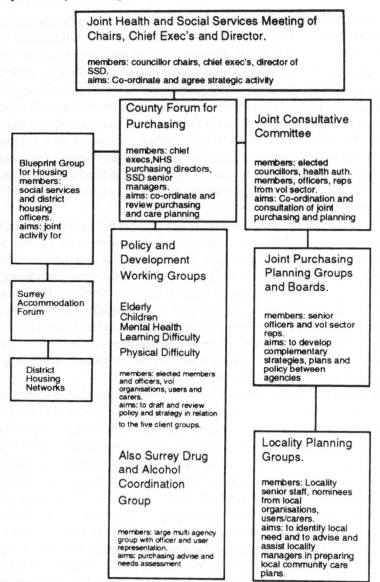

**Figure 4.5 Surrey Community Care Plan:
consultation structure and process, 1994-1995**

*Source*: Surrey County Council (1994) Surrey Community Care Plan.
1994-1995, pp. 18, 19, 122.

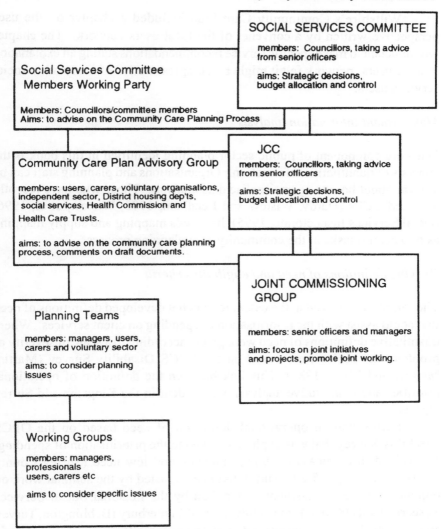

SOCIAL SERVICES COMMITTEE

members: Councillors, taking advice from senior officers

aims: Strategic decisions, budget allocation and control

Social Services Committee Members Working Party

Members: Councillors/committee members
Aims: to advise on the Community Care Planning Process

JCC

members: Councillors, taking advice from senior officers

aims: Strategic decisions, budget allocation and control

Community Care Plan Advisory Group

members: users, carers, voluntary organisations, independent sector, District housing dep'ts, social services, Health Commission and Health Care Trusts.

aims: to advise on the community care planning process, comments on draft documents.

JOINT COMMISSIONING GROUP

members: senior officers and managers

aims: focus on joint initiatives and projects, promote joint working.

Planning Teams

members: managers, users, carers and voluntary sector

aims: to consider planning issues

Working Groups

members: managers, professionals users, carers etc

aims to consider specific issues

**Figure 4.6    Wiltshire Community Care Plan:**
**consultation structure and process, 1994-1995**

*Source:* Wiltshire County Council (1994) Community Care Plan, 1994-1995.

Wiltshire's Community Care Plan included a chapter on the user perspective written by a convener of the local users network. The chapter was reluctant to make specific service recommendations stating an explanation that the users' network felt it might be unrepresentative of many other social services users.

## Management information analysis

One core component of public sector planning identified in this book is the analysis of quantitative information. Organisations and planning staff can be unclear about how to operationalise data analysis. Those who have recently analysed CCPs (Hardy, Wistow and Leedham, 1993; Wistow, et al, 1996; Social Services Inspectorate, 1995) list needs mapping and supply mapping as two central tasks in the community care planning process.

## Working definitions of need and eligibility criteria

The sample was mixed in the extent to which it developed definitions of need that could assist with the prioritisation of spending on client services. Where quantitative definitions of need were given, according to a scale of severity of problem, the scales were based on the OPCS Disability Survey (Martin, Meltzer and Elliot, 1988). This link between the definition of operational priorities and quantitative analysis was evident in the Kingston and Surrey reports.

Surrey had an operational definition of need based on the OPCS Disability Survey that was explicitly linked to the prioritisation of spending. It involved three measures, high, moderate and low need (Surrey County Council, 1994, pp. 25-27). Surrey has been assisted by the seminal work on population needs assessment undertaken by the Personal Social Services Research Unit (PSSRU) at the University of Canterbury (Bebbington, Turvey and Janzon, 1996). Kingston referred to the same three eligibility criteria (Kingston, pp. 37, 120), but did not relate these measures explicitly to its own operational, case management policy.

Other authorities did not document a quantitative method that was related to priorities. Richmond listed priority definitions of need, but these were not directly linked to a quantitative methodology (Richmond, Appendix C). The impression was given that these priorities were being operationalised by assessment staff. Bromley used similar categories, but its discussion of their use was not comprehensive (Bromley, p. xvi). Greenwich (pp. 97-104) had eight pages of text explaining its priority bands and eligibility criteria in some detail. Priority bands are discussed for each client group, but the same five point ordinal scale is used for each. The Isle of Wight listed three priority groupings, but these were defined in terms of social services response rather than clients' disabilities or needs. For example, priority 2 is defined as: 'if resources permit.' (Isle of Wight, 1994, p. 30)

Wiltshire's approach to need prioritisation also gave pragmatic examples of what it considered to be high priorities. Their list of high priorities (Wiltshire, 1994, p. 51) includes criteria such as: immediate very high risk of personal safety; cannot be left alone; carer under severe stress. Another criterion in the same list reads 'requires prompt intervention'.

In summary, only two authorities of the 14 sampled were demonstrating an integrated quantitative methodology for needs assessment and priority rating (Kingston and Surrey).

*Population needs data*

All the plans available included some reference to general secondary population data (Table 4.2). Most often this was taken from the 1991 OPCS Census, but in some cases this had been refined by local authority planning projections that would incorporate Register General population counts. Thirteen plans developed more detail than population counts, also offering some simple analysis of age structure.

Tabulation of the census statistics on long term limiting illness was a popular addition and used by six authorities. Less common was the addition of social deprivation indicators such as those utilised by Southwark (p. 9). Three authorities included basic data on unemployment in their area, implying that higher levels of unemployment are related to higher demands on social services. Seven authorities included some reference to data on the ethnic mix of their local populations. Six London authorities included some reference to differences in the ward (local geography) characteristics of variables such as age structure. Croydon include two ward based statistical maps.

There was a lack of any attempt to analyse and model the association of social deprivation and long term illness. For example standardised measures of long term illness and mortality were not referred to. This is despite the fact that social deprivation is known to have an association with increased rates of long term illness and early deaths (Whitehead, 1992; Gould and Jones 1995; Senior, 1995; Wilkinson, 1996; Dorling, 1997; Drever and Whitehead, 1997). Local authorities also avoided comparing themselves with neighbouring authorities, despite the range of comparative performance data available from the Department of Health each year.

Only four authorities presented locally acquired data in the body of a plan as evidence of the background mapping of need. For example, Greenwich included a local acquired survey on those with suffering from a learning difficulty (p. 55). More frequently plans referred to the intention of using locally acquired data in the future. The inability of authorities to provide their own quantitative information in the sections on analysis of need was a notable limitation of the plans.

*Assessment and supply side data*

London boroughs seemed better at utilising locally acquired supply data in the body of their main reports than shire counties. An exception here was the Isle of Wight which included analysis of its own care management assessment statistics. Richmond upon Thames included quite detailed local statistical summaries in an appendix, taken from the year 1993-1994. Kingston included local data analysis in its summary of community care needs of the borough (1994, chapter 5). Greenwich integrated local client referral statistics into its discussions of specialist group needs, as did Bexley - to a lesser extent. West Sussex listed available service places in the statutory sector, rather than focusing on client referral statistics. In general there was a lack of data on the numbers requesting assessment and the numbers of assessments carried out in response. Authorities were more likely to present inventories of service places and outputs.

Service output data was usually presented in an inventory format, without any analysis about what it meant for costings. This was surprising, given the problem for local authorities of rationing resources and increasingly having to charge for services. Without explanation of the political and economic constraints on resources there is a danger of further raising expectations for services which cannot be provided.

*Explanations about implementation and organisational process*

Planning in a complex public sector environment needs to include strategies for adjusting internal organisational systems and culture. This is important if an organisation is to construct a process that can deliver the desired output. Arguably such matters are for the internal consideration of organisations and agencies and not necessarily relevant to be published in a CCP, but there is a counter argument. If organisations and agencies are to maximise their use of outside bodies and markets they need to be communicating their own operational structures.

This is particularly relevant to local authorities because they are subject to relationships with numerous external systems. If prospective independent providers are to be confident of a supply of work, they need to understand the mechanics of case management and at what point in an organisation funding decisions are to be made (Forder, Kendall and Knapp, 1996). In general the plans surveyed here did not give much space to explaining administrative and organisational change and there was only a small degree of such information within most documents. Seven plans had an explanation of care management and how it was to progress (See for example the Isle of Wight, p. 15; Southwark, pp. 30-31). Wiltshire (1994, p. 12 and Appendix F) included some basic information on the proposals to reform local government structure in its area.

## Market System

### Financial information

Almost all the plans studied gave some background presentation of the community care special transitional grant (STG) and how this was to be made available to the relevant authority. In four CCPs this information was isolated from the remainder of the social services budget, a fact that could mask the full picture of a social services department's purchasing activity (see Bexley, p. 9; East Sussex, p. 5; Wilshire, p. 29; Richmond, p. 99). Southwark (p. 18) also listed its Community Care Grant expenditures separately from its general PSS budget, with a small footnote explaining that the figures were also incorporated in the general social services budget later.

The most integrated and comprehensive of the background financial information provided was in the plan supplied by Kingston upon Thames (Kingston, chapter 8). This demonstrated a concise analysis of a range of economic inputs and outputs.

### Costed examples

Surrey and Kingston were unique in linking their definitions of prioritised need alongside costed examples of individual care packages (Surrey, figure 15, p. 53; Kingston, pp. 117-120). This gives a key indication to independent providers about how to set reasonable and realistic prices.

*Budgets actual and budgets forecast*

Thirteen of the plans included budget summaries. All included budget forecasts for 1994-1995. The East Sussex plan was the only plan that did not include a budget summary. Sometimes budget information was left for the appendix (see Wiltshire, Appendix G; Isle of Wight County Council, 1994, pp. 119-122), but this was not always the case. The London Boroughs of Bromley (1994, pp. 27-29) and Kingston (1994, pp. 113-114 ) provided such statistics in the main body of the report. Greenwich (pp. 11-13) included an integrated summary of local borough, social services, housing and heath authority expenditures. Chelsea (pp. 13-15) had a similar integrated summary.

Eight of the plans included a comparison with the budget from a previous year (Bexley, 1994, p. 9; Bromley, 1994, p. 24; Croydon, 1994, p. 7; Kingston, 1994, p. 112; Isle of Wight, 1994, p. 119; Richmond, 1994, p. 101; Wiltshire, Appendix H). Where these were provided they constituted an important source of general information that could add considerable sense to statistics on the use of the Community Care Special Transitional Grant (STG). Kingston's plan offered a concise summary in chart format that allowed significant detail for those wanting to understand the balance of funding. This allowed the reader to assess the context of growth or cuts in expenditure levels. Wiltshire included an appendix where three year's financial summaries were compared (Appendix H). This included out-turn statistics for 1992-1993.

*Grants and loans*

The availability of information on grants and loans paid out in support of independent service provision and development was variable. Some information was hidden in the detail of charts and figures listing developments for specific client groups (for example see West Sussex County Council, 1994, p. 55). This has the disadvantage of not being particularly accessible to new providers and user groups trying to establish how to get funding. It leaves authorities open to the criticism that only privileged groups who are in key policy networks get access to funding opportunities.

Social services departments were resistant to the introduction of compulsory competitive tendering in social care, but it would have had the advantage of making such payments more open and accountable. None of the plans seen were explicit in advertising the availability of grants, loans and contracts. Surrey made it clear in its chapter on purchasing that it had recently increased grants and published a diverse list of organisations to whom it was currently paying grants (Surrey, p. 97), but this gave no indications of possible grants available in the future.

*Local market research*

There was little evidence of authorities engaging in substantial quantitative market research. User based consumer research was more likely to be qualitative and informative, sometimes indistinguishable from the consultation meetings that has evolved. Four authorities mentioned user based surveys briefly (East Sussex , p. 46; Greenwich, pp. 55-56; Kingston, p. 67; Surrey, p. 65). Apart from Greenwich's life planning register, these methods received little coverage suggesting either they were not seen as invalid indicators or they were viewed as of little substantive significance.

Quantitative consumer based research is an undeveloped area that needs to take more centre stage in the social care market in coming years. Market research is a sophisticated method that can inform authorities of real consumer preferences in the planned and managed social care market (Jeffrey, 1997, p. 30).

*Charges*

There has been some discussion recently of social services charging policy in academic studies and the variations and inequities between local authorities (Balloch 1994; Baldwin and Lunt, 1996; Kempson and Bennett, 1997). Only three of the plans surveyed discussed local charging policies, this despite the requirements laid down by the Department of Health (1992a). The Isle of Wight (p. 3) plan made a short reference to charging in its introduction alongside a discussion of a resource shortfall, but the details of how the policy might evolve were not discussed . The Richmond plan included a paragraph on charging policy on page 93, with no substantial information given. Kingston (p. 121) provided the most information on charging, one full page of text. This included details of actual charges likely to be made and in what circumstances. Charging policy is likely to be one of the areas of most concern to service users and therefore one might expect to see more information on charging policies available. One key strategy that local authority social services committees use to cope with cuts in central government grant and increased demand from the local community is to increase the local charges for domiciliary and day care, these being service areas where the authority has substantial powers to change rates of charge without reference to central government (Baldwin and Lunt, 1996). The lack of information in CCPs about this issue raises questions about the use of the documents by councillors and managers. Difficult local political issues might be avoided in the hope that opposition and lobbying groups are not given information to assist their cause.

*Evidence of commissioning and purchasing*

The majority of the plans sampled devoted considerable space to intentions to increase joint commissioning with local health authorities and this was clearly a major priority for most social services departments. There was little in the way of rationale as to why this was a good strategy, what the outcome benefits might be and conversely the possible dangers of narrowing the number of purchasers in the market place. (Le Grand, 1991; Hoyes and Means, 1991; Le Grand and Bartlett, 1993). Restricting the number of purchasers might reduce the quality and motivation of providers, if prices are fixed inappropriately. Alternatively, good communication between Health and Social Services offers an opportunity to provide integrated health and social services that are not duplicated inefficiently. Conversely, a lack of communication might result in one service assuming that the other is commissioning - when it is not. Joint commissioning with health authorities appears to be one of the earliest embedded logics in CCPs, it being inherited from earlier and concurrent central government policy documents (Department of Health, 1989; Department of Health, 1990; Department of Health, 1995b). The CCPs show some diversity in their approach to joint purchasing.

Bexley's plan mentioned the establishment of a specific joint fund to purchase on behalf of elderly people with mental infirmities (Bexley, p. 15). This is described in the plan as having the purpose of protecting the needs of this group through the maintenance of high quality services. Thus joint commissioning for specific client groups may be a useful check on market forces, given that for high need groups, unpopular with the market, poor quality and abuse might more easily occur in a competitive environment (Le Grand, 1991;1993).

In contrast, Chelsea's approach to joint commissioning was much broader, it being seen as an integrated sharing of plans and budgets between health and social services, so that: 'agencies offer a complementary range of services' (Chelsea, p. 11). This shows joint commissioning as an intervention that ensures a diversity of supply, rather than focusing on regulations to protect an 'at risk' client group.

Other authorities see joint commissioning as more global, it being at the top of the planning and policy implementation hierarchy. For example, Greenwich, East Sussex, Surrey and the Isle of Wight put emphasis on how health and social services will plan organisationally and act together on almost all matters, including reference to organisational structures. But there is very little information easily available in these plans on what this approach means in terms of budget control, devolved budget expenditure and actual cost factors. West Sussex is more conservative and pragmatic (perhaps realistic) in its approach, preferring to put emphasis on building-up the existing good network of joint finance and planning (West Sussex, p. 12), and it also lists joint finance expenditure in its section on resourcing (op cit, p. 73).

Kent, Wiltshire and Kingston take a more devolved approach. Wiltshire describes a scheme for the joint purchasing of social care for older people based at GP practices in Trowbridge and Malmesbury (Wiltshire, p. 11) and Kingston puts emphasis on its grassroots development of multi-disciplinary assessment teams (Kingston, 1994, p. 23).

Joint commissioning was rarely explicitly linked in the published plans directly to counsellors or radical ideas about involving direct consumer participation. Counsellors were involved more directly in Greenwich (as discussed previously) and the Isle of Wight (p. 13). In the Wiltshire plan (p. 36) a voluntary sector representative in a joint commissioning team is quoted as saying: 'My main concern is that too few people are involved in the consultation process...many of the people in most need are not reached by organisations, do not attend meetings or complete forms.'

*Market strategy and the sharing of economic intelligence*

It was not easy from any of the plans to gain a concise and clear insight into the local authorities' intentions for future purchasing in the private social care market place. This kind of information is a prerequisite of Department of Health (1994a) guidance. Often if such an intention was stated it was hidden in the detail of the report. For example, in the midst of a chapter on 'Responsibilities for Planning and Providing Services', Greenwich lists seven specific services that it will need to purchase from the independent organisations in the coming year (1994, p. 18). There is no detail about how purchasers would like to see these services developing, the type of purchasing contract likely to be used or clues about how much money is likely to be available. An interested party would be left to rummage in the remainder of the report for clues from the budget statistics and organisational descriptions.

Croydon (1994) makes a more clear and specific point of advertising its purchasing intentions at the end of each section of analysis of key client groups. The intention statements include estimated funding. However, there is no detail about the kind of contracts likely to be used and whether grants might be paid towards development costs.

About half of the chapter on purchasing in the Surrey plan describes purchasing intentions with some degree of detail given, but there is a sense of the intentions having been realised (which might discourage new interested parties from applying). No authority sought to offer a costed overview of the economic activity of the private care market in its area, although basic volume counts of the units provided were given in three plans - as lists of resources.

## Discussion

There are methodological problems with using plans as a source of evidence about real local authority planning. They are in effect one manifestation of an iceberg, where the real mass may be of a different shape and drift. But published documents are, none the less, what local areas use to advertise their planning both to the local community and to some extent central government and because of this they are an important source of data. A degree of covert planning and policy is likely, but the bulk of direction cannot be hidden and will need to be presented, at least in part, in the published plan.

A study of the content of published plans does uncover some evidence about the process used to gather information and the concurrent evolving of a strategy. The activities of information gathering, the planning process, and publication of a plan are entangled (Bryson and Roering, 1988, p. 32). The strategic planning which resulted is at least partly related to the published plan made available.

The sample of plans studied here are notable for their managerial and organisational presentations of simple quantitative volume need and the qualitative feedback from user and carer consultation systems.

### *The dominance of the managerial system and logics*

As evidence of planning, the plans studied reflect a managerialist system as dominant over a political one. Their focus is a limited analysis of social care needs, market provision, and the emerging organisational changes of the social services department. There is only minimal integration of this analysis into a political synthesis and a central-local strategy for the medium and longer term (Department of Health, 1995a). The plans contain little discussion or description of conflicts over competing and limited resources, at a time when this has been a key feature of local government policy. Where such accounts were made, they were the exception. For example the chair of the Isle of Wight social services committee discusses the particular problems of reduced central government grant (1994, p. 1).

In contrast to the one example above, the survey of plans suggests an isolation of councillors from the plan making process. At best councillors have a limited involvement and this implies a weak strategic overview. They spend little time in the process and only attend high level periodic strategic meetings (Audit Commission, 1997). The managerial system appears to dominate the formulation of plans, including the consultation process with users which is designed to give voice to the users of community care and enable them to influence the strategic process. Named local politicians could only be identified in a minority of plans (n=5). Named senior managers were more likely to be identified with the plans (n=11). When seeking to analysis the documents as a form of communication between authors and readers (Atkinson and Coffey, 1997, p. 61) the plans are predominately a communication from local authority managers to the other actors in the social care market, that is users, carers, and independent sector service providers. Local authorities own role in the market place is diverse and fragmented. It includes purchasing on behalf of users and providing some services. The inability of plans to articulate focused and specific market strategies suggests some conflicts of interest, both internally - within the local authority - and in their relationship with outside bodies.

The logic of the market system is still rather dislocated from the text of the plans with documents appearing unclear as to the extent to which local authorities need to both curtail and stimulate market forces and how to begin making such market management decisions. The plans are not enthusiastic statements of a market system, for example they do not explicitly advocate competition, price competitiveness and consumerism, but the implicit tone is that a mixed market of supply will create quality and choice for users.

This suggests that social services managers are struggling to make sense of the increased marketisation of social care services that has followed the 1990 NHS and Community Care Act (Wistow, et al, 1993). Managers are struggling to adjust to an enabling role where their relationships with bodies outside of the organisation, that is, users groups, co-purchasers and providers is of growing importance (Leach, Stewart and Walsh, 1994, pp. 234-235). Despite the guidance from the Department of Health (1993b;1993b) that authorities should move directly to consulting with independent sector providers in the CCP process, in addition to consulting with users and carers, there is little evidence of this happening in the documents scrutinised.

*Strategic management and planning*

The managerial dominance in the new local authority planning process has resulted in the current textual structure of CCPs. This contextual structure can be broadly described as a four stage process: simple strategic summary, quantitative needs based assessment; supply based assessment (that is, service location and availability) and finally, market intervention and financial management. It is these four emerging stages that are the focus of the new local planning typology. The last of the stages is the least developed in plans. The stages have evolved incrementally. In part, plans have evolved at a local level (hence the local diversity in which the main contextual themes are covered). The themes of the plans are also the product of Department of Health policy and guidance. There is an implicit 'intextuality' (Atkinson and Coffey, 1997, p. 55) linking the recent history of central government community care policy documents. For example, the words 'choice' and 'quality' are key concepts in both central and local documents. Only occasionally is this 'intextuality' made explicit (Kingston, p. 15).

It was surprising how little the text of local plans was explicitly linked and referenced to national policy and policy documents, given the national contingencies that limit the scope for local action. This again is evidence of the dominance of managerialism over the local planning process where the logic of new managerialism encourages public organisations to see the policy environment as micro, internal, apolitical and subject to simplified efficiency and performance criteria (Clarke, Cochrane and McLaughlin, 1994). The managerial text creates its own definition of the social care sector where 'quality' and 'choice' are available to those in high priority need. The text therefore encourages readers to simplify the complex parts of the social care process (Prior, 1997, p. 67), persuading them to accept that 'choice' and 'quality' can only be available in the worst of circumstances.

The dominance of a managerialist logic on the process and form of plans reflects political intentions to use public management to impose a market and consumer based policy (Walsh, 1995). This logic may increasingly have to adjust to reflect a more holistic public service orientation with a new culture of public responsibility and representation (Self, 1993; Stewart and Clarke, 1987; Leach, Stewart and Walsh, 1994). The influence of supply side marketisation logics on CCPs is not exclusive and notions of demand planning (based on state subsidy and the management of public expenditure) have also had some influence on the evolution of CCP. Arguably what is now needed is to bring the activity of public expenditure planning back to the forefront of the national strategic agenda (Joseph Rowntree Foundation, 1996). The current local CCP system reinforces the time and space dislocation of local government from central government in its managing of social care. The timing of local elections does not relate directly to political and policy timetables at the central level. Spatial dislocation results because local government does not have direct access to central government decisions that effect social care, such as benefit, grant and taxation decisions. These time and space dislocations from strategic policy are reinforced by the permanence of textual documents (Prior, 1997, p. 76). Local permanent texts can be subsequently undermined by later policy changes from a different political government.

*National strategic planning*

Central government has not evolved a parallel strategic planning process and the focus of change has been almost entirely at the local level. This is in marked contrast to the national social care planning systems of the 1960s and 70s (Hambleton, 1986, p. 164). A method is needed to clearly link central government ministers with the policy decisions they take, for example a statutory requirement to publish a policy planning document on specific areas of government activity that goes beyond the basic budget analysis of public expenditure. The requirement to publish a yearly statement on central government objectives and outcomes for community care would be a useful catalyst to cross-departmental activity in addition to allowing government a vehicle for publishing what it sees as its achievements (Griffiths, 1988). There is, perhaps, a precedent for this, given the publication of the Health of the Nation targets and educational performance targets for schools. Choice and quality will be limited if there is inadequate long term national financing policy that ensures that individuals have either the insurance or taxation subsidy to enter the social market place.

*Needs based planning*

Certainly Griffiths and subsequent legislation and guidance have reintroduced a needs based planning typology into the evolution of local community care policy. But this new needs based planning typology is more complex than its predecessors. The previous national plans used only simple quantitative definitions of need and supply, based on supply based assumptions about what people would need. The increasingly presence of markets in the supply of social care to the public, introduces a diversity of supply. This is related to the premise that need itself is diverse and not homogeneous. Such qualitative assumptions make needs based planning in the social care market more complex. Quantitative analysis has to become more sophisticated and approximate this diversity.

This new phase of needs based planning requires some fundamental re-thinking on the definition of need and how best this can be understood in the new policy environment of community care (Hudson, 1997). Most authorities have so far only considered local need in the sense of 'relative priorities' and limitations have been placed on the definition of need because of resource constraints imposed by central government.

The survey of local plans shows that the published approaches to needs based planning are not sophisticated. Most only use basic data. The more advanced examples in this survey were from Kingston (1994) and Surrey (1994) both of whom utilise the information on severities of disability available in the 1998 OPCS Disability Survey. Surrey tries to use its quantitative model of need to estimate shortfalls in resourcing and unmet need. It refers to this as 'gap analysis' (Surrey, 1994, pp. 24, 47). Kingston also makes a limited attempt at this kind of analysis. The Kingston plan (1994, p. 120) concludes that estimates of such unmet need illustrate that: 'a considerable proportion of local people in need will be cared for by family, friends and neighbours and make little or not call on Social Services. Also the cost of providing a more universal service as this calculation shows is beyond the capacity of the local authority.'

The working priority of SSDs has been to prioritise the rationing of subsidised services. In effect, the planning process for the majority of local authorities is still dominated by the rationing of supply, rather than starting with a fundamental analysis of the relationship between need and demand. Local authorities pragmatic response has to be understood in the context of its relationship with central government. The local SSD is heavily dependent upon central block grant in order to provide a subsidised element of market supply. This makes it difficult for local authorities to encourage increased demand and take up of services.

More surprising in this climate is the fact that the new localised assessment of need is only weakly linked to unit costing given central government concerns with using market logics to inform the choice of supply.

The plans surveyed that had started to cost demand and needs (Surrey and Kingston) were able to create a much clearer contextual account of how the new policy environment is working and the difficulties created by a lack of demand side finance.

*Supply planning*

The analysis of market supply in relation to costs was minimal, and little active analysis was made of expenditure, apart from isolated figures on the transitional community care grant (STG), the social services budget summary, and ad hoc costing of certain provider services. Authorities avoided comparing their performance with neighbouring authorities, although a substantial range of data is available.

Plans failed to make clear and concise statements about purchasing intentions that would be meaningful to the independent sector, that is, the charities and businesses wishing to embark on service developments (Department of Health, 1993b). Often market strategic information on grants and contracting policies was sparse and rather hidden in the mass of more descriptive information. There were no examples of a clear local economic strategy. For example, statements from an authority that a certain volume and costed value of respite care is needed in the coming years. Current discussions between central and local government about the concept of 'best value' are likely to lead to all local authority departments publishing more transparent information about the purchase and supply of services (Department of Environment, Transport and Regions, 1998a).

Croydon (1994, p. 2) did make some attempts to move in this direction and the plan states in the introduction :

'Unless providers know what we, the purchasers, want they will not be able to develop a wider range of services in Croydon that will offer more choice...Our aim is to develop our annual plan so that it will reflect a three year vision of where purchasers wish to see their funding targeted. This plan does not achieve that goal, but we have set ourselves three years to develop our expertise in this aspect of our planning.'

The Croydon plan does offer some limited planning intentions for key client groups for the next financial year and these include some proposed costing (op cit, p. 22).

Social services do have dialogue with potential providers, but the lack of readily available public information about market supply developments and the value of contracts entered into, suggests that well organised large companies and trusts might all too easily establish a 'special relationship' with senior purchasers, while smaller charities and cooperative user groups are excluded from economic power and influence. Knowledge and information is an important source of power in itself and the big operators are able to afford their own market research and lobbying. It would be particularly useful to see plans addressing a section on how a small local operator could make a business plan and discuss it with the major purchasers, perhaps with examples being given. Plans could also be used to advertise grants that are becoming available for service development. Otherwise potential suppliers are dependent upon existing knowledge of the organisational systems and politics.

## Management consultation and public participation

One of the key features of the plans surveyed was their determination to demonstrate consultation with users and carers. But a consultation structure does not necessarily result in user preferences actually being met. How the managerial consultation logic of the plans evolves into a 'new consumer politics' (Mulgan, 1994) or user participation is not clear. Consumer politics requires consumers to have an economic power to withhold or change purchasing behaviour and this power is not widely available in the social care market.

Previous theories help explain the presence of a cultural barrier between a managerial consultation system and the process of political participation. Kakabadse's (1982) analysis of the hierarchy of cultures pervading the work of social services departments, proposes three different cultures as influencing different layers of the organisation. At the top is a power culture, constructed of the games and compromises, where counsellors interact with high level officers. In the middle tier is a role culture that is preoccupied with focusing on organisational stability, bureaucratic process and what is required of staff. On the front line of the organisation is a task culture that tries to achieve complex social outputs. The cultural types of power, role and task are derived from Handy (1991).

Domain theory also proposes three different types of organisational behaviour in the public sector; the policy domain, management domain and the service domain. Again, the management domain is seen as dominant in the middle section of a public sector organisation. It is characterised by a technocratic bureaucracy that uses hierarchical forms of control and structure, with a tendency to adopt linear information systems (Kouzes and Mico, 1979).

These theories also explain why the implementation of community care planning appears mostly as an expression of the management domain. It has essentially been established in the middle part of social services organisations and has only weak links with the major strategic decisions of councillors and chief officers.

This suggests that the old forms of political accountability are still dominant in social services departments and the new forms of accountability of power sharing with user groups, and offering market power to consumers are still under developed. Some anecdotal evidence from user groups also suggests that they experience the reality of a separation of the political system from the managerial system. One user in a mental health user group in East Sussex for example had found that it was necessary to lobby councillors when a deadlock was reached in the managerial consultative system. It was recognised that such political representation could have much more conclusive results, in terms of political game theory - either all was won, or all lost. If the extra resources were won, the group might be temporarily ostracised from the managerial consultation process because of its political moves. The last point shows that the political and managerial systems do overlap and that some new kind of system transformation can take place if actors permit it.

A complex systems analysis of this type of tension proposes that order can come out of the tension between sub systems, and that the tensions in the strategic process can be optimal. The elements of disorder need more understanding, if it is to be possible to create a strategy that includes the public viewpoint.

> 'Essentially, participation can be seen as either a means of arriving at decisions more efficiently, or as a manifestation of movement towards a participatory democracy...efficiency criterion will tend to lead to practices which reinforce the status quo in relationships between the professional, the elective representative and the public, the application of greater democratization criterion will tend to cast them in completely new roles.' (Benwell, 1980, p. 71)

If such a process is to be resolved satisfactorily the tensions need to find adequate expression through contact between the systems involved. Kauffman (1995) has called this inter-system communication 'patches'. Stacey

(1995, p. 488) prefers the term 'networks', where the informality of inter-system contact is defined by an emergent order and localised rules of engagement: 'random local rules of behaviour can result in emergent order at a global level, and whether there is order depends upon the degree of connectedness between elements of the network.'

A complex systems analysis suggests that long term structures cannot themselves be functional and that structures need to transform more readily to accommodate the current needs of actor groups. Another alternative solution would be to set up a new political planning structure that works alongside the managerial system, where councillors and outside stake holders are linked directly in the formulation of strategy. Part of the attraction with this method is that it might free the managerial system to perfect its analysis and information input more. But this also creates a dual structure where analysis and synthesis might not be linked in the best optimal manner.

Adding a new representative tier to local government where only a few individuals represent users and carers at high level meetings is at best only a partial solution to the participation issue. Research in Scotland has argued that this type of structure and process results in a group of 'pseudo-councillors' (Jeffrey, 1997) who are not fully accountable to the ballot box and party systems. Instead what is needed is a variety of parallel or heterarchical patches where community participation is able to feed directly into the various types of strategic planning and needs analysis. Citizen's juries offer one method for a group of representatives to deliberate with elected members and officers over specific policy issues. Market research opinion surveys and referendums taken from random samples of the local population can also provide more general evidence about local opinion on specific issues.

All this indicates the time scale needed for the culture change of moving from a predominately public sector monopoly, where professional and bureaucratic power has dominated in the middle mass of the organisation, to an inter-organisational process, where power and responsibility is shared in less institutionalised structures between all stake holders. In such a changing environment, condensing analysis and strategy into published plans is not a simple process, and will always be somewhat superficial. But nevertheless the correct balance between generality and detail needs to be sought.

Brodie (1994) cautions that the current community care planning system has become too divergent with its multitude of objectives and systems to satisfy. Hudson (1997) summarises the vast range of information that SSDs have to consider placing in the text of their CCPs in relation to statutory guidance. Brodie (1994) asks whether two or even three separate types of planning activity and publication are needed. The key question here is the extent of market and operational detail needed by a public audience. Would it be enough to merely indicate where more detailed information can be obtained? But this ignores the fact that the key readers will have a stake in what the detail embraces; users and carers, potential providers and the like. If these groups are to be empowered in order to take their place in the market, a significant goal for local authorities is to communicate valuable market information in an understandable and empowering manner. Only then will the economically poorer users and carers with less experience in business stand any chance of finding a foothold in the market place.

The danger with separating the current CCP process is that the political activity will continue to be remote and formalised and not successfully integrated. Brodie (1994), writing from the local authority management point of view, is concerned that plans have taken up resources and energies that should be devoted to the production and analysis of information. Producing written plans can become dysfunctional to on going strategic planning activities. Certainly there is little evidence from the survey of plans that the present emphasise on producing plans is linked to in depth information analysis and high quality strategic thinking. Alternative diagnoses and prognoses are not referred to. Planning needs to include a range of activities, and be able to encompass uncertainty and contradiction (Mintzberg, 1994; Bochel, Bochel and Page, 1995). It does need to have links with political, managerial and market systems.

Accepting a simplified definition of the CCP might lead to simplified planning activity. This would not increase an understanding of complexity. It might further reinforce a false economy of logic that relies on limited data. The lesson of previous policy planning is that planning is fragmented when confined to tight boundaries of politics and management systems. Alternatively, in some situations planning activities could join these systems quite explicitly: 'planning documents rarely exposed real political choices for elected members and the public...the planning process should be amended to concentrate on conflicts of interest amongst groups in the community' (Clapham, 1984, p. 49).

Some of the disorder of the current system of plan production and strategic activity is to be welcomed, if it is more dynamic and pragmatic in result. Rather than attempting to create simpler structures and models, a creative transformation of the existing systems and structures is the preferred organisational solution. The danger with explicitly encouraging a dichotomy of published managerial needs analysis versus ongoing political strategic thinking is that the organisational separation could suppress important conflicts of interest by not allowing sufficient inter-organisational patches through which views and logics can be expressed and compromises openly negotiated. Mintzberg (1994a, p. 201) says: 'to argue that politics interferes with the practice of planning is to ignore the political effects of planning on the one hand and the positive effects of politics on the other.'

The complexity paradigm of strategy development in open systems proposes that order can paradoxically come about from the chaotic collapse of old systems (Stacey, 1995). As old systems breakdown an informal cross communication of ideas between them leads to new solutions. Community care planning needs to focus on getting the activities of information collection and information analysis done - rather than seeking to find a perfect organisational structure for the production of plans.

The analysis of 1992-1993 and 1993-1994 plans by Wistow, Leedham and Hardy, 1993 (see also Hardy,Wistow and Leedham, 1993) both end with statements about the need for local community care planning to be as much a process as an end in itself. Commenting on what they describe as 'planning for planning' they remark: 'it is a continuous process, within which plans are only intermittent outputs; and second, that it is a prospective exercise aimed at both anticipating and shaping the future' (Hardy, Wistow and Leedham, 1993, p. 61).

If information collection and analysis is to be undertaken by managers it requires a substantial shift to occur in the current balance of how much time social services managers currently spend managing the user consultation process, towards the better management of complex information and its on going analysis.

Counsellors need to spend more time consulting with users, rather than being tied entirely to formal committee processes (Audit Commission, 1997). Small working briefings between management planners, councillor strategists and user representatives are likely to be a better instrument for integrating strategy and analysis, rather than an over-reliance on the traditional committee system (Essex, 1996).

In a rejection of the managerial organisational processes that deliver public sector plans, Healey (1990, p. 29) comments: 'far too much emphasis had been placed on the technical and analytical aspects of plan making and far too little on the political processes through which policy ideas are debated and negotiated into a broadly-based agreement on values and directions.'

But in terms of the content of the CCP observed in this chapter, middle managers appear to have been unable to develop the complex analysis of information necessary because they are managing strategy development. Again this leads to an argument for more direct involvement from councillors in the consultation process. This would allow middle tier social services managers to become more expert at the information analysis role. Such a realignment of roles does not necessarily have to contradict the complex systems hypothesis about the need for systems to converge and transform. Patches of inter-system communication would still be critical for the optimal integration of strategy development with managerial analysis.

Before the formulation of current community care policy, Glennerster (1980, p. 369) proposed a not dissimilar hypothesis, namely the need for a local social services strategy to be carved out of the competing rationalities of politics, professionals and consumers. His particular concern was that budgetary restraint could heighten the conflict between these logics, a finding also confirmed by Ferlie and Judge (1981).

A complexity theory analysis of organisations dictates that some instability between systems and logics is required, but that this instability is managed between some ultimate boundaries, if optimal solutions are to be found (Kiel, 1994; Stacey, 1995). Clapham (1984) has suggested that planning should openly acknowledge competing strategies, so as to inform debate. This is similar to Cartwright's (1991, p. 53) proposal that planning should present 'an ensemble of forecasts' to deal with chaos and uncertainty, and Healey's (1993) more recent contribution which defines public planning as a process of debate.

Managerial analysis does not currently make sophisticated quantitative arguments in CCP documents. At best the models used are descriptive of resource constraints and limited choices. A transformed planning process, where system structures are less institutionalised, might allow managers to present a variety of statistical arguments that will help inform political debate and the search for alternative strategies. Summaries of the findings of such analysis could be presented in plans.

## Conclusion

This chapter has evaluated the content of CCPs to see if their content provides evidence about the nature of the separate systems of management, politics and market and the interaction of this systems with planning activity. In conclusion the dominant system is the local authority management system, which is driven by an 'economy of logic' best described in terms of the NPM

(Hood, 1991) ethos now well documented (Pollit, 1990; Clarke, Cochrane and McLaughlin, 1994; Walsh, 1995; Clarke and Newman, 1997).

This NPM logic attempts to uses rational management science to implement market disciplines into public service areas. Simple financial and activity indicators are seen as the best method for attributing efficiency values to public sector activities and complex social interactions and inequities are largely ignored.

> 'In so far as new public management is limited to transferring management insights from business administration to the public sector it is not really new at all. In fact, it is concerned with the micro-economic issues of the public sector. This means that the discussion has a limited application for the issue of governance in a complex environment.' (Kickert and Koppenjan, 1997, p. 390)

A managerial emphasis on producing plans has not resulted in adequate creative analysis and modelling, and the focus on managerial consultation with external groups has distracted activity from both adequate information analysis and open strategic debate.

It is unlikely that an organisational structural solution can be found that assists community care planning. Stacey (1995) one of the key proponents of the application of chaos and complexity theory to the study of organisations has said that in is futile to look for the perfect structure as a solution and that it is better to get on with strategic thinking. A process that encourages adequate activities of analysis and synthesis will require the appearance of spontaneous and divergent patches of communication between different systems. Such patches are described in the language of organisations as, task forces, networks, project management and working groups, being based on informality, self-organisation and self-regulation. This is different to the old administrative entity of local government based on formalised committees and sub-committees. The challenge remains how to make these methods accountable (Taylor and Hoggett, 1994).

Organisational structure was the traditional technique by which the public sector tried to integrate the collection and analysis of data with the strategic planning of chief officers and councillors. If complexity theory shows that rigid and permanent structures cannot cope with such a task, the emphasis for planning moves to arranging the best temporary activities and concentrating more on getting the actual process of analytical and strategic integration, at any one point in time, correct. Essex (1996, p. 166) says: 'there are many advantages to members and officers working in partnership while respecting one another's responsibilities.'

Kauffman (1995, p. 28) places doubt on the ability of order and structure to solve complex human problems. He talks of: 'an orderly regime where poor compromises are found quickly, a chaotic regime where no compromises are ever settled on, and a phase transition where compromises appear to occur at the phase transition between order and chaos.'

A planning structure must change readily and the focus must be on getting the right blend of activities done in any one time and place (Fisher, 1998, p. 251). In modern, complex situations, the collation, analysis and updating of information becomes critical if a policy process is to perform at an optimal level.

# 5 Planning and the Social Care Market

## Introduction

It has been identified that one of the three systems in which community care planning operates is the market. The influence of markets on local authority social care planning has increased, in that while monetary forces inevitable had some indirect effect on planning in the past, via activities like Joint Finance and the purchase of services from the voluntary sector, in recent years markets have become more influential on service provision.

> 'This shift will require managers in SSDs to develop a whole range of new skills...It will also require them, and their political masters to make strategic decisions about the nature of and mix of service provisions that is most appropriate for their community.' (Osbourne,1990, p. 3)

The actual process of formulating a strategy and implementing it requires activity from political and managerial actors. To use Kontopoulos' (1993) terminology, marketisation is the 'totalizing logic' at work on social care structures. New public managerialism (NPM) seeks to use market values and structures to achieve output efficiency (Hood, 1991; Walsh, 1995). In this chapter the nature of planning intervention in the market is explored. Is management of a market compatible with planning activities?

> 'Since a market system is a "spontaneous order" monitored by its feedbacks, it conflicts with a rational order shaped by targets...In varying degrees, planning is intended to compensate for the inadequacies or faults of market processes.' (Sartori, 1991, p. 98 )

> 'In theoretical terms, this emerging concept of a 'planned market' occupies an intermediate position between command-and-control planning systems, on the one hand, and pure neo-classical market systems, on the other.' (Saltman and Von Otter, 1992, p. 16)

Historical evidence provides little help when state planning machinery is asked to increase the use of market mechanisms to achieve efficiency and choice in the delivery of public services. But market spontaneity is now seen by many, at least in part, as the solution to creating a diversity of supply. The key challenge for government becomes the analysis and subsidy of market entry.

> 'The central issue is the balance between the use of straightforward market process and planning. Unregulated markets are unlikely in most cases. What we have at present are often markets in which there are a few individual customers and limited use of the price mechanism.' (Walsh, 1995, p. 163)

The chapter assesses the manner in which a social care market structure can be actively planned and managed if a policy is to be equitable, in addition to efficient. What is proposed is a planned approach to a social market for social care, as an alternative to a 'drift' towards a market that is supposed to organise itself. This book defends planning, arguing that it can be a realistic and complex process that helps provide optimal policy solutions.

In this book the term 'marketisation' is preferred to privatisation. In a social market place market forces are used to deliver choice and diversity, but the market system is not fundamentally private - in the sense that it is operated independently, or secondary to, state management and planning. In a social market place market forces are used to encourage choice and diversity, but the state intervenes to ensure equity of opportunity for purchase between rich and poor. Laing has proposed that the 'social market' model of marketisation is appropriate for the purchase and provision of social care products (Laing, 1993).

## Markets in Social Policy

Confidence in markets is founded on the ability of the price mechanism to distribute supply in relation to demand, with it achieving this function more efficiently, effectively and equally than alternative methods of social coordination and distribution. Faith in the market to deliver a social policy objective like near full employment was one central feature of neo classical economics. This political 'faith in markets' as the only means of delivering efficiency and public choice was paradoxically not impervious to state influence on markets. For example the continued selling of council houses, alongside a state policy of mortgage tax relief, inflated and distorted both the demand for property and credit to finance their purchase. The Government was indirectly subsidising the housing market through mortgage income tax relief. When the market collapsed it left a legacy of bad debit. Policy to provide rest home beds in the private sector rather than the public sector distorted the provision of residential care at the expense of home care, with much of the funding of the private provision still paid for by government (Audit Commission, 1986). Despite the privatisation and marketisation of social structures the state remains 'entangled' in these newly expanded markets.

## Complexity Theory and Markets

Complexity theory rejects the notion of a market equilibrium and an inherent price stability (Waldrop, 1993; Ormerod, 1994; Elliot and Kiel, 1997a). Planning must focus on an appropriate understanding, manipulation, management and regulation of evolving market systems. The most fundamental and erroneous underpinning of the totalizing logic of marketisation was the neo-classical belief that market equilibrium would self regulate developments (Ormerod, 1994).

> 'A more accurate assessment of economic reality would allow for the fact that those stabilising forces do not operate. If that is the case, then there is no single equilibrium point for the economy, but a multitude of potential equilibrium points.' (Elliot and Kiel, 1997b, p. 71)

This error can be explained with reference to the importance in complexity theory of time as a partial determinant of order. Waldrop (1993, p. 37) summarises the new economics of complexity in contrast to neo-classical economics. He states that complex economics is based on the self organisation of biology rather than the equilibrium of physics and it focuses on the diversity of individual people rather than the rationalist-determinist idea of people all being the same type of consumer. Recent research into the ability of people to consume social care as a market product suggests that people do not conform to a simple market rationality in their attitude to care (Baldock and Ungerson, 1994; Baldock, 1997; Parker and Clarke, 1997).

Having denounced equilibrium, complexity economists diverge, forming a contrast between those who continue to defend the totalizing logic of marketisation as the best policy amongst uncertainties (the neo-Austrian complex economic theory, Parker and Stacey, 1994, p. 81) as contrast with the complex political-economic model of Allen, Clark and Perez-Trejo (1992).

Complexity writers who argue that markets are the best method of allocating resources accept that equilibrium does not exist, but cite the development of the Austrian school in its distinctiveness from neo-classical economics.

'In Austrian thinking, economies move predictably to equilibrium only if information is perfect or complete. Only then will all individuals acts be coordinated, leading very quickly to no surpluses or deficits in markets. In practice, in economics information is not complete and actions are not perfectly coordinated, so surpluses and deficits are not perfectly coordinated, so surpluses and deficits can exist for some time.' (Parker and Stacey, 1994, p. 89)

There is a problem in the explanation 'for some time'. Time is a critical dimension to complexity theory in that it is highly probably an event will occur in the future, but it is not known when it will occur. The consequence is to plan for a range of short term scenarios. The juxtaposition of neo-Austrian economics and complexity theory is inadequate because of the inability to define with any clarity how long the market will take to clear to something near to equilibrium. This uncertainly over the time span necessary undermines the neo-Austrian Complexity account.

It is possible to defend the use of descriptive macro economic planning models as a method governments can use in the management of complex economic systems. Quantitative economic information can be presented on a range of social and economic variables so as to assist government intervention for the public good (Allen, Clark and Perez-Trejo, 1992).

The contrast here with neo-Austrian thinking is a belief that a minimum state can partly understand its entanglement with a market economy. Neo-Austrians are cynical about purposeful government intervention. They suggest that state management and planning is likely to distort market behaviour more than the market is likely to distort itself. This reflects a dualism of state and market where the activities of state and market are separated in terms of cause and effect - hence the state can be blamed for its effect on the market. In this book it is proposed that in the modern complex world the boundary of state and market is not rigid, rather the two systems are increasingly entangled. The juxtaposition of neo-Austrian economics and complexity theory is inadequate because it is based on a dualism of state and market. This book argues that such a dualism is erroneous.

Marketisation is one example of the entanglement of state and market. The state's desire to increase the use of market forces in the supply of public goods has necessitated a state promotion of market types. The activity of the state promoting market activity becomes a market distortion. For example, governments have arguably under priced state assets as they have been sold to the private sector. This creates undervalued new markets (that were previously a state monopoly) which displace investment and economic resources from markets that previously existed. It is not only government regulation of markets that distorts markets. Pro market government behaviour can disturb natural market processes. It is not possible to completely separate the two entangled systems. Politics, state and market as modern systems of social coordination cannot be separate and explained as closed systems. They are adaptive and open systems (Capra, 1996). They are inter-dependent and the tensions between these three systems needs to be understood in these terms, rather than by simple explanations of cause and effect. Where exactly the three systems overlap is difficult to map and is changing over time. Some key patches of system interaction and activity can be identified, for example, activities like budget setting and establishing financial rules and regulations.

Privatising governments of the 1980s were in this sense equivocal - highly active politically, rather than passive to market forces (Marsh and Rhodes,1992). The government's entanglement with markets was not well understood or planned. In the post war tradition, intervention through distorting government actions continued, but the effect of such distortions was not readily acknowledged by a government which claimed it believed in minimal state intervention. This allowed distorting actions to be unmanaged in their effect. In the social care market, small changes in residential care rules for the payment of social security in 1980 lead to exponential and unplanned growth in the state funded provision of private rest home beds for the next 15 years. Domestic and domiciliary home care was largely neglected (Audit Commission, 1986).

The premise here is that all modern governments, even those that are ideologically pro market, inevitably have to try and understand and plan their own intervention and entanglement in the market. To deny such a role is counter productive. Planning cannot be based on single linear models and assuming one determinist future, rather it seeks a full analysis of information and possible scenarios of what might happen (Allen, Clark and Perez-Trejo, 1992). Similarly within the social care market, local authorities must face the reality of their own entanglement in the local market place and seek to understand it.

*Bringing back market forces*

Given their ideological confidence in markets, government ministers of the 1980s were keen to experiment with public choice notions of bringing 'internal' market forces into the public sector to counteract state and professional monopolies. Hence a range of 'marketisation' strategies was applied. These varied from the planned market of the NHS and Next Steps agencies, that were predominantly built on internalised purchaser and provider separation, to the compulsory external contracting of local services (like refuse collection) where there are potentially multiple private providers. Between these types is the approach of the social care market where the aim is to have both internal public providers and external independent providers.

In a recent review of global privatisation, published in *The Oxford Economic Journal*, Boycko, Shleifer and Vishny (1996) argue that privatisation is in many circumstances economically efficient, because it makes it difficult for politicians to distort productive activity. Their model is based on classical economic theory of competitive profit maximisation that neglects the complexities of public or semi public goods (or merit goods) which are non-excludable, non-rejectable and have external social costs and benefits. In the 1970s, when rational economics was being applied increasingly to an analysis of public expenditure, Williams wrote of the requirement for economists to also consider the 'complex notions of externalities and merit goods' and not to provide a 'simplistic interpretation of demand' (1974, p. 71). Because of these complexities the application of market forces to public service transactions has lead to use of the term 'quasi' markets by Le Grand (1991 ). This is because the markets being developed are not open competitive markets, but significantly distorted by a structural difficulties. The privatisation of British Rail is one such example. Passenger carrying companies have to purchase a contract with the rail maintenance body Railtrack, they have no choice to run their trains elsewhere.

Within the public sector the move from bureaucratic structures to market structures has much to do with a new prioritisation of what social and economic values are important. Evolving social logics associated with marketisation have placed concerns about equity and social justice as less important, whilst efficiency has become paramount. Le Grand and Bartlett (1993, p. 14) comment: 'there is nothing caring about wasting resources. And it is the avoidance of such waste that is the prime motivation behind the efficiency considerations in any area, including those that form the welfare state.' They proceed to define efficiency in language that is more pragmatic for the welfare state:

> 'A drive for efficiency...could become simply an excuse for cost cutting, regardless of the impact on the quantity or quality of the service provided. A second concept of efficiency, known to economists as product efficiency, does

not suffer from this problem. For this explicitly relates the costs of a service to the quantity and quality of service provision.' (p. 15)

It is because markets in the public sector are structurally imperfect that they have to depend on new conceptual forms of organisation and management, sometimes in the form of unelected committees, or the political activity of local government, to regulate their limitations. Therefore utility regulatory bodies currently limit the price rises for telephone, gas and water charges. There is insufficient competition for these markets to be permitted to set their own prices. Price fixing takes place when SSDs purchase residential social care at fixed annual rates, to prevent the escalation of profits on the supply side (Wistow, et al, 1996, p. 151; Laing, 1998).

## Public goods and semi-public goods

The most obvious examples of public goods are those goods that are non-excludable and non-rivalrous, because by their nature they are accessible to others, for example parks and roads. More contested as public goods are the goods provided by the welfare state post 1945, such as medical care and education. Whilst these can be exclusive and rivalrous and provided only to selecting individuals by the market place, they are not 'rejectable', in that in a modern society when people are very ill, or lacking in education, they have to obtain these products to take part in society, and cannot abstain from their purchase. Cultural norms require families to look after the education and health needs of their partners and children, regardless of wealth. Therefore health and social care is both a private and public good, or a semi-public good. In the modern social context these goods are non-rejectable. Semi-public goods like social care are sometimes referred to as merit goods, because while they are strictly speaking not shared equally by the public, they possess important social and collective benefits for society that are greater than the needs of the individual consumer.

Neo-classicists accept that public goods are inevitable in some circumstances. The central issue becomes how can the public's choice and accountability be maximised (Self, 1993, pp. 36-43). But neo-classicists dispute the appropriateness of some economic activities which have been defined as semi-public goods (or merit goods) in modern society and attempt to push the frontiers of state involvement back.

# The Application of Market Logics to Social Care

*Social costs and money economics*

Market costing of social care facilities starts with an understanding of the monetary concepts involved. Firstly products and outcomes of a social value have to be given some kind of financial value. This book refers to this process as 'social costing'. What is disputed in this book is the extent to which the market alone can do this efficiently.

*Kinship logics and care*

Not all behaviour that carries a social cost can easily be converted into a financial cost. Not all social care does take place primarily in a market landscape or consumer system, it is argued here that much social care is not logically or culturally perceived as being market activity that responds to the logics of the price mechanism (Clark, 1996).

Social care can be observed as operating in a primary landscape system of kinship, where families, neighbourhoods and other sub-cultural groups have complex cultures of loyalty and reciprocity (Bulmer, 1987). Here decisions about when and where to provide care are remote from economic rationale. Sub-logics of class, family, and geography will be entangled in the logics of kinship care. The possible nature of this interaction is shown in Figure 5.1. Kinship care is also entangled with state, political and market behaviour. The kinship system is entangled with the market system, rather than being separate from it by clear boundaries, and it becomes necessary to understand the patches where the two merge and are inter-connected.

Classical economic rationality suggests that market prices normally resemble the social cost of an activity, that the social cost of kinship care will make some contribution to the calculation of market price of care, providing that market activity has not become distorted by government behaviour. In this book it is proposed that complexity theory challenges the simplistic notion of this economic rationality, proposing instead that the relationship between kinship logics of what social care is costing, has an unstable and unpredictable relationship with market logics of pricing (Taylor-Gooby, 1998).

This is especially so in a society where there is much social change and diversity of systems and culture, and numerous sub-logics in operation. It is proposed that there is some 'bounded instability' (Stacey, 1995) in the relationship between kinship assessments of the cost of social care and actual

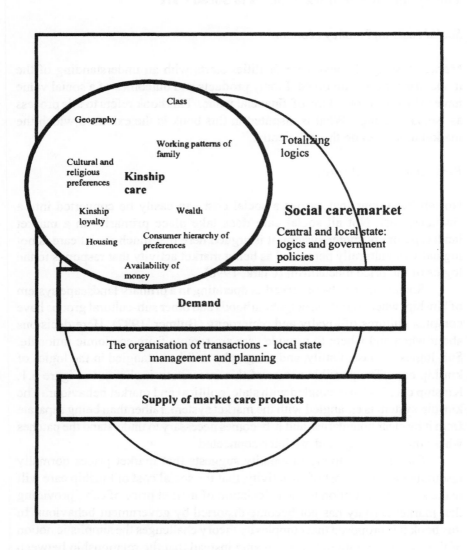

**Figure 5.1  Systems of kinship care**

market prices. This fluctuating boundary is defined by the differing qualitative social comparisons that actors make. It is proposed that at any one time, kinship and market cultures do interact to form a quantity of market demand for social care, but that over time the relationship is relatively unstable and unpredictable.

## *Bounded instability: social care costs and conversion to monetary value*

In a manufacturing business costing is the means by which accountants measure the cost of purchasing items necessary for production over time and add on a profit calculation so as to generate a market price. This is often referred to as 'cost plus' accounting (Bottle, 1996). In a stable market, price should be marginally higher than the costs of production and related to the forces of demand and supply. When stable market forces are not structurally possible, government costing of units of activity also becomes a means by which priority and value is given to the allocation of a unit of supply in relation to demand.

Public choice theory is concerned that the level of public goods provided has exceeded real social value and real social cost (McLean, 1990; Self, 1993). For public choice theory this hike in costs reflects an over supply and an increase in unrealistic public demand. This process is fed by government intervention and fiscal financing that distances inefficient costs from individual people. A hypothetical example of such a public choice economic analysis of a social care transaction follows.

In Table 5.1, Family X have an older relative living with them. The social costs are large, but many are difficult to put a financial value on (Knapp, 1993, pp. 10-13). Nevertheless Table 5.1 shows a hypothetical list of annual costs.

It is immediately apparent that the family is not bearing the cost of all items and some are borne by others. The older woman pays most using her own pension. The fixed state cost of a single person pension could theoretically be added to the state expenditure columns in both scenarios, but it is a fixed cost to the state that does not change over the two scenarios - so it has not been added. It is possible to calculate an alternative provision in Table 5.2 (Scenario 2) to see what happens to the public costings. Imagine that the couple learn that the older relative is entitled to a place in a rest home paid entirely by the state because she has no housing equity or savings in her own right. The cost implications are set out in Scenario 2. The price set by the care home is £14,000 per year (fixed to get the maximum in state benefit top up

**Table 5.1    Scenario 1, informal care costs:**
            **older person living with daughter and family**

|                              | Family  | State   | Employers | Older Relative |
|------------------------------|---------|---------|-----------|----------------|
| R=Room rent                  | £ 2000  | £ 1300  |           | £ 2000         |
| P=Power & Service costs       | £ 600   |         |           |                |
| SW=Stress costs at work       |         | £ 100   | £ 400     |                |
| SM=Stress costs, medical      | £ 50    | £ 450   |           |                |
| HMC=Home medical care         |         | £ 1000  |           |                |
| F=Food and social needs       | £ 200   |         |           | £ 1600         |
| Totals                       | £ 2850  | £ 2850  | £ 400     | £ 3600         |

Explanations.

**R** A room that used to be rented out to a student, is worth £4000 a year to the family and £1,300 to the inland revenue. The relative now pays £2,000 to the parents for rent and this is exempt from taxation. The family loses £2,000 and the state £1,300.

**P** Additional power and phone costs borne by the family and not charged to the relative.

**SW** Stress causing lost days at work for couple. These costs are borne by the government and employer in the form of sickness benefit with no costs for the couple.

**SM** Cost of medical help for stress. Only prescription charges are borne by the daughter and family. Professional fees are paid by the NHS.

**HMC** Cost of Home medical care for elderly relative, ie: GP and nursing visits etc (Paid by NHS).

**F** Food and social needs is arranged rather informally in this family; but they estimate that the older person carries most of the cost from her own pension, with the family contributing about an additional £200 per year.

**Table 5.2     Scenario 2,  older person moves to rest home: costs**

| | Family | State | Older Rel | Empl'r | (Price charged) Rest Home. |
|---|---|---|---|---|---|
| R=Room rent | -£2000 | -£ 1300 | £ 3500 | | £ 3500 |
| P=Power & Service costs | -£ 600 | | £ 500 | | £ 500 |
| SW=Stress costs at work | | -100 | | -£ 400 | |
| SM=Stress costs, medical | -£ 50 | -£ 450 | | | |
| HMC=Home medical care | | £ 1000 | | | |
| F=Food and social care | -£ 200 | £ 8400 | £ 1600 | | £ 10000 |
| T=Travel for visits | £ 300.00 | | | | |
| Totals | -£ 3700 | £ 7550 | £ 5600 | -£ 400 | £ 14000 |

Explanations.

**R**  The room can be rented out to a student again and is worth £2000 more a year to the family and £1,300 to the inland revenue. The older relative now pays £3,500 to the rest home for their rent of their room.

**P**  Extra power and phone costs borne by the family are now  saved, a similar payment has to be made by the older relative to the rest home.

**SW**  The Stress that caused lost days at work for couple. is terminated These costs are no longer borne by the government and employer in the form of sickness benefit.

**SM**  The termination of the stress related illness for the carers also saves treatment monies.

**HMC**  There is no change in the cost of Home medical care for the older relative, ie: GP and nursing visits etc (Paid by NHS).

**F**  The family saves on its food and social care costs, but the state and older relative inherit a much more substantial bill from the rest home for these services.

against the permissible charge on the woman's pension). She agrees to go. The net cost to the state is £7,550, even when tax revenue is raised on the renting of the room she vacates and NHS costs for the stress caused to the daughter and her family are cut. The older relative has substantially less economic freedom because she is required to commit almost all her pension to the costs of the care home. The family are better off and the daughter's employer marginally so - due to the cessation of working time lost through stress. The state loses the most.

This example is hypothetical and not based on real prices or costs. But it serves to illustrate the point that public choice theory seeks to make. The subsidy that the state is willing to pay to the rest home distorts the whole situation. It will lead to an over demand and supply for residential home care - when home care costs are comparatively less.

An alternative analysis is that the state's rationing may lead to an unrealistically low financial cost being placed on certain social costs in the domestic care Scenario 1 (Table 5.1). In effect there might be a psychological advantage to the carer in avoiding the financial value of the social costs, because of the personal stress and guilt involved in facing up to all that is being lost and cost. In the domestic care example (Scenario 1) the family only estimated that social care and food cost them £200 per year. This in itself illustrates the imperfection and problems of social opportunity costings and how such costs will vary according to personal definition. This family does not assess the care and food costs as very great. They were buying in bulk for the rest of the family, and as regard to social contact, they were planning to be at home and together much of the time.

Another family in the same situation might refuse to accept such a low value on social cost and see their own life as so disrupted that it becomes imperative to pay someone to come and sit with the relative on most days. This would push the social opportunity costs up greatly and make them more comparable with the rest home. Individual psychological factors such as loyalty, guilt and personal ambition begin to enter into the rational economic calculation, but these are extremely difficult to generalise to other families and carers.

In conclusion, social opportunity costs are subject to quite wide fluctuations according to personal choice, class, culture and expectations. Economic rational choice can be shown to be relatively diverse and unpredictable when applied to social care. Certainly the relationship between social costs and real costs is relative and not absolute. Some common shared rationalities exist, but there are also important individual differences. Different individual people tend to cost differently, with some placing more relative price value on the social labour cost of domestic caring than others. It is proposed that in the language of complexity theory the relationship between social costs and real costs is one of 'bounded instability' (Stacey, 1995). If the social care market is to succeed in balancing efficiency with equity it requires a valid conceptualisation of such costing and thereby the appropriate pricing of social care services.

There is one final point to be made here. One social costing effects another. For example the price costing of the rest home will have effected psychologically the social costing of the family's care. This again serves to illustrate that costing is socially constructed and not scientifically rigid or solely reductionist. Costs are a social phenomena: all costs and their associated prices interrelate and none is an entirely independent entity. Entanglement is again a key feature. Actors are constantly having to make comparative judgements about different individual items and priorities of purchase. While there may be some trends and national similarities in these comparative consumer judgements, there is also a large degree of individuality and instability between actors (Taylor-Gooby, 1998). This partial presence of a consumer rationality that establishes some boundaries within which a range of individuals behave differently, can be viewed as similar to Stacey's (1995) idea of bounded instability.

## *Market prices and public service charges*

This leads to a definition of financial cost, whereby money cost is the socially and economically constructed calculation of combined resource costs. In a pragmatic sense it will need to include capital, revenue and transaction costs, although in the public sector government may carry some of these in the form of an implicit subsidy and not pass them onto the user.

In manufacturing industry resource costs that underpin pricing are likely to be relatively tangible and predictable when compared to the intangible problems of costing social care. In private manufacturing industry price over time usually needs to be greater than combined resource costs over time, to generate a profit. For a short time management decisions can be taken to lose profit, or even sell below cost, on selected items for reasons of market strategy. This will partly depend on the diversity of products manufactured. Time is a critical variable in making sense of monetary economics. A loss over three months might be turned around to a profit over six months.

The traditional logic of business economics is that over time a supply company must make a profit and that profit must be based on the financial cost of production, plus a margin for profit. But this logic assumes that people will pay a price for the product that meets the 'cost-plus'.

Whether or not actors will do this in reality depends on a number of complexities, including social context and the stability of the social environment. An alternative logic is to ask people in any one context and social environment how much they are willing to pay financially for a product, in other words what financial value do they symbolically put on the product? Here the business economist is moving to a logic of 'price-minus' (Bootle, 1996). Price calculation starts with the social context of the price that the consumer is willing to pay.

The business then tries to work out if it can produce the product at that price by analysing the unit costs of production (op cit). Given the level of price fixing in the social care market, it is likely that providers are influenced by the price-minus approach to costs and profits (Wistow, et al, 1996, pp. 89, 110; Laing, 1998). Public purchasers of care also have to give consideration to the comparative social context, knowing that many individuals will not chose to spend their money on social care, but will prefer to spend their money on other items.

In the public sector there has often been a logic applied that price paid can actually be lower than financial cost. This is because the government is willing to discount a price for reasons of equity and to increase 'positive' market activity, especially in goods like education and health care. Here 'charges' are defined as the proportion of a calculated cost that a public service passes on to a user. Therefore public charges can be much lower than real market prices. Goods like health and social care products are seen as of social merit and so the government attempts to reduce their price in order to increase access.

The PSS have a tradition of charging below the market cost in order to achieve equity and take up of social care provision. When assessing charging policy PSS have the difficult task of assessing what proportion of costs to pass on in charges and also whether or not to charge a flat rate to all users, or means test according to the principles of equity. Means testing raises the cost of the service because of the bureaucracy of completing the means test (Joseph Rowntree Foundation, 1996). By implication a means test might also raise the charge set.

Many people do not associate social care with the need to consume and they do not make social care purchases alongside other every day comparative economic decisions about consumption. Often a social and family crisis suddenly forces actors into the social care market. Actors instantaneously have to make large financial and emotional decisions that they find difficult to put in any comparative economic context (Baldock and Ungerson, 1994). They may look to the state and social services to help them understand this context and for guidance on how to behave appropriately.

The under consumption by actors of social care products is supported by evidence in the Office of National Statistics Family Expenditure Survey (1994, 1997). Table 5.3 shows that a reduction in the average household income of retired people reduces their capacity to consume the extra domestic help they need when they are older and have more need. Although those aged 75 and over are spending more on domestic help as a percentage of their total expenditure than any other age group (3%) , the amount in terms of spending power is small, because of their low average expenditure (£139.00 per week).

*Planning as an economic analysis and synthesis*

Given the imperfect rational nature of social care markets both local and central government must make a continuing assessments of the market's functioning. It is argued in the remainder of the book that there are three critical areas to be addressed in the content of plans and planning; the management of transactions; structural inadequacies of supply, and the relationship between human need and market demand. The last of these is the most neglected in the current planning process and therefore both chapters six and seven focus on demand side planning.

## The Management of Transactions

*The price mechanism and social care transactions*

In a market based system demand for volume cannot be divorced from prices because the market is used to allocate resources and price is the methodology invoked to achieve the best distribution of supply. In a traditional free market, if there is a lack of supply, then price will be high. If supply is abundant then prices will be lower. In the social care market inelasticity of demand may occur due to consumers underestimating the social cost (or real social value) of social care in comparison with other consumer preferences. Actors are trying to postpone payment on social care as long as is possible, so as to make other more 'positive' consumer choices such as material purchases, or

**Table 5.3    Expenditure on domestic help, 1993-1994 and 1995-1996, average weekly expenditures per age group, head of household**

| 1993-1994 | | Age of head of household | | | | |
| --- | --- | --- | --- | --- | --- | --- |
| *average weekly expenditure* | >30 | 30-49 | 50-64 | 65-74 | 75+ | All |
| on domestic help (£) | £ 1.37 | £ 3.53 | £ 1.23 | £ 1.58 | £ 2.03 | £ 2.30 |
| gross expenditure (£) | £ 258.61 | £ 344.86 | £ 302.01 | £ 191.65 | £ 121.73 | £ 276.68 |
| % spent on domestic help | 0.5 | 1.0 | 0.4 | 0.8 | 1.7 | 0.8 |

| 1996-1997 | | | | | | |
| --- | --- | --- | --- | --- | --- | --- |
| *average weekly expenditure* | | | | | | |
| on domestic help (£) | £ 1.73 | £ 3.81 | £ 1.41 | £ 1.44 | £ 4.11 | £ 2.74 |
| gross expenditure (£) | £ 269.94 | £ 360.66 | £ 309.83 | £ 198.40 | £ 139.00 | £ 289.86 |
| % spent on domestic help | 0.6 | 1.1 | 0.5 | 0.7 | 3.0 | 0.9 |
| standard error (£) = +or - | 10 | 3 | 9 | 14 | 5 | 4 |

*Source*: Office of National Statistics, 1994;1997. Crown copyright.

retaining savings and equity levels for children. People will 'reject' the product of social care as long as they can, until it is not longer rejectable because of their severe ill health.

Evidence submitted to the House of Commons Health Committee (1995, pp. 43-44) by the British Geriatrics Society for Health in Old Age argues that providing care at lower levels of disability is vital if unnecessary deterioration and severe disablement is to be prevented. This implies that a higher take up of lower level care might lead to a decrease in demand for intensive community and residential care at a later date (House of Commons Health Committee, 1996, p. lvii). This argument is supported by research into the implementation of home based community care services (Davies and Challis, 1986). People who do not have access to help with social tasks at the onset of a serious illness may relapse and deteriorate more quickly than those who have access to such services. While relatives may be able to provide a high level of emotional and physical support, professional staff may be better trained to give advice that prevents aggravating the illness and they may see warning signs that enable medical treatment to be administered before a deterioration. If people tend to deny their need for care when they first become ill, general income benefits are unlikely to stimulate much increased expenditure on social care unless they are set at much increased rates or a specific voucher, redeemable for care, is given. The Family Expenditure Survey (DSS, 1994; 1997) shows how unpopular domestic care is relative to other consumer products. For lower income groups this lack of desire and inability to consume domestic social care is likely to be exacerbated by poverty. A re-analysis of the data collected by the OPCS national disability survey of 1988 by Bebbington, Turvey and Janzon (1996) concluded that only about a quarter of people over 65 years of age who experience low levels of disability were receiving social services. Recent research into healthy life expectancy in England and Wales suggests that:

> 'while people are continuing to encounter disability creating conditions at a similar rate, the most severe levels of disability are being successfully contained. If these trends continue, then in the future as the number of elderly people increases, there will be more with minor problems, though the demand for services for severe disablement may not necessarily increase.' (Bebbington and Darton, 1996b, p. 1)

This research was based on longitudinal analysis of the General Household Survey. The limitations of this data are discussed by Bone (1995).

The findings imply that the government must address the strategic issues of equity, access and consumer rejection of social care products, if prevention is to continue to be successful.

In a social market place the government will want to modify the extremes of this instability of demand to achieve a degree of equity and a socially acceptable balance of distribution (Knapp, et al, 1994, p. 147). To achieve this it intervenes in the market place, purchasing supply on behalf of individuals, or by giving them the means to purchase, or save for later purchase, themselves. In effect this is an attempt to persuade people not to 'reject' social care as a consumer choice. Government subsidises the purchase of social care either directly or indirectly through fiscal policy.

*Preference inelasticity*

The inability of those in need to enter the market and express their need and preference for a social care product in relation to a rational comparison of other consumer products can be described as 'preference inelasticity'. If the government does not intervene many people will avoid the market place choosing, or having, to bear the opportunity costs of providing family care themselves. Social care will be rejected as a market commodity. This ability of social care consumers to avoid expressing demand is likely to be partly related to the severity of long term illness and partly related to income and wealth. Actors in higher income groups seem more likely to express demands for care in the current market place, at lower levels of need (Baldock and Ungerson, 1994; Laing, 1993).

Where government does not intervene to increase the likelihood of a preference being made for a social care product there will be externalised social costs. Minor disabilities will deteriorate more quickly (House of Commons Health Committee, 1995). Another implication of a natural, localised system of informal care as seen in the developing world is that population growth occurs because families seek to have large numbers of children so that they can be adequately looked after when they are older. Home care might also be dysfunctional to the developing and developed economy in other ways, with skilled workers being unavailable to the economy because they are caring. In order to intervene government has to distort the market place, so as to make economic choices associated with social care more attractive to people.

The degree to which social care should be equitable and redistributive is debated and subject to political disagreement, but what seems certain is that all political parties will seek to intervene in the social care market to some extent and thereby displace costs across society away from the suffering, so that the relative economic burden is shared.

The government needs a degree of national centralised planning to deal with the preference inelasticity of demand, the inability of people to choose to spend money on social care. An association between social care and a lack of preference is likely to be related partly to sub-culture, consumer attitudes and relative wealth. If social care is determined by market price alone many will chose not to enter the market. The poor, who are most likely to fall ill and die early (Whitehead, 1992; Bebbington and Darton, 1996b; Dorling, 1997; Wilkinson, 1996), are more likely to reject social care products until their health is so poor that the products are no longer rejectable.

In a social market the role of the state in assessing costs and influencing prices is critical, because cultural preferences create demand inelasticities that distort price and lead to low levels of market activity. Conversely, at certain points in time, when older people's lives are in severe crisis, they are vulnerable to abuse from the profit incentives of the market place.

This illustrates the need for government to plan for vertical equity rather than concentrating on unit product efficiency alone. To deny the need to deal with vertical equity undermines the resulting product efficiency, because of a loss in consumer pressure (Netten, 1993). An explicit goal of the social care market must be to get all relevant peoples into the market place and thereby increase total market size. The burden for doing this should not fall predominantly on local authority purchasing structures. Central government fiscal redistribution, cash transfers and regulation of local state activity are important policy vehicles. Central government national planning is as important as local planning.

## Planning and Market Transaction Analysis

Wistow et al list six types of demand transaction. These are: coerced collective demand, uncoerced or voluntary collective demand, corporate demand, uncompensated individual consumption, compensated individual consumption and individual donation. These can be located with examples.

1. Public professional transactions. A care manager purchases a service on behalf of a user.
2. Voluntary professional transactions. Voluntary sector purchases a service on behalf of a user.

     3. Private Company transactions. A company purchasers a service on behalf of an employee.
     4. Private consumer transactions. A private individual purchases.
     5. Subsidised consumer transactions. A Person uses a government benefit to purchase service.
     6. Private Gift transactions . A person purchasers a service for an older relative.
     (1993, p. 34.)

These are the different types of market transaction where need is translated into actual market demand. Given the concerns in this book about low levels of market activity and the poor choosing to reject social care products, the public sector has a crucial role to play in encouraging new transactions in the social care market place.

     The economic cost of facilitating a transaction between demand and supply is a vital dimension in understanding the fundamental characteristics of organisations (Williamson, 1985). Williamson proposed that organisations often exist to lower the cost of transactions. Organisational structures in the 1960s and early 1970s tended towards larger corporate types with the aim of using size to cut transaction costs by economies scale. More units of function were added to the permanent structure of organisations so as to achieve economies of scale. For example, an outlying small component supplier might be purchased and brought into a company so as to reduce the insecurities and legal costs of negotiating annual contracts with the supplier. One reason for removing transactions from the market place and bringing them into an organisational, bureaucratic structure is a lack of clear information to determine price and a resulting price instability.

     The privatisation policies of the 1980s saw something of a reversal of this trend with large organisations tending to split into linked but smaller core elements. In social services creation of the purchaser-provider split indicated a belief that economies of scale could become inefficiencies of scale if rigid organisational procedures developed that protected the power base and status of those within the organisational process, this over and above focusing on the end product and outcome of the service.

     It might be argued that Williamson's theory does explain the trend towards the logic of marketisation in that he cited transactions as being primarily driven by economic criteria of efficiency. Large efficiency gains subsequently become inefficient because they grow to represent unaccountable power bases. These power bases have to fragment to become more accountable to individual units of expenditure.

Critics of Williamson work have pointed to its oversimplified application and a need in particular to examine the difficulties in locating what forces are really within or outside of an organisational system (Clarke and McGuinness, 1990). Take for example a simplistic market transaction analysis of professional social work engaged in a professional assessment of what products should be purchased for a social care user. Professional assessment might be seen as an expensive method of managing the transaction between demand for, and supply of, social care. Public choice theorists might be suspicious of the power base of professional social work and its ability to extract money and payment from the transaction process, by claiming specialist knowledge and expertise about what a users needs are. For Williamson (1985) the critical point is that social work secures an additional economic activity between users and providers that otherwise would not take place. Without the social worker the user would not find and purchase the service they needed. The cost of employing social workers to manage the transaction adds value and this is at least equal to the value of the extra market activity generated. Similarly, one must be sure that alternative methods of transaction facilitation cannot do the job more efficiently, for example advertising social care provision in the local press.

Complex analysis of social care as a product render this kind of transaction analysis as only partially useful in explanation. An additional point of complexity is that social work offers a crisis counselling product itself, during the assessment and transaction process (Hoyes, et al, 1994, p. 28). Those who have fallen long term ill are encouraged to come to terms with their needs and are supported in the psychological hardship they experience (Baldock and Ungerson, 1994). In this sense the transaction process is not just raising the number of the quantitative total transactions achieved (by bringing more people into the market place), but also provides a crisis counselling and befriending product. Social Work care management is contributing to the social definition of supply and demand as outlined earlier in this chapter (Figure 5.1) and culturally redefining when and how it is appropriate for an individual to make an economic assessment of social care, rather than one based on kinship loyalty and family life. Social workers can give actors 'cultural permission' to enter the market landscape.

Williamson's (1985) model also ignores the social externalities of the wider social benefits generated by the professionalisation of transactions. These are the development of specialist knowledge, increased employment diversity and increased wealth and well-being of society. These external benefits to the professionals involved in the transaction have to be contrasted carefully with the benefits to the recipients of the immediate transaction.

A key determinant of favouring an organisational transaction over a market one is that something of value is added in the process of removing the transaction from the market place to an organisation, but the problem is that the process of adding value may be complex and include external social benefits that are not immediately obvious. Williamson identified that the solution was not as simple as either choosing a larger organisation to absorbed the transaction element, or leaving the transaction in the market place. He proposed that organisational structure could be changed quite significantly to prevent rising transaction costs before it was necessary to consider privatisation and market separation of the transaction. One alternative form of organisation he proposed was the divisional form of organisation based on specialist function and the use of profit centres.

Organisational analysis of transactions is simplified, but it makes an important contribution to the progress of satisfactorily analysing transactions in the social care market. This book has shown the difficulty with generating a satisfactory elasticity of price, due to social and structural problems that undermine market demand. One of the most fundamental problems is that social and cultural factors prevent need being predictably transferred into market demand. If such instabilities of demand and price elasticity encourage the removal of social care transactions into a state organisational process, there become associated issues of difficulty about the partial use of pricing and charging by these organisations.

*Prices and charges in the personal social services transaction process*

For some of the reasons outlined above the history of pricing in social services is problematic. Judge and Matthews (1980a, p. 107) criticised personal social services pricing policy for being illogical in its policy objectives. 'The present use of charges is replete with inconsistencies, variations, conflicts and anomalies, and there is a clear case for rationalisation at the earliest opportunity.'

The above authors demonstrated how charges have originated on an ad hoc basis across a range of services and with little central control exerted on the level and equity of prices set. In the 1970s only charges for residential care had significant central controls placed upon them (this is still the case today), although these did account for the greatest proportion of money raised for personal social services through charges.

Disquiet about the increased use of charges to maintain service provision in the economic crisis of the 1970s lead to a substantial review of the use of charges by the Layfield Committee, this discussed by Judge and Matthews (1980a,1980b). As a result of their discussion they concluded:

'(1) the need for more accurate and consistent information about charges to be made available;
(2) the desirability of consolidating legislation to cover consumer charges....
(3) the rationalisation of anomalies and variations in charging policy and practice.' (Judge and Matthews, 1980a, p. 6)

The inconsistency and irrationality of certain local authority charging practices is still documented in the 1990s (Balloch, 1994; George, 1995; Harvey, 1995; Baldwin and Lunt, 1996; Kempson and Bennett, 1997). Harvey (1995) found that charges were inequitable regionally, with large variations in means testing and actual amounts charged. George (1995) questions whether authorities know the organisational transaction costs they are incurring by means testing.

Research for the National Institute for Social Work and the Joseph Rowntree Foundation (Balloch, 1994; Baldwin and Lunt, 1996) focused on non-residential charges and found similar concerns about equity and effectiveness. This research showed that local authorities were often including welfare benefits when assessing means to pay for services. This raises important issues about what combined central and local government policy hopes to achieve when making a mixture of transfer and subsidy payments and the need for coordinated central and local government planning. In effect, central government is paying a benefit to encourage a social care purchase that is then means tested by local government against a charge for a partly subsidised service. One government policy may be undermining the other.

Setting charges at the right level and alongside consistent central and local economic policy is likely to be critical to the success or failure of the social care market in meeting need. Analysis of the component parts of the market, at central and local level, is critical to the development of a strategy and synthesis that can deal with the complexities involved. A major review of the cost of continuing care published in 1996 concluded that government partial charging and pricing in order to raise the efficiency of social care transactions was largely misplaced and tended to raise transaction costs (Joseph Rowntree Foundation, 1996).

Planning needs to address the relative advantages and disadvantages of raising the cost of transactions by professionalisation of assessment and the costs of implementing individual costing and charging. Is extra demand facilitated by professional involvement and is there evidence that need is better related to supply? There is a need to show that the social work assessment adds value to the final service output. Users need confidence that the professionalisation of such transactions does not remove the value of what is ultimately available to the user, or removes the user from access to the product altogether, because few resources remain to provide a service output.

The potential instability of price transactions in the social care market is in part based on the unreliability of information available at time of purchase (Lapsley, 1996, p. 116). Forder, Knapp and Wistow (1996, p. 212) describe social care as 'experience goods' where people demanding a service have little idea what it is they are wanting until after they have had a chance to experience it and this creates a 'principal-agent' problem where the purchaser has less information about the good or service than the provider. This is partly an indication of the intangible nature of social care goods, with the difficulty in resolving how outputs (like beds provided) relate to quality of outcome (experience of being cared for in the bed). Social work assessment and transaction management therefore has a potentially important 'value added' role in creating confidence and trust in the quality of products available.

*Contracting, quality and regulation*

Supply side product efficiency requires the monitoring of quality. Quality can be ensured by stating adequate detail in a contract that requires evidence of the maintenance of minimum standards. It can be a contractual agreement that a provider service will monitor its own client satisfaction levels and performance and provide feedback to purchasers. Independent government inspection also contributes to quality maintenance.

The monitoring of quality is crucial to the success of the market and requires adequate contracting (Le Grand, 1991, p. 12). Contracts must state clearly who is responsible for on-going information that can substantiate quality, but contracts themselves can raise transaction costs (Common and Flynn, 1992; Le Grand and Bartlett, 1993 pp. 26-30; Wistow, et al, 1996).

Contracts can consider the aims of the service, details of the physical resources available, the intended results and outputs, quality standards and arrangements for monitoring and inspection. Contracts need to get beyond costing agreements to definitions of quality and clarify specifications that can help deliver quality products. This can involve evaluative research and the training of social care staff employed in the provider agency.

Regulation and contracting is best developed in collaborative mode so that negotiation is not adversarial and expensive. Hard negotiation may reduce the number of suppliers willing to work with local authorities (given their control of the majority of purchasing and ability to fix prices). Adversarial contracting can also inflate transaction costs (Common and Flynn, 1992; Walsh, 1995; Flynn, Williams and Pickard, 1996; Wistow, et al, 1996).

It is not sufficient for a government to depend on market forces alone to deliver social care to the population. Similarly public managers cannot build transaction and quasi market structures as a solution, but should see them as only a partial means to an ends. Managerial analysis of these structures and systems and how they effect social care outputs and outcomes over time and space becomes imperative. The building of inter-organisational networks based on trust and partnership is critical to avoiding an unnecessary focus on legalism, structure, bureaucracy and standardisation (Flynn, Williams and Pickard, 1996).

In a comprehensive assessment of the transaction issues in the social care market Forder, Knapp and Wistow (1996) and Wistow, et al (1996) conclude that there are five key elements to the social care transaction: structural losses due to too much market power on the demand or supply side; informational losses where open information is not readily available to both demand and supply sides; excessive bargaining costs where purchaser and supplier over compensate for a lack of information at the point of contract; costs of selective intervention created by a demand side organisation distorting a market activity; and costs of regulation. Wistow, et al (1996, p. 142) conclude on the impact of these issues for planning and strategic thinking.

> 'It follows then that a market might be 'managed' in order to change its regulatory framework and to reduce these losses, that is to minimise transaction costs...in evaluating social care commissioning or purchasing we should examine how alternative arrangements might reduce transaction costs and how they might influence structural and informational imperfections.'

An on-going analysis of the details and evolution of social care transactions must be one part of a complex government planning information system. This is best done at a local level, with experiences shared nationally. There is likely to be much local diversity. It is unlikely that static analysis of the interaction of these complex effects can be generalised easily over time, place and between service types. This confirms the need for planning analysis systems in the new social planning environment to be spontaneous, evolving and based on network structures that respond easily to changing demands.

**Supply Planning**

Given the dominance of the logics of marketisation, efficiency and choice on the NHS and Community Care Act 1990, much of the initial focus of SSDs has been on planning more diversity in the supply services. This was also influenced by the Conservative Government's requirement in 1993 that SSDs should spend 85% of the Community Care Special Transitional Grant (STG) on services in the independent sector. Davies and Wittenberg (1996, p.33) state that: 'the initial priority for reform was, however, almost entirely given to tackling the structures and philosophies which most directly influenced supply.' This focus on supply planning was indicated in chapter four where the study of planning documents showed minimal needs analysis and more emphasise on developing a diversity and choice of supply, and setting policy objectives about how the diversity of local supply could be increased and targeted at priorities.

*The development of supply diversity*

In 1991 research evidence showed that local authority managers and councillors felt there was an insufficient number and quality of independent providers for the growing social care market to function (Wistow, et al, 1993). Two years later, in follow up research, there was more confidence in the supply of private and independent rest homes but a belief that there was insufficient supply competition in the areas of domiciliary care and short term respite care (Wistow, et al, 1996, p. 44).

*Planning contacts with suppliers*

The initial design of the post 1990 social care market suggested that monopolies would not be a problem, given the emphasis on diversity of provision allocated on the basis of individualised assessment. If authorities seek to purchase services in bulk so as to keep down their transaction costs, monopoly providers might emerge that are in a strong market position to force up prices against deteriorating quality (Le Grand and Bartlett, 1993, p. 26). For this reason it is argued by some that block purchase should be limited to those services where there is an under supply. In a recent survey of local authorities Wistow, et al (1996, p. 89) found that most authorities preferred the idea of spot contracting to block contracts. This is probably based on the assumption that spot contracts permit more market adjustments between demand and supply factors over time in circumstances where individual need is highly variable. But this assumption ignores the transaction costs of always attempting an adequate and detailed costing of individual need during the assessment stage of case management. It is doubtful whether such a rational and scientific assessment of cost and need is really possible (King and Llewellyn, 1996, p. 135). Spot contracts can also create uncertainties for the supplier, based on short-termism, that might undermine their ability to provide a high quality of care. The decision about block and spot contracts requires a detailed local assessment of the market place and stability of suppliers available.

*Structural imperfections in cost*

The initial costs of providing new services is higher than subsequent provision. This is because new services will need financial capital to establish themselves and this includes surplus start up capital costs, such as building acquisition, information technology and furniture etc. In order to facilitate the growth of new services local authorities might anticipate paying some start up grants or low interest loans, especially if sufficient finance does not come from the private sector. Such a shortage of capital was a concern when rented housing provision was encouraged in the private sector in the later 1980s. The Business Expansion Scheme (BES) created significant tax break incentives to private providers of rented housing.

The experience of the development of private rest homes in the 1980s shows that where widespread government subsidies are available to reward private initiative, new social care services will develop and that the private sector will permit capital costs. In a public lecture to West Sussex Social Services Department in 1994, Professor Norman Flynn estimated that a large proportion of all private rest homes started in the 1980s were paying up to a third of their profits in the service of bad debts on negative equity. In effect this is revenue that, if purchasers commit to alternative competitor homes, could be spent on providing a higher quality of care. Local authority purchasers should therefore be concerned about independent sector capital and revenue funding ratios. In some cases this gives charitable provision an advantage over private bodies. Charitable providers can get access to funds in ways that the private sector cannot, for example public charitable donations and tax exemptions on profits. This can allow it to carry higher costs than a private sector provider (Forder, Knapp and Wistow, 1996) and thereby provide greater quality (Wistow, et al, 1996).

*Cream skimming*

The term 'cream skimming' has been used by Le Grand (1991, p. 14) to illustrate the danger that the supply of services for severely disadvantaged users may be avoided by the market place because of the expense and logistic problems involved. This must be counteracted by the payment of generous subsidy to specific and high needs services. There is some precedent for this in child care where social services have a tradition of meeting quite high fees for specialist therapeutic communities who able to help the most disturbed of children.

*Motivation of suppliers*

The motivation for establishing such therapeutic communities is often as much altruist as economic, it coming from interested and concerned professionals who want to work in a higher risk environment. This suggests that the motivation of supply actors in the social care market is likely to be quite diverse and cannot be assumed to be purely for rational economic gain. A suspicion by the public purchaser of independent providers is not justified by research (Hardy, Young, Wistow, 1996, p. 6). Historically both public and private have provided both high and low quality resources and mode of ownership is unlikely to be a reliable predictor of outcome quality. The motivation of suppliers in the social care market is diverse and not easily attributed to simple economic behaviour (Kendall, Forder and Knapp, 1996; Wistow, et al, 1996, pp. 96-97, 109).

*Supply inelasticity*

In some types of provision, historical advantages were created prior to marketisation in areas where there has been a lack of alternative provision and small numbers of prospective users. This can create difficulties for new businesses who want to compete. Those who need high levels of social care and cannot live in any sense independently, for example people with severe learning difficulties, have little flexibility or choice about expressing their demand elsewhere. This means that there is more risk that an established provider can move towards monopoly and inflate prices. Conversely in geographical areas where a single state purchaser dominates over individual private purchase, quality might be undermined by fixing prices too low (Laing, 1998).

Labour and capital resource constraints can be created by a range of factors, often outside of the immediate sphere of the social care market, for example the implementation of a minimum wage, EU rulings on employment and government job programmes. Shortages of labour and capital, or rising labour and capital costs, can make it more difficult for new businesses to compete with existing and established ones. Similarly the availability of volunteers can effect the cost and availability of labour (Forder, Knapp and Wistow, 1996).

Specific parts of the social care market will be more subject to supply inelasticity than others. The market for residential care for older people is now functioning in a competitive supply mode in many rural and suburban areas of the country. Despite some initial concerns about a lack of competition in the domiciliary care market , a recent survey of the market for domiciliary care for older people concluded that competition was now 'relatively healthy' (Forder, Kendall and Knapp, 1996). But some specialist function services, such as residential care for those with severe learning difficulties and domiciliary care for those with high needs appear less likely to respond to market competition. Choice might be limited to only one or two specialist providers, or alternatively supporting a partner or parent at home. In these situations government and its agents have to make a careful assessment of what is a reasonable economic cost to pay for the service, as it cannot be assumed that the market will generate a realistic measure of price with ease.

## Supply Side Management

The current mixed market for social care has two generalised features. The market is providing some services that demonstrate adaptability to the market environment on a large scale. Private residential homes in the south east of England are one example. In other circumstances newly developing services and more specialist services require nurturing from local government.

### *Supply side subsidies*

Local authority domiciliary care is a good example of a service that has been previously subsidised at the point of supply and provided by local authorities. There are many regional variations in output levels (Department of Health, 1996; Boyne, 1997) and a diversity of means testing and flat rate charging. The problem with flat rate subsidies is that they are not effective at dealing with vertical equity and tend to benefit the rich the most. This is because a flat rate charge gives all actors, whether rich or poor, the same allocation of subsidy. Means testing only one particular type of supply can add to the distortion of choices. For example, differences in the ratio of means tested subsidy for domestic home care as compared with residential care might act as a perverse incentive for one over the other (Joseph Rowntree Foundation, 1996, p. 22) For this reason means testing is better undertaken on the demand side of the market equation, in assessment of a cash or voucher payment, before a choice is made about supply, so that a means test does not then adversely effect the choice of service.

Subsides can also be directed at the direct funding of provision. They can be targeted at internal SSD services, or paid to the voluntary sector as block grants to encourage service start ups, or used to fund at source a large proportion of particular type of service. Supply side subsidies should reduce the direct costs to the user. The danger is that they decrease efficiency by protecting inefficient operators and maintaining artificially high cost factors. If this is the case the subsidy becomes dysfunctional and the benefits are erroneously passed to employees and entrepreneurs rather than users. There is pressure on government provider units to reduce their unit costs when compared with the voluntary and private sector (Department of Health, 1997a).

*Supply side management and planning*

Supply side management can be used to correct weaknesses in the market place. An example would be to pay a subsidy that encourages an existing provider to modify a service. A rest home might be asked to leave a proportion of its beds unallocated, so that they can be used for respite care. This can inflate the cost of individual units of respite care over what it might be, but cost might still be cheaper with this method than financing the start up for a new unit. Quality of the provision would also have to be considered. When such decisions have to be made a pragmatic cost benefit analysis has to be applied. Shropshire's Social Care Enterprise Agency offers one example of a supply side management initiative. Here the aim has been to support small new initiatives in the independent sector by providing a subsidy of free business advice and support (Kimber, 1995). Supply side management and planning has to be related to local analysis, given the variance in market conditions between areas.

## *Planning for providers*

Local authorities can also help providers to adjust to market requirements, by making their purchasing plans clear (Department of Health, 1992b;1994a) and creating a culture of information and trust (Department of the Environment, Transport and Regions, 1998a). In recent years some authorities have reported a lack of supply competitiveness in domiciliary care. Wistow, et al, 1996 (p.145) say that in such cases: 'limitations on supply were not so much due to the costs of market entry as to the lack of local authority commitment to making sufficient funds available, paying reasonable rates, or making their purchasing intentions known.'

Social care planning must include communicating good information to the supply side provider or potential provider (Department of Health, 1994a).

## Conclusion

It has been argued that 'rivalrous' competition is not a stable feature of the social care market and that this is prevented by inequalities of wealth distribution, differences in cultural expectation and the cultural inability of people in a material consumer society to face the issues of illness, death and dependency.

It is argued in this chapter that the social care market is one in which the ability of market forces to meet demand and supply is unstable. Human attitudes to social care are not as rational as classical economic and public choice theory suggest. Many individual people will not save for their future suffering (Parker and Clarke, 1997). It has required large scale historic state intervention to provide financial wealth for people in retirement, through state and employer based pensions. Adverts for private pensions and even long term illness insurance focus on the positive things that can be done when the policy pays, like taking a holiday, this rather than the need for care when ill and disabled. The take-up rate for such insurance policies is low (House of Commons Health Committee, 1996, p. xiv).

The traditional mechanism for ensuring social care of older people and those with a long term illness was family attachment, having a large close-knit family who would feel under obligation and responsibility to provide care. Industrialisation, globalisation and the process of modern capitalism continues to destroy these social bonds. The pressure to have many children for protection in old age leads to over population and a drain on the earth's ecological resources. Adult children who are unable to move away from home so as to work and study, lose educational and labour market opportunities. Social care becomes in part a 'public good' or 'merit good'.

Theoretical need for social care is prevented from being transferred into actual demand because of poverty and people's cultural inability to access the market place. Many people choose to reject the idea of being consumers of social care, until there is literally no choice but to seek help. This has lead to a tendency for supply to dominate with people accepting what they can get in a final crisis. Demographic changes increase the demand for high priority care. By spending state subsidy in the private market, namely private rest homes, in the 1980s, government policy succeeded in producing some supply competition.

Because some people seek to acquire basic low priority social care through families and local networks rather than by monetary transactions, home care products do not relate to the market mechanisms of price determination particularly well. It is argued in this chapter that the price determination of informal social care becomes subject to what complexity theory calls 'bounded instability' (Stacey,1995). Families assessments of social care costs will relate in part to their own peculiar attitudes, their understanding of the welfare state and their own position in the labour market and the cost of giving up work (Baldock and Ungerson, 1994).

Market cost and price mechanisms have partial value in making care products and the rationing of resources more efficient, but they cannot improve general levels of access to social care, or the macro social-efficiency of social care policy. In a market place for social care separated from state management, there is a particular problem with inequality feeding inequality. A free market is likely to lead to poor people making low self assessments of their own domestic social care costs. Such cost assessment renders it impossible for the poor to enter into the choices of the active market place which they perceive as too expensive. For this reason government intervention in a market has a responsibility to define costs , prices and charges that reflect the true value of social costs borne by carers (Netten, 1996). A challenge to social care market planners in the late 1990s is to confront the disincentives people face that persuade them not to act as consumers of social care and to give a just financial reward to those who do undertake the family task of providing care.

The focus of local authorities on planning the supply side of the social care market is partly because they do not have the control over resources to alter demand side financing in relation to need. The achievement of increased consumer participation and equity in social care is possible in planned ways, but it requires central planning.

First, central government could seek a general redistribution of wealth via central and local redistributive taxation. But there is also no guarantee that general reductions in relative poverty will have a positive effect on the social care market. Consumer preference might still dictate that individual consumers do not choose to spend a proportion of their wealth on social care. This is because of the relative low preference status that social care products seem to possess when ranked on a scale of consumer preferences.

Second, there could be a planned redistribution between spatial areas by changing the allocation of central government grants and varying levels of local tax and charges. This method has proved difficult historically to target effectively at those most in need. Areas targeted for help by government are often constructed from large geographies and these geographies have a large range of inequities within them (this approach to planning is discussed more widely in chapter seven).

Third, the government can plan national policies specific to the inequities in demand and supply of social care, using insurances, benefits and vouchers to subsidise demand.

*A policy synthesis and strategy*

In an extensive review of the possibilities for paying for a future social care system, Oldman (1991) concluded that subsidy was inevitable. The resulting debate is at what governmental level and with what mechanisms this subsidy should be generated.

Much recent debate has focused on the appropriateness of a policy to encourage people to take responsibility for saving themselves towards social care. The Conservative Government in 1996 proposed state subsides of private insurance schemes where people would protect themselves from the means test and having to sell their property as part of the means test (Secretary of State for Health, 1996). Commentators stated that these insurance policies were unlikely to be available to many in the population, thereby increasing the inequity of policy (House of Commons Health Committee, 1996; Richards, Wilsdon and Lyons, 1996). Such a policy also only represents a medium to long term planning solution.

Planning interventions must focus on both demand and supply. The least developed aspect of these combined policies is the need to coordinate a national programme that places demand side equity as a priority alongside the supply side goals of choice and efficiency. It is clear that the full policy strategy cannot be planned by local authorities alone but needs the political and strategic lead of central government.

The independent review of continuing care published by the Joseph Rowntree Foundation in 1996 comes closest to an adequate complex national plan for social care, but it is not a government document. This proposes a separation of care and accommodation costs, where care is funded universally via a specific tax, similar to national insurance. This tax based insurance would be invested in a fund partly independent of government and managed by an independent public body, so as to prevent the identified monies being spent elsewhere in a political crisis. Accommodation funding would be means tested. Social care provision would continue to be diverse and provided by the independent and state sectors, with day to day purchasing involving local authorities and users. The purchase of social care would be universally guaranteed by the national pool of specific national insurance based taxation payments.

Effectiveness and equity can be linked. 'The optimum lies somewhere between the endpoints of hierarchy and pure markets though its identification may be as difficult in practice as in principle' (Wistow, et al, 1996, p. 168).

A market strategy will not be effective if the humanistic aims of a social policy are failing. Planners must aim to increase the levels of activity in the social care market, achieving less consumer rejection of social care products. The fact that people wait until they are so ill that they cannot 'reject' social care goods, only confounds their inability to make consumer choices and adjust to the role of economic and physical dependency. Rejection of social care goods can also lead to an escalated demand being expressed at a later date, because the progression of long term illness has not been prevented and treated (House of Commons Health Committee, 1996, p. lvii, paragraph 2).

In the remainder of this book the focus is on two particular activities of planning analysis that are important to the successful programming of a strategy which will achieve equity and the creation of adequate levels of subsidised demand.

In chapter six the book examines the requirement for better government planning of need and demand, given the weakness identified with the current models of planning analysis in chapter four, and the need for planners to grapple with the demand realities as argued in this chapter.

In chapter seven the focus is on an analysis of the SSA (Standard Spending Assessment). This is a key point of overlap between the managerial, market and political systems. The SSA is a planning activity that primarily concerns central government politicians and managers, involving them in using a rational calculation that distributes public expenditure resources for the local purchase of social care. The SSA calculation is evaluated as a method for planning the distribution of resources.

# 6 The Planning of Need and Demand

## Introduction

In this chapter the book argues that both central and local government must focus their planning strategy on increasing access to the social care market because of the current evidence that there is a large amount of unmet need (Bebbington, Turvey and Janzon, 1996). This is human need which has not been expressed as demand in the market place. Chapter four showed how Kingston and Surrey Social Services had begun to make some attempts in their CCPs to estimate unmet need using a basic quantitative analysis. This chapter presents a quantitative model that seeks to measure general need levels in an SSD authority area. The model is based on secondary data sources and the results can be compared with SSD output statistics to examine the possible occurrence of unmet need. While this model was being developed, some other similar models were being developed by other research units. There is an absence of publications available to describe these models, possibly because they include commercial information, although the early developments of the Social Services Research and Development Unit at the University of Bath and the application of their model to Gloustershire SSD are discussed in Wright and Kerslake (1994). Subsequent implementations of the University of Bath model to Cheshire SSD are discussed by Bebbington, Turvey, and Janzon (1996, pp. 13-14) who also discuss the development of their own model.

After developing a model in this chapter, some of the demand side structural weaknesses of the market provision of social care are further explored. The extent to which planning can assist the management of these problems is discussed.

## The Relationship between Need and Demand

Needs based planning requires that the quantitative and qualitative need of the population are measured and accurate measurements made of prevalence and incidence (Department of Health, 1993a). With regard to beginning the task of needs assessment, some national studies have been particularly helpful, for example, the OPCS (Office of Population Censuses and Surveys) prevalence of disability survey (Martin, Meltzer and Elliot, 1988), the OPCS (1996) prevalence of psychiatric morbidity survey and the 1991 Census, which included a measure of the prevalence of long term illness.

Total volume measures of prevalence are only one estimate of need. These can be compared with actual incidences of requests for help at social services departments and provider agencies and qualitative accounts of the diversity of choices that people express. Baldock and Ungerson's (1994) study of the local social care market in Kent showed that people with broadly similar physical needs expressed their needs differently, in accordance with culture and market expectations. At the individual level of the consumption of social care, the relationship between need and demand is diverse. Not all social needs will be expressed as demands on services.

In previous text on the definition of need, Bradshaw (1972) and Forder (1974, chapter 3) discussed a number of theoretical definitions. Need can be measured as basic minimum standards, where some residual measurement of allocation is accepted. It is common for SSDs to only allocate state help for social care services to those judged to be a high priority on the basis of eligibility criteria, applied by professionals. Because of the restricted funding available to local authorities for state based purchasing of care, eligibility criteria have become increasingly important to the policy definition of need. Need defined by minimum standards is similar to 'normative need' where need is defined by experts and a desired standard operationalised (Bradshaw, 1972; 1994).

Need can also be assessed with reference to comparative need, this being, average or relative quantitative definitions, where the burden of resources are allocated to those with above average requirements for resources. Some resources might still be given to those falling below the required measurement. Statistical indicators are used to operationalise comparisons between people and spatial areas. Comparative need can be based on national criteria, such as indicators in the OPCS disability survey with its definitions of severity of disability based on WHO (World Health Organisation) classifications. The allocation of social care using such a measure is likely to be difficult given the fact that people with the same physical condition require a diversity of service provision because of their culture, and by implication an allocation based on a high degree of individual preference (Clark, 1996).

Need could also be defined in terms of whether it is expressed, or felt or not, hence Bradshaw's (1972) concept of 'felt need'. Research like Baldock and Ungerson's (1994) shows that certain social groups, namely the middle classes and more socially articulate, are more likely to express 'felt need' and create demands on the system.

> 'Provision based on felt need would require a wide dissemination of knowledge, and indeed a much greater openness about the criteria for decisions than most of those concerned with the provision of social services, professions, administrators and representatives are generally prepared to show. But one may be up against a much deeper attitudinal problem among potential consumers of the social services, whose belief in the possibility of change may be stunted by long experience of deprivation and of failure to achieve successful change.' (Forder, 1974, p. 52)

Forder also mentions need as defined by 'specific techniques' of supply, where judgement of need is based on which service is seen to be providing a professionally desirable output. This supply based definition contradicts the philosophy of demand side empowerment advocated by the community care reforms and is close to Bradshaw's (1972;1994) definition of normative need. The philosophy of needs assessment in the community care policies designed in the last decade suggest that need should be met on the basis of what is expressed and felt by users, but the implementation of community care policy has focused on the means testing and rationing of people's access to services. The driving logic of recent policy management has been the economic argument that need does not function consistently as a demand side concept (Bradshaw, 1994, p. 48) and instead the focus of policy should be on setting priorities with limited resources, or in other words assessing 'relative needs' (Williams, 1974, p. 70).

But the simplified use of rationing and priority setting, when services face expressions of felt need, has unintended policy effects. If users are faced with the prospect of charges after being made subject to an assessment and means test, their own rationality about what they need might change. They may no longer wish to express their need for care, preferring instead to struggle on themselves with family and friends.

Expressed and felt need are inconsistent over time and place, and influenced by the social context. Baldock and Ungerson's (1994) work suggests that some people may never express their need to social services or the social care market because they do not have the consumer knowledge and power to do so. Cultural capital (Bourdieu, 1993) becomes a key component of how needs are felt and expressed. Wealthier and better informed citizens have higher expectations in the social care market than the poor and are more likely to express their demands earlier in the course of an illness.

The definition of need cannot be measured entirely as a reductionist individual concept. There must be a sense of collective expression in needs based planning. Normative and comparative standards must be assessed alongside individuality. The measurement of inequality and inequity becomes important (Bradshaw, 1994). A 'dual strategy' that encompasses individual expressions, group political representation and rational methodological principles is proposed by Doyal and Gough (1991, p. 310) : 'we have argued that our theory of need points to a dual polity, just as it does to a dual economy. The dual strategy flows from a concept of need which is rational, consensual, dynamic and open-ended.' This is a working definition of need that can comprehend social complexity.

The difficulty with defining and measuring need illustrates the problems of needs based planning on the demand side of the social care market. Measurements of need are possible, but they do not guarantee the facilitation of demand in the market place. The facilitation of actual demand requires planned intervention from politicians and managers. Some writers prefer to define need by demonstrating evidence that shows how needs have been met by service provision (Davies, Bebbington and Charnley, 1990; Sanderson, 1996).

*Theoretical need and demand*

Quantitative volume calculations of long term illness offer important background information, but improving their ability to become reliable and valid indicators of actual demand is more problematic. For example, it is possible to calculate a prediction that there will be a fixed number of people with severe disabilities, but research cannot assume a normative need of particular services without asking clients about their own ideals and choices, as this would undermine much of the philosophy of the community care reforms. Offering a choice of services is a clear policy objective. Quantitative secondary data and calculations yield estimates of *theoretical demand* but not *actual demand*.

*Actual demand*

Measurement of *actual demand* will encompass more detailed local calculations and user feedback. This will include local internal surveys of users and carers and supplementary qualitative research. Actual demand expressed relates closely to costing, pricing and charging, as if purchasing power is not available to users, their demands cannot be translated into actual supply. The measurement of actual demand needs to be sensitive to the reality that measurements of demand expressed in a social care market at any one time may not be consistent with actual supply. It cannot be assumed that a service being supplied is really the service that was required. The monitoring of social worker assessments and the expressions users make at the time of assessment becomes another important point of information collection if actual demand expressed is to be successfully measured. At present there is a lack of data available on social worker assessments at a local and national level.

Actual demand expressed may not come to the attention of the local state purchasing process for a number of reasons. Private, independent funding will be available to a minority and prevent their need to call on social services. The exact measurements here are unclear. Kreitzman (1996) predicts that approximately 30% of social care transactions are privately financed. In 1995 28% of people living in residential homes in the independent sector were entirely self-financed (Joseph Rowntree Foundation, 1996, p. 15, Table 16). In some cases it is possible that these users may still have had an original assessment and referral form local authority social services. The availability of benefits like attendance allowance and disability living allowance will facilitate some actual demand in the independent market place that local social services are not directly aware of.

The actual level of demand that exists at anyone time is partly related to the available supply of money, or suitable credits, to purchase care. Government subsidy or indirect subsidy will partly determine this, given what has been argued about the limitations of social care as a market commodity.

Four types of user participation in the care market are proposed by Baldock and Ungerson (1994): consumerism, welfarism, privatism and clientalism. Only welfarism and clientalism showed a tendency to make demands on state purchasing, with the later group exhibiting low levels of assertiveness and being passive recipients of what purchasers offered. Baldock and Ungerson discovered from interviewing users in Kent that welfare consumerism is not easily undertaken by all clients, many exhibiting more passive or public sector avoidance strategies because of previous assumption about how the welfare state operates. The privatism group tried to avoid the market place and state purchasing completely, preferring family and neighbour, kinship based care. Those users who exhibit low levels of participation in the market are in danger of reducing the overall aggregate actual demand. Equally there is a danger that local authorities will bias their supply side to fit estimates of actual demand based on low levels of participation.

This leads to a third definition of demand, *demand realism*, in which a balance is struck between theoretical ideals and strategic practicalities. *Demand realism* will place more emphasis on the availability of resources and ways in which to encourage people to see social care as partly their responsibility in partnership with the state. *Demand realism* is a combination of theoretical demand and actual demand, that can acknowledge the under consumption of social care and set reasonable objectives about how to increase levels of participation in the social care market that are consistent with individual and collective needs.

## The measurement of theoretical need

This next part of the chapter evaluates the relationship between theoretical demand and actual demand in the old shire county of East Sussex and its implication for planners. Since this research was completed the shire county of East Sussex has been subdivided into two administrative areas; Brighton and Hove Unitary Authority and East Sussex County Council.

## Demand and Need Indicators

The introduction of local CCPs in the NHS and Community Care Act 1990 brought with it the requirement that local authority social service departments should seek to estimate demand for their resources within their area of jurisdiction (Department of Health, 1993a, 1993b). Some local authorities were better prepared than others, having built up quite sophisticated arrangements to monitor research and development of some years standing. Many local authorities have utilised the United Kingdom census and this continues to be a widely used source of secondary information for local authority and health service planning (Champion, 1993).

The market approach to social care requires that sophisticated information systems be developed that can support the valid and reliable costing, planning and management of services (Audit Commission, 1992). It is possible for SSDs to spend vast amounts of money on purpose built information systems without first adequately considering the information that they require if they are to plan and manage the local community care market effectively. This is a point made by David Browning of the Audit Commission in his evidence to the House of Commons Health Committee.

'Where you get software off the shelf it may not fit your needs and there is a past history of packages of this type costing a great deal of money and failing to give what people want. My own view is that the problems are not really in software. It is actually the design of the information. Once people have done that they can often use fairly readily available databases and spreadsheets to facilitate the supply of data. So rather than rushing into vast investment in expensive software systems they need to be very clear that readily available packages are not able to do the work and only then make these investments.' (David Browning, Associate Director of the Audit Commission, House Commons Health Committee, 1993b, p. 11, paragraph 187)

## The 1991 census and base population tables

Given that the results of the 1991 census became available in 1993 - close to the publication of the first round of local authority plans - they have quickly become incorporated into planning.

Local population tables operationalised from the census local base (LB) and small area statistics (SAS) can be disaggregated to ward level and also transposed into larger district, county and regions (Dale and Marsh, 1993). Much of the information is recorded in its 100% format direct from the census count, but some of the variables with a large number of categories, such as occupation, are reduced to a 10% sample of the total census. It is estimated that about 2.2% of the national population failed to be counted in the census (Middleton, 1997). The census is still high quality data with reduced sampling errors when compared to large national surveys like the General Household Survey (GHS).

The reliability of the census as an estimate of population has been question by King (1989) who demonstrated the alternative use of local register general population statistics, when supplemented by OPCS data and used for prediction purposes. King has shown that when calculating central government grants for local services the use of actual registrations for the community charge was preferable to the census, despite the numbers failing to register. His method reduces some of the difficulties of 'capping' excess local expenditure on the basis of local population statistics that later prove to be wrong estimates.

## SARs (Samples of Anonymised Records)

For the first time individual and houschold data from the 1991 census was also compiled into the SARs (Sample of Anonymised Records), a statistical database that is not restricted to the census office tabulations and allows for more complex analysis and modelling. The SARs are based on 2% sample for individuals and 1% for households. It is not possible to identify individuals or household addresses because the smallest geographically area of location and analysis is restricted to district council geographic boundaries. All local county and metropolitan borough boundaries, hence SSD boundaries at April 1994, can be computed. The SARS represent a rigorous national sample with reduced sampling error when compared to the much smaller alternative national surveys (Dale and Marsh, 1993). SARs data is used in the next chapter.

*Long term illness*

The 1991 census included an indicator of the occurrence of long term illness that can be computed in small local areas. This variable is available in the LB, SAS and SAR formats. One of the simplest ways to estimate basic overall demand for community care services is to utilise the measure of long term illness, as operationalised by the 1991 census. Evidence of this was seen in some of the CCPs examined in chapter four (Table 4.2). The 1991 census was the first census to attempt a measurement of long term illness. Question 12 of the census asked: 'Does the person have any long term illness, health problem or handicap which limits his/her daily activities or the work he/she can do?' (Dale and Marsh, eds, 1993, p. 367). Underneath the question is the instruction: 'include problems which are due to old age?' This instruction was included to try and increase the reporting of disability by older people, since the earlier OPCS survey by Martin, Meltzer and Elliot (1988) revealed that older people tended to under report the incidence of long term illness. Populations adjustments to both the OPCS measure of Long Term Illness and the OPCS (1988) measure of disability can be made using more recent population data (Champion, 1993).

*The General Household Survey (GHS)*

The GHS is operationalised every other year and is based on a sample of approximately 10,000 people; or 0.016% of the population. Although this introduces higher sampling error than the SARs, more detailed information is collected in the GHS on disability and caring, but only periodically.

*The OPCS survey of disability (Martin, Meltzer and Elliot 1988)*

Within SSDs, another method for assessing community care demand is to use the 1988 OCPS survey of the prevalence of disability (Martin, Meltzer and Elliot, 1988). Examples of the use of this survey were identified in the review of CCPs in chapter four. Both Kingston and Surrey had used information from this disability survey. Similarly academic models developed by the PSSRU (Personal Social Services Research Unit) at the University of Kent and the SSRADU (Social Services Research and Development Unit) at the University of Bath have used this data in their models (Bebbington, Turvey and Janzon, 1996; Wright and Kerslake, 1994).

The OPCS disability study was an important prevalence survey into the occurrence of disability in the general population. It adds considerable detail unavailable in the GHS and census. Using a similar sampling frame to the GHS it identified the rates of disability on the basis of physical type (Martin, Meltzer and Elliot, 1988, p. 26, Table 3.12) and scale of severity (op cit, p. 22 Table 3.7). It also provides details of occurrence by gender and region (op cit, pp.22-23, Tables 3.7 and 3.9). The scales of severity have been used by some SSDs (for example in the Surrey CCP, 1994-1995 and the Kingston CCP, 1994-1995) and also by the PSSRU planning model (Bebbington, Turvey and Janzon, 1996). The authors of the OPCS 1988 disability study compare their findings with the GHS, 1985, and found that the GHS over-estimated prevalence up to the age of 74. Thereafter it underestimated the prevalence amongst the oldest citizens (Martin, Melter and Elliot, 1988, pp. 20-21). These differences were linked to the reliability of the questions that were not standardised over the two studies. The different findings are quite large. The GHS (1985) concluding that 139 adults aged 16-59 per thousand suffered a disability or long standing illness compared with the 58 adults per 1,000 for the same age group recorded by the OPCS.

Table 6.1 compares the concurrent validity of three possible measures of the incidence of disability in the general population, comparing the GHS, 1985, OPCS Disability Survey, 1988, and 1991 census. The 1991 census is broadly consistent with the OPCS Disability Survey, with the GHS (1985) being the most inaccurate. Therefore it is reasonable that the disability severity estimates of the OPCS Disability survey can be imputed onto census tables.

**Table 6.1    Concurrent validity of disability prevalence studies**

| Study | 16-PA | PA | All ages |
|-------|-------|------|---------|
| Census, 1991 | 6.9* | 36.8 | 12.3 |
| GHS, 1985 | 13.9 | 39.9 | 20.8 |
| OPCS, 1988 | 5.8 | 35.5 | 13.5 |

Note:          Percentage estimates of the occurrence of long term illness
               in the total population. These tables are for Great Britain. The
               1991 census estimates that 1% of the GB pop are resident in
               medical and care establishments. *Includes 0-16 year olds.

*Source:*      All census figures shown here omit communal establishments and
               are taken from OPCS, 1994, Table 4. Crown copyright.

An example of computing OPCS (1988) estimates of disability prevalence
onto census tables to estimate local authority demands for community care
services is given by Wright and Kerslake (1994). One problem highlighted in
the Wright and Kerslake article is an inability to calculate the occurrence of
multiple disabilities, something that they say the OPCS (1988) survey did not
do. Nevertheless the OPCS (1988) work does distinguish a 10 scale severity
of disability, which includes some calculations of multiple problems. In
particular the OPCS severity category of 7 or more indicates the occurrence
of a multiple disability (Martin, Meltzer and Elliot, 1988, p. 12). Bebbington,
Turvey and Janzon (1996, pp. 13-14) report that Wright and Kerslake have
moved beyond these initial operational problems.

The measure of severity of disability used in the OPCS (1988) disability
study is sophisticated in its methodology and allows for detailed interpretations
of need that are not permitted with the single factor measure of long term
illness used in the GHS and 1991 Census. An ordinal severity score is allocated
to each person with a disability in the sample, this resulting from their scores
on ten different sub-factors where each sub-factor could receive a maximum
score of 13.

The sub-factors are: locomotion, reaching and stretching, dexterity,
seeing, hearing, personal care, continence, communication, behaviour,
intellectual functioning (Martin, Meltzer and Elliot, 1988, p. 10). The
researchers found that severity of disability from the 10 sub-factors could be
predicted as equally as reliably by only taking into account each respondents
worst three scores (op cit, p. 12). These three separate scores were combined

using the formula: 'Worst +0.4 (second worst) + 0.3 (third worst) to give the combined factor of 'severity of disability'.

Approximately 100 skilled 'judges' were used in the allocation of severity marks. All respondents who have scores of 13 or more must have a multiple disability because 13 is the maximum that can be obtained on a one disability sub factor (op cit, p. 12). This leads to the conclusion that any one with a combined factor score of 7 is suffering from a multiple disability (see op cit, pp. 14-15) and by implication they suffer a considerable impairment. Some respondents with combined factor scores of less than 7 will also be suffering from less serious multiple disabilities.

## The Theoretical Demand for Care

*Severity of disablement and predicted needs*

If people with a severity score of 7 or more are suffering from a multiple disability this is likely to be a significant and reliable indicator of severe need. These will be the clients in most relative need, although the study makes it clear that by no means all will be confined to institutional or residential care and many will prefer and receive community care.

The OPCS (1988) disability study indicates the kinds of disabilities that are most likely to lead to a person living in an establishment (op cit, p. 35). These are: locomotor, seeing, personal care and intellectual functioning. Conversely the disabilities least likely to be observed in residential establishments are problems with reaching and stretching, dexterity, consciousness and digestion.

The study predicted that some 510,000 individuals in Great Britain would be suffering form a severity score of 7 and greater whilst still living in a private household. Of all household residents, 43% with a score greater than 7 are over 75 (op cit, p. 27, Table 4.1). The remaining prevalence of such severe disablement within households is almost equally shared between the 60-74 and 16-59 population groups.

An important variable to consider alongside age is gender. In Britain there are more than twice as many disabled women as men in communal institutions (op cit, p 22, Table 3.6) and there are three women for every two men who are disabled and resident in a private household. These proportions are further compounded in the older age groups, where women outlive men. Women make up almost twice the number of those with a score of 7 and above in the 75 and over age groups living in private households (op cit, p. 27, Tables 4.1 and 4.2). According to the survey there are four times as many women than men over 75 and living in institutions with severity scores over 7.

The decision about whether a person will chose residential or nursing home care will often depend on the availability of a resident carer. Men are likely to die before female partners and many of these women identified in high need of social care will therefore not have a domestic carer to look after them, they having been left alone by a male partner. This is one demographic reason for predicting a constant demand for residential care, before more complex and unpredictable considerations like the growing divorce rate and improved health care are understood.

The OPCS disability survey can be used to design bands of relative need, similar to the kind of prioritisation categories identified by social services departments in the survey of plans analysed in chapter four. In chapter four it was seen that the most popular number of relative need categories was three.

For example Surrey has the categories; high, moderate and low need (Surrey County Council, CCP, 1994, p. 23), although some other authorities had five. The OPCS severity category 7 is proposed in this thesis as a useful point to predict those of high priority need requiring home or institutional services, partly because it is identified in the OPCS own work as the point at which people are recorded as having clear multiple disabilities (Martin, Meltzer and Elliot, 1988, p.12). Similarly medium priority is proposed as those cases receiving OPCS scores between 3 and 6, whilst low priority will be those with a score of 1 or 2 (see Table 6.2). Table 6.3 computes the numbers of people falling into each of the three priority categories nationally, these based on the OPCS 1988 calculations.

In their review of the progress of the SSRADU model at the University of Bath, Bebbington, Turvey and Janson (1996, p. 13) report that Wright and Kerslake's (1994) model now operationalises OPCS severities 9-10 as 'severe' and OPCS severities 4-8 as 'significant'. This rationality appears to be based on the limited resources available to local authorities and the likelihood that those with the greatest needs will have to take up the most resources. It is argued in the model developed in this chapter that it is preferable to include a relatively wide band for high priority (OPCS, 1988, severities 7 - 10) because population needs based planning should include theoretical estimates of need that include unmet need, rather than being based at the start on supply side assumptions about limited resources. The rationale behind the ranking system in the model developed in this thesis is that social services departments need

## Table 6.2 Need for services: priority ranking

| Rank | OPCS (1988) equivalent severity score |
|---|---|
| High | 7-10 |
| Medium | 3-6 |
| Low | 1-2 |

*Source*: Based on Martin, Meltzer and Elliot, 1988, OPCS, Crown copyright.

## Table 6.3 Estimates of the number of disabled adults by severity and age groups, Great Britain

Severity/priority ranking
Totals (establishments and households)                    (thous)

| Age group | All Disabled | low (1-2) | medium (3-6) | high (7-10) |
|---|---|---|---|---|
| 16-59 | 1925 | 665 | 892 | 368 |
| 60-69 | 1334 | 538 | 565 | 231 |
| 70+ | 2942 | 833 | 1251 | 858 |
| Totals | 6201 | 2036 | 2708 | 1457 |

Communal establishments only                    (thous)

| Age group | All Disabled | low (1-2) | medium (3-6) | high (7-10) |
|---|---|---|---|---|
| 16-59 | 70 | 6 | 19 | 45 |
| 60-69 | 36 | 5 | 9 | 22 |
| 70+ | 317 | 17 | 82 | 218 |
| Totals | 423 | 28 | 110 | 285 |

*Source*: Based on Tables 3.6 & 3.8, pp. 22-23, OPCS, 1988. Crown copyright.

broad targeting zones for their plans, these being working classifications that allow resources to be targeted without unduly reducing the discretion of local purchasers and social work assessors. It is clear from the qualitative examples of severity rankings given by the OPCS (Martin, Meltzer and Elliot, 1988, p. 13-15) that cases do vary in their social and psychological impact. However sophisticated the quantitative methodology used, actual field allocation from one ranking to another will be somewhat subjective and arbitrary, this especially so when field social workers are allocating the classifications, rather than focused researchers. Therefore by reducing the severity criteria to three categories it is not the intention to undermine the validity of the OPCS, 1988, 10 points, but merely suggesting that three ordinal points are sufficient for planning social services delivery. Flexible need bands should be used so that maximum discretion is accredited to the front line care manager. The realities of social service CCPs scrutinised earlier suggests three such categories are likely to be workable in the field.

The 1991 census measure of long term illness did not record severity of disablement. The census did tabulate the long term ill living in households, as shown by Table 6.4. The differences in age categories available from the published tables in the two studies makes direct comparison difficult, but broadly the two national counts can be seen as similar. This is more clearly validated where the age groups are at their closest; those of pension age in the census, compared with those over 60 in the earlier OPCS survey.

It is proposed that the census can be used to gain a more localised geographical picture of total prevalence of disability, based on the census long term illness measure (estimated as equivalent to the OCPS (1988) severity scores 1 -10). The severity scale predictions can be applied by using the OPCS (1988) survey's regional and national severity ratios.

The OPCS disability survey did make some attempt to control for regional variations. Total severity categories 1- 10 were cross tabulated with geographical regions (op cit, p. 23, Table 3.9). The two regions used of interest to this thesis are the GLC and South East (Table 6.5). These regions are shown to have less prevalence of disability than other areas of the country. East Anglia has rates of prevalence broadly similar with the GLC and the south east, except that it has remarkably low levels of high priority severe disablement (severity categories 7-10). The South East has one of the lowest incidents of disability in Britain and the OPCS table 3.9 (op cit, p 23) confirms that this lower incident relates specifically to the severity categories 7 - 10. The relationship is less clear in the lower disablement categories where regional differences are more complex.

## Table 6.4 Frequency of disability in Great Britain by age and residence in households, 1991 census

GB Household population base.            54,054,534

                                             % of age group.

|  |  | % of age group |
|---|---|---|
| All ages with long term illness (households only) 16+ | 5335247 | 12.35 |
| 16-PA | 2280926 | 6.93 |
| PA+ | 3720759 | 36.77 |
| 75+ | 1856643 | 48.72 |

*Source*: OPCS(1994) 1991 Census Key Statistics for Local Authorities, GB, HMSO. Crown Copyright.

Check against OPCS, 1988                  Confidence interval

|  |  |  | Confidence interval |
|---|---|---|---|
| (households only) 16+ | | 5780000 | +/- 161000 |
| 16-59 | | 1855000 | |
| 60+ | | 3924000 | |
| 70+ | | 2626000 | |

*Source*: Martin, Meltzer & Elliot/ OPCS (1988) The prevalence of disability among adults. HMSO, based on table 3.3, p. 18. Crown copyright.

**Table 6.5  Estimates of prevalence of disability among adults by region and severity category**

(Cumulative percentages)

Total population 16+

| Severity | GLC | S. East | GB |
|---|---|---|---|
| 7-10 | 3.3 | 3.1 | 3.3 |
| 3-10 | 8.4 | 8.7 | 9.5 |
| 1-10 | 12.5 | 13.2 | 14.2 |

Population in households 16+

| Severity | GLC | S. East | GB |
|---|---|---|---|
| 7-10 | 2.7 | 2.4 | 2.7 |
| 3-10 | 7.6 | 7.9 | 8.8 |
| 1-10 | 11.7 | 12.4 | 13.5 |

*Source*: Martin, Meltzer & Elliot/ OPCS (1988) The prevalence of disability among adults. HMSO. Crown copyright.

*Combining 1991 census and OPCS 1988 disability survey material*

The methodology used in this thesis to estimate theoretical demand for social care services is to combine the OPCS (1988) disability ratios with more detailed local census tables. There are clear statistical weakness with such a model, in particular there will be the possibilities of errors in variation when predicting tables for local areas based on regional or national disability ratios. Regional and national variations in severity may not be strongly correlate with the unavailable local variations in severity. The model has to progress on the assumption that the ratios at regional and national level will be valid with smaller local long term ill populations. Bebbington, Turvey and Janzon (1996) have proposed an alternative method that is based on correlating census variables with a re-analysis of the original OPCS (1988) disability survey data. While this method does give additional local reliability, the method requires considerable extra time and resources that may not be available to the majority of local authorities. The method also relies on synthetic estimation and over time the validity of the model may break down if local social needs variables do not continue to be strongly correlated with the original disability data. First the method proposed here is demonstrated using national estimates, before moving to a local model.

Table 3.6 (Martin, Meltzer and Elliot, 1988) in the OPCS disability study estimated that the number of disabled older people (those with an OPCS score of 1 and greater) in the total national population of those over the age of 75 was 2,119,000. In Table 6.6 it can also be seen that 1,837,000 of these individuals were resident in households.

It is possible to compare this with the national 1991 census table for long term illness in households that records 1,885,300 people over the age of 75 as suffering some degree of severity of long term illness (Table 6.6). The numbers are close enough to assume that the 1991 census measure of long term illness approximates the entire OPCS categories 1 - 10. By implication it is reasonable to compute the severity ratios operationalised by the OPCS (1988) disability survey onto actual census counts of long term illness.

It is known from the 1991 census that there is significant local variation in the incidence of long term illness being reported (OPCS, 1994). Using the census for a base long term ill population when assessing local populations is more reliable. For example whilst the percentage of the population of people 75 and over with long term illness was recorded at 44% in East Sussex, it is 49% nationally, a 5% variation. This degree of variation will not be fully picked up in the national and regional tables calculated by the OPCS disability survey (Table 6.5).

Even where localised sub-samples of the 1988 data are available through the national data archive, confidence intervals will be large as the sub-samples of the survey become much smaller at county level. It is more satisfactory to use the census for total long term illness counts at local level and to then calculate a prediction of the incidence of severities.

Some variance errors will accumulate in doing this because national and regional ratios are being applied to local circumstances, but the model has the advantage of starting from a more robust count (not sample) of total disability in the local area.

In the national example in Table 6.6 it is predicted that 33% of all the long term ill over 75 fall into the severity 7 and over, this taken from the OPCS (1988) disability survey (Martin, Meltzer and Elliot, p. 22, Table 3.6). The ratios of severity on the right hand side of Table 6.6 are then applied to the more recent census counts of the total long term ill population. The 1991 census counts that there are more people aged over 75 residing in institutions than the 1988 OPCS survey. The definition of medical and care establishments in the census is remarkably similar to the communal establishments surveyed in the 1988 OPCS survey (op cit, p. 46). The proportions of over 75s in

**Table 6.6    Prevalence of disability and severity of cases, 1988-1991, Great Britain**

**OPCS, 1988 predictions**            (thousands)
Severity category predicted (1-10)

| | Totals | Low 1-2 | Med 3-6 | High 7-10 | % Low | Med | High |
|---|---|---|---|---|---|---|---|
| GB population (0ver 75s) with disability | | | | | | | |
| Communal establishments | 282 | 14 | 71 | 197 | 5 | 25 | 70 |
| Households | 1837 | 499 | 828 | 510 | 27 | 45 | 27 |
| Total | 2119 | 513 | 899 | 707 | 24 | 42 | 33 |
| % | 100 | 24 | 42 | 33 | | | |

Note:    Over 75s.  Severity predictions using OPCS, 1988 and up-dated with Census 1991.

*Source*:  Martin, Meltzer & Elliot, p. 22, table 3.6. Crown copyright.

**Census revision**            (thousands)

| | |
|---|---|
| Census total GB population (over 75s) | 3870 |
| Census residents with long term illness (over 75s)(households only) | 1885 |
| Census residents over 75 (Medical and care establishments) | 368 |

*Source*:  OPCS(1993) LBS L04. and OPCS(1994) *1991 Census Key Statistics for Local Authorities*, GB, HMSO Crown copyright.

(thousands)
Severity category predicted (1-10)
OPCS(1988) ratios

| | Totals | Low 1-2 | Med 3-6 | High 7-10 | % Low | Med | High |
|---|---|---|---|---|---|---|---|
| GB population (0ver 75s) with disability | | | | | | | |
| Communal establishments | 368 | 18 | 92 | 258 | 5 | 25 | 70 |
| Households | 1885 | 509 | 848 | 527 | 27 | 45 | 28 |
| Total | 2253 | 541 | 946 | 743 | 24 | 42 | 33 |
| % | 100 | 24 | 42 | 33 | | | |

institutions increased since the mid 1980s because of the increased take up of social security funding for residential homes. Table 6.6 shows the increase in institutional care during the late 1980s. This is confirmed by a third source of concurrent validity, the Department of Health's statistics on residential care. These statistics for elderly and younger disabled people show a 38% increase in beds for all ages between 1983 and 1993, with a large 70% increase for the 85 and over age group (Department of Health 1994c, p 8). There was some suggestion that the average length of stay was decreasing with local authority homes increasing their short stay admissions from 67% of admissions in 1983 to 83% in 1993 (op cit, p. 13). But by 1993 local authority homes only accounted for 27% of the total residential beds available.

The base line population of over 75s has also increased since the OPCS (1988) disability survey was taken in the mid 1980s. These facts help us to explain the increase in over 75s in medical and care establishments evident at the 1991 census, over and above the 1988 survey prediction.

**Analysing Theoretical Need and Actual Demand in a Local Area**

This chapter now examines a quantitative model of social care demand in East Sussex. The model is based on the method proposed in the first part of this chapter. The aim is to examine the mismatch between theoretical demand and actual expressed demand in the social care market. This research took place before the Unitary Authority of Brighton and Hove was established in 1997, and the data refers to the previous shire county of East Sussex.

# East Sussex

*Background*

East Sussex had an average population size for an English shire county with a population total very close to the shire mean average (Department of Health, 1994c). However, in comparison with other English shires there was a high incidence of social needs.The county had a high incidence of unemployment (according to the 1991 census) with a rate of 8.4 %, compared with the English shire county average of 7.5%. Population tables published by the Department of Health (1994c) for June 1991 and based on the 1991 Census show that the county had a higher proportion of those aged 75 and over than any other shire county. In addition, it had the second highest rate of pensioners living alone when compared with other shire counties.

The rate of pensioners living in rented accommodation was lower than the shire mean average, as was the age standardised incidence of long standing limiting illness amongst pensioners Department of Health, 1994c). Both these indicators imply that the large number of pensioners was in part compensated for by a higher distribution of wealth amongst older people than might be expected nationally. The area is known as a popular retirement centre and the ability to move areas during retirement is in part facilitated by wealth - a less likely occurrence for the poor who suffer higher rates of morbidity (Law and Warnes, 1982).

East Sussex was unusual for a shire county, in that it had the combined features of a relatively high government standard spending assessment for the personal social services (Society of County Treasures 1994) but a county council that spent at below this advisory rate for personal social services, and did so consistently between 1992-1994 (Department of Health, 1994c and 1995c). In 1996 East Sussex spent slightly more on personal social services than its PSS SSA, the first time this had happened in the 1990s (Department of Health, 1996).

An examination of the detail of the East Sussex 1994-95 PSS SSAs shows that the calculation for elderly domiciliary services is higher in comparison to other shires than its assessment for elderly residential services (Society of County Treasurers, 1994). 1992 output statistics show that the county had an above average number of total residential beds for the elderly over 75 (Department of Health, 1994c). The majority of these were in private homes, supported by social security expenditure prior to April 1993 and increasingly financed by users, their families and the local authority. East

Sussex also had relatively high internal local authority elderly residential home expenditure, this was inflated by high unit costs for its own elderly homes. These costs were the second highest of shire counties in England in 1991-1992 (Department of Health, 1994c). Perhaps as a result, its domiciliary services are supplied at an output rate below the shire average. The number of home help hours received during the same year by all client groups aged 75 and over stood at 11 per capita, whilst the shire average was 22. Similarly the number of meals served during the year for all client groups per capita aged 65 and over was 3.6 with the shire average being 5 (Department of Health 1994b, Key Indicators of local authority social services 1991-1992). These problems were compounded by the county's discretionary division of finances between children and adult services which favoured child protection work more than some neighbouring shire counties (East Sussex Social Services Department, 1994a, p 18; Chartered Institute of Public and Financial Accountants (CIPFA), 1994).

**Demand Assessment**

The next stage is to outline the county's population and develop some general indicators of theoretical demand.

*The choice of population data*

Table 6.7 summarises county population data from key statistical sources. The key difference between these statistics is the incongruous table for the 75-84 age group with the Registrar General's mid 1992 estimates, as used for the calculation of the 1994-1995 SSA (Society of County Treasurers, 1994), being approximately 30,000 below the 1991 census and 1994 Department of Health tables. For the purpose of modelling in this book census data is validated against East Sussex County (1994) Council planning department data. All the sources in Table 6.7 agree that the number of people in the 75-84 age group is declining in the early 1990s, but the over 85s are increasing. The County Council predictions of population changes for East Sussex are shown in Table 6.8

*Age adjustments to the census and OPCS data*

The following method is applied to develop a model of total theoretical

**Table 6.7  East Sussex population statistics compared**

county totals

Census 1991 local  base statistics

| Ages | 0-17 | 18-64 | >65 | 65-74 | 75-84 | >85 | >18 | Total |
|---|---|---|---|---|---|---|---|---|
| Totals | 133593 | 395492 | 199362 | 79215 | 99892 | 20255 | 663999 | 690447 |

*Source*: 1991 Census LBS, Crown copyright.

Registrar general mid 1992 estimates

| Ages | 0-17 | 18-64 | >65 | 65-74 | 75-84 | >85 | >18 | Total |
|---|---|---|---|---|---|---|---|---|
| Totals | 142185 | 415325 | 163045 | 78903 | 61692 | 22450 | 578370 | 720555 |

*Source*: 1994/1995 SSA Calculations, Society of County Treasurers.

Department of Health projections for 1994, based on 1991 census

| Ages | 0-17 | 18-64 | >65 | 65-74 | 75-84 | >85 | >18 | Total |
|---|---|---|---|---|---|---|---|---|
| Totals | 156304 | 399447 | 217305 | 80799 | 92900 | 23091 | 730399 | 752540 |

*Source*: Department of Health, 1994b, Crown copyright.

**Table 6.8 Population age bands: count adjustment**

East Sussex      45 and over

| | 45-64 | 65-74 | 75+ | All ages |
|---|---|---|---|---|
| Population change % | 9 | -6 | 5 | 4 |

Note:    1991-1994 based on 1992-1997 estimates.

*Source*:  East Sussex County Council.

demand. The first table used is the OPCS census count of all residents who suffer from a long term limiting illness. This is calculated from table L12 and L13 in the local base statistics. The data is provided at 100% count. The data is then adjusted for population change in the period 1991-1994 using the East Sussex figures in Table 6.9. Such a calculation assumes that within a given age range the proportion with a long term illness will be constant over the short to medium term.

**Table 6.9    Comparison of surveys and their prediction of long term illness (LTI)**

| Data source | LTI 16-59 | %LTI | sub pop |
|---|---|---|---|
| National | | | |
| GHS 1985 | *51724* | 13.9 | 372114 |
| Martin et al, OPCS, 1988 | *21583* | 5.8 | 372114 |
| Local | | | |
| Census 1991 | 26973 | *7.2* | 372114 |

| Data source | LTI 60+ | %LTI | sub pop |
|---|---|---|---|
| National | | | |
| GHS 1985 | *84216* | 35.5 | 237227 |
| Martin et al, OPCS, 1988 | *94654* | 39.9 | 237227 |
| Local | | | |
| Census 1991 | 73567 | *31.0* | 237227 |

| Data Source | LTI 85+ | %LTI | sub pop |
|---|---|---|---|
| National | | | |
| GHS 1985 | *11910* | 58.81 | 20255 |
| Martin, et al, OPCS, 1988 | *15779* | 77.90 | 20255 |
| Local | | | |
| Census 1991 | 13890 | *68.70* | 20255 |

Note:   1991 East Sussex, with comparison controlled by age ranges
Figures in italics are imputed figures calculated in this analysis.

*Source*:   Population tables for East Sussex are based on 1991 age groups, Census LO2. All data used here is Crown copyright.

This calculation of total residents with long term illness is then assumed to be equal to the OPCS (1988) disability survey prediction for disability types 1- 10. At a national level the sample provides severity ratios that are also categorised in age structures. Next the OPCS severity ratios are applied to the local census long term illness tables on the basis of the 1988 OPCS national calculated ratios for the distribution of severity scores within households and institutions, and sub-divided by age structure (using Martin, Meltzer and Elliot, 1988, Tables 4.2 and 4.8). The separate proportions of severities applied to households and institutions is not relevant in this exercise because the aim here is to map total theoretical demand (not where services should be supplied) and the household and institutional severity ratios are combined (see later Tables 6.15 and 6.16)

This uses the methodology developed earlier in the chapter.The smallest spatial calculation of the OPCS Disability survey severity ratios is United Kingdom regions. It should be noted that the severity ratios applied to the local census counts are from nationally calculated ratios, not regional ratios. This is because the national ratios give additional information on the relationship between severity of disability and age structure that is not available in the tables of regional ratios.

*The choice of disability statistics*

Table 6.9 tests the hypothesis that concurrent validity exists between different government long term illness studies. In Table 6.9 total estimates of long term illness in East Sussex, are shown as predicted by the 1991 census, the OPCS (1988) disability study, and the GHS (1985). Note that the age group sub populations here are taken from the 1991 census, not the later Department of Health population tables (1994c). Table 6.9 compares the census counts for long term illness in East Sussex with the national disability ratios predicted by the OPCS 1988 survey and the GHS 1985, where all the ratios are applied to 1991 census age group population counts.

The OPCS (Martin, Meltzer and Elliot, 1988) disability survey bears close resemblance to the census data for 16-59 year olds, but there is an over estimation by the 1985 GHS as identified by Martin, Meltzer and Elliot (1988). The GHS does, however, appear to underestimate the occurrence of disability for those aged 60 and over.

*Unique features of possible demand in East Sussex*

The differences in Table 6.9 can be explained. It should be remembered that the GHS 1985 and OPCS (1988) prevalence ratios, are taken here from national estimates, they being imputed onto 1991 local census population tables. This is how the predicted rates of actual long term illness (the numbers in italics in Table 6.9) are arrived at. In contrast the 1991 census row (Table 6.9) is constructed entirely from the local self-reported occurrence of long term illness.

In this East Sussex example the census recording of total long term illness in the population over 60 is lower than both the GHS and OPCS (1988) survey, because of its sensitivity to real local divergence from national trends. It is a more reliable measure. It is hypothesised that East Sussex has less long term illness than might be expected because of intervening social variables. The local divergence is because East Sussex is a comparably wealthy county with relatively low numbers of older people living in rented accommodation. Assuming that poverty does partly determine the early onset of long term limiting illness (Whitehead,1992), need in East Sussex will be less than in poorer areas of the country. Another important local feature is the reduction in localised older people, those between 75-85, as predicted by population documents (see for example I and S Unit, East Sussex Social Services, 1994 and the Department of Health, 1994c, p. 14). The use of local census tables allows important local divergence from the national averages to be observed.

The OPCS 1988 survey report shows that when regional differences are taken into consideration then the south east has less total prevalence than the national rates, prevalence likely to vary from the national rate by approximately -1% (see Martin, Meltzer and Elliot, 1988, p. 23, Table 3.9 and also Table 6.10 in this chapter), but the survey cannot detect divergence in more localised areas. This again confirms the validity of spatial census counts and the local divergence from national prevalence. Another 1991 census document confirms this. It shows that long term illness in households (not including institutions) was reported as 3.5% below the national levels in East Sussex for those of pension age and over, and as much as 4.5% below for those aged 75 and over (OPCS, 1994). The strength of the local census counts in illuminating local divergence from the regional and national norm is clear.

Table 6.10 allows for the regional south east (not national) ratio of all levels of prevalence from the OPCS survey to be computed. Here the OPCS 1988 severity ratios are slightly underestimating the total prevalence of long term illness counted in the 1991 census. This is likely to be caused by a simple random sampling error in the OPCS 1988 survey that has to be expected to produce small variations from other concurrent surveys.

**Table 6.10   Total estimates of the prevalence of long term illness (LTI)**

| East Sussex, prevalence | Total | Pop base | % pop LTI |
|---|---|---|---|
| *Actual counts of LTI* | | | |
| 1991 census | | | |
| LBS tales L12-L13/LO2 | 103906 | 690447 | 15.0 |
| Total residents in households and institutions with LTI | 100920 | 690447 | 14.6 |
| *Predictions* of LTI | | | |
| Martin et al, OPCS, 1998 | *91139* | 690447 | 13.2 |
| GHS 1985 | *143613* | 690447 | 20.8 |

Note:   Comparison of the concurrent validity of three studies, East Sussex. Numbers in italics are the predicted and imputed figures, calculated from the ratios.
Martin et al, OPCS, 1988.

*Source*:  OPCS, 1988, p. 23, controlling for SE adjustment. Crown copyright.

*The long term ill in communal establishments*

The Census (OPCS, 1994) shows that East Sussex had nearly twice as many residents living in institutions than the national average in 1991. It is hypothesised that many of these suffer from a long term illness. Tables 6.11 and 6.12 reveal that there is a discrepancy with where the 1991 census and OPCS 1988 survey are locating residence of their respondents. The census finds that there are 85,359 people aged 16 and over who suffer from a long term illness and live in households (Table 6.11). Even if this is adjusted for population growth we might expect it to be only marginally higher by 1994-1995. Table 6.12 shows that by calculating the OPCS 1988 total disability prevalence rates for the south-east using 1994 population projections gives

## Table 6.11   Distribution of long term illness (LTI), all severities institutions and households, ages 16 and over

|  | Households | | | | Institutions | | | | All |
|---|---|---|---|---|---|---|---|---|---|
|  | 16-59 | 60-75 | >75 | Total | 16-59 | 60-75 | >75 | Total | Total |
| Brighton | 6238 | 5887 | 5671 | 17796 | 641 | 402 | 1223 | 2266 | 20062 |
| Eastbourne | 2810 | 3754 | 4587 | 11151 | 391 | 614 | 1901 | 2906 | 14057 |
| Hastings | 3622 | 3408 | 3291 | 10321 | 398 | 483 | 1662 | 2543 | 12864 |
| Hove | 3232 | 3673 | 4275 | 11180 | 245 | 366 | 1913 | 2524 | 13704 |
| Lewes | 2729 | 3670 | 3626 | 10025 | 227 | 179 | 1066 | 1472 | 11497 |
| Rother | 2482 | 3890 | 4835 | 11207 | 240 | 252 | 1580 | 2072 | 13279 |
| Wealden | 3542 | 4528 | 5609 | 13679 | 356 | 246 | 1176 | 1778 | 15457 |

Note: The definition of an institution in the 1991 Census is broad and includes medical and care establishments, prisons, hostels, caravans and boats. Nevertheless, further examination of these tables shows that for the 75 and over age group of LTI 10521 people were resident in institutions only 524 were resident in medical or care institutions.

*Source*: 1991 Census LB12, Crown copyright.


## Table 6.12   Severity of disability and prevalence ratios in the south east, imputing Department of Health, 1994, population projections

| (Households and Institutions) | | | (16 and over) | | Institutions |
|---|---|---|---|---|---|
| Severity Category | Occur in SE (% in pop) | Number (cumulative) | Occur in SE (% househ'ds) | Number h'holds (cumulative) | Number ins (cumulative) |
| 10 | 0.5 | 3740 | 0.2 | 1496 | 2244 |
| 9-10 | 1.3 | 9724 | 0.8 | 5984 | 3740 |
| 8-10 | 2.1 | 15708 | 1.5 | 11220 | 4488 |
| 7-10 | 3.1 | 23187 | 2.4 | 17952 | 5236 |
| 6-10 | 4.3 | 32163 | 3.5 | 26179 | * |
| 5-10 | 5.8 | 43383 | 5.0 | 37399 | * |
| 4-10 | 7.3 | 54603 | 6.5 | 48619 | * |
| 3-10 | 8.7 | 65075 | 7.9 | 59091 | * |
| 2-10 | 10.4 | 77790 | 9.5 | 71058 | * |
| 1-10 | 13.2 | 98728 | 12.4 | 92750 | 5979 |

Note:   Total population aged 16 and over = 747983; *=unavailable.

*Source*: Martin et al, OPCS, 1988, table 3.9, p. 23, Crown copyright.

an estimate of disabled people in households of 92,750. The difference does not appear to be significant.

More problematic differences in concurrent validity occur when one examines the estimates of those who are long term ill and living in institutions (Tables 6.11 and 6.12). The 1991 census counts 15,561 people compared to the OPCS 1988 prediction of 5,976. Here the local variation invalidates the OPCS 1988 estimate. It is concluded that the OPCS 1988 survey has misplaced some of its prediction, with the movement into private rest homes of the late 1980s which moved some of those predicted to be household disabled into institutions. The 1988 OPCS survey was operationalised in the mid 1980s, before the national residential care homes population had reached its peak (Department of Health, 1994d).

Tables 6.13 and 6.14 show the census records for residents in medical and care establishments in East Sussex. Not all residents considered that they had long term illness, especially those living in housing association premises. These are presumably individuals with a high degree of independence and less willingness to diagnose themselves as ill. By combining the information from these tables with Table 6.11 it is possible to calculate that between three and four thousand adults who are long term ill are in fact living in other types of institutions, for example: defence establishments, prisons, non-housing association hostels and lodgings and ships.

To summarise thus far, the methodological prospects for predicting local theoretical demand are good. Local 1991 census counts of the long term ill can be combined with OPCS 1988 severity ratios. Problems develop when trying to locate where the long term ill are living, as it seems that location is fairly unstable over time. This is not surprising, given the nature of long term illness, and the need for the severely ill to enter institutions at short notice, either for a short or a long stay. Location of the long term ill is also likely to reflect changes in cultural expectation and government funding policy. It is not the intention of this demand side model to prescribe the location of long term ill in households or institutions. Rather the three funding priority bands suggested, based on the concepts of low, medium and high severity, should allow for the potential of choosing the appropriate purchase of home care and residential care, dependent upon choice and carer availability. The discovery that the OPCS 1988 Disability survey is locally inaccurate in its estimation of how much supply is generated by institutions is not important. A model of theoretical demand is primarily concerned with the use of the 1988 OPCS survey to predict proportions of severity within a local population with disabilities. The model is not at present concerned with using the survey to

**Table 6.13   Residents in medical and care establishments, East Sussex**

|  | Total | 16-PA | PA-74 | M>75 | F>75 | Total>16 |
|---|---|---|---|---|---|---|
| All medical and care est | 13000 | 1573 | 1528 | 1837 | 7990 | 12928 |
| NHS Psychiatric | 111 | 63 | 18 | 7 | 23 | 111 |
| NHS other | 527 | 181 | 57 | 62 | 225 | 525 |
| Non NHS psychiatric | 34 | 9 | 6 | 4 | 15 | 34 |
| Non NHS hospital | 42 | 33 | 5 | 3 | 1 | 42 |
| LA homes | 1199 | 200 | 149 | 191 | 643 | 1183 |
| Housing Assc accom | 408 | 122 | 33 | 40 | 205 | 400 |
| Nursing homes, private | 3564 | 133 | 372 | 621 | 2437 | 3563 |
| Residential homes, private | 7115 | 832 | 908 | 909 | 4441 | 7090 |

*Source*: 1991 census, LO4, Crown copyright.

**Table 6.14   Proportions of residents in medical and care institutions who diagnosed themselves as suffering from a long term illness (LTI), East Sussex**

|  | Total | LTI | % |
|---|---|---|---|
| All medical and care est | 13000 | 11893 | 91 |
| NHS Psychiatric | 111 | 101 | 91 |
| NHS other | 527 | 502 | 95 |
| Non NHS psychiatric | 34 | 34 | 100 |
| Non NHS hospital | 42 | 41 | 98 |
| LA homes | 1199 | 1146 | 96 |
| Housing Assc accom | 408 | 289 | 71 |
| Nursing homes, private | 3564 | 3480 | 98 |
| Residential homes, private | 7115 | 6300 | 89 |

*Source*: 1991 census LO4, Crown copyright.

predict where these proportions will be living.

Tables 6.15 and 6.16 show the national disability severity ratios for households and institutional populations based on the OPCS (Martin, Meltzer and Elliot) 1988. Although the distribution of severities between these two locations has changed since 1988, it is hypothesised that the total distribution of severities across a combined household and institutional population is unlikely to have changed substantially in a relatively short time span (Kreitzman, 1996, pp. 51-52), although it is also acknowledged that the relationship between standardised morbidity and standardised mortality is difficult to measure over time with methodological precision (Robine and Mathers, 1993). One recent report proposes a small decline in the prevalence and severity of long term illness in the last decade (Bebbington and Darton, 1996b).

The immediate research problem is how to impute the ratios of OPCS severity scales onto the local data, given that the OPCS (1988) Survey report calculates the proportions of severity ratios attributed to each age band separately for households and institutions.

This is done by imputing the severity and age band ratios from household and institutions in the OPCS 1988 in parallel, so as to make the ratios proportionate to the household and institutional location evident in the 1991 East Sussex census tables. Once that the two sets of ratios have been applied to census data the resulting figures can be summed. This inevitably leads to some degradation of the data, but it provides an aggregate method for capturing the overall ratio of priority need bands in proportion to age, regardless of whether people were previously ill at home or in institutions. The aim in doing this is to remove the residential error of the OPCS 1988 survey ratios.

These are the calculations behind the final model of theoretical demand for social care for adults in East Sussex presented in Table 6.17. The key part of this table is the final summation, remembering that at this point in the analysis it is not the intention to prescribe service supply to a household or institution, but merely to aggregate all possible demands. The age band tables have been adjusted to take account of East Sussex County Council population estimates. The final model of theoretical demand shows that of 102,559 long term ill in East Sussex, 30,168 will be of low need, 43,002 of moderate need and 29,372 in high need.

## Table 6.15  Disability severity ratios by age group, households

Households, GB

| | Low | Severity Medium | High | |
|---|---|---|---|---|
| Age range | 1-2 | 3-6 | 7-10 | |
| 16-59 | 0.35 | 0.47 | 0.18 | 1 |
| 60-74 | 0.41 | 0.43 | 0.16 | 1 |
| 75+ | 0.27 | 0.45 | 0.28 | 1 |

N=9998

*Source*: calculated from Martin et al, OPCS, 1998, table 4.2, p. 27, Crown
copyright.

## Table 6.16  Disability severity ratios by age group, institutions

Institutions, GB

| | Low | Severity Medium | High | |
|---|---|---|---|---|
| Age range | 1-2 | 3-6 | 7-10 | |
| 16-59 | 0.05 | 0.25 | 0.70 | 1 |
| 60-74 | 0.11 | 0.29 | 0.60 | 1 |
| 75+ | 0.05 | 0.25 | 0.70 | 1 |

N=4000

*Source*: calculated from Martin et al, OPCS, 1988, table 4.8, p. 33, Crown
copyright.

**Table 6.17    Model of the demand for community care in East Sussex**

Total long term ill (LTI), 1991 census, adjusted for 1994 population.
        Applied priority ratings (using Table 6.15 and 6.16)

|  | Households | Low | Medium | High |
|---|---|---|---|---|
| 16-59 | 25641 | 8974 | 12051 | 4615 |
| 60-74 | 27370 | 11221 | 11769 | 4379 |
| 75+ | 33488 | 9042 | 15070 | 9377 |

|  | Institutions | Low | Medium | High |
|---|---|---|---|---|
| 16-59 | 2598 | 130 | 649 | 1819 |
| 60-74 | 2415 | 265 | 700 | 1449 |
| 75+ | 11047 | 552 | 2762 | 7733 |

|  | Summation | Low | Medium | High |
|---|---|---|---|---|
| 16-59 | 28239 | 9104 | 12701 | 6434 |
| 60-74 | 29784 | 11487 | 12469 | 5828 |
| 75+ | 44535 | 9594 | 17832 | 17110 |
| Total | 102559 | 30186 | 43002 | 29372 |

**Table 6.18    East Sussex residential care: all client groups, numbers in residential care institutions and those supported by the local authority, 1994-1995**

|  | 18-64 | 65-74 | 75 and over | Total (18+) |
|---|---|---|---|---|
| June 94 pop | 421312 | 79904 | 79904 | 581120 |
| *% in residential care* | *0.1* | *0.7* | *8.1* | *1.3* |
| No in res care | 585 | 559 | 6472 | 7616 |
| No supported | 134 | 160 | 1278 | 1572 |
| week cost per supported res | £437 | £254 | £254 | |
| cost per week | £58558 | £40640 | £324612 | |
| cost per year | £3045016 | £2113280 | £16879824 | £22038120 |

Notes:   The unit cost table used for 18-64 age group is the table for
        Learning Difficulties, indicator UC21, Dept of Health (1996b).

*Source*: calculation made using data supplied by Department of Health (1996) Key
        indicators of local authority social services. Government Statistical Service,
        Crown copyright.

**Actual Demand for Services**

The next task is to try and predict how much theoretical demand is being expressed as actual demand on services. It is necessary to recall at this point some assumptions made in earlier chapters. It is hypothesised that certain groups, like the poorer long term ill, will under consume and not demand services. Here theoretical demand is high, but actual demand postponed. People cope as long as they can, until there is a crisis, and then the maximum of state resources are spent on both assessment and provision. This feature is most likely to exist in areas with large traditional working class and rented housing populations, especially when these sub groups have a demographic bulge in the over 75s and over 85s. Census data on the distribution of long term illness by social class, tenure, and age, can assist in the prediction of these specific issues, as will be demonstrated at the end of the next chapter.

*Actual demand and service provision*

Secondary information from the Department of Health provides an indication of what social services departments are actually providing in relation to theoretical demand. At present total requests for help and assessment are not publicly available and therefore actual demand cannot be easily separated from actual provision. Data on the number of assessments carried out is likely to be made available in the future (Department of Health, 1994b). At present there are methodological problems with the reliability of data collected by local authorities and passed to central governments and then reused in a number of formats. Aggregated unit costs, in particular, are not likely to be a valid means alone for making policy decisions (Kelly and Bebbington, 1993; see also the discussion in Department of Health, 1996, Table U1, p. 5)

When a number of data sources are evaluated to understand actual provision it can be seen that current SSD purchasing is unable to sustain any notion of universal provision to meet all theoretical demand and it becomes clear why the use of priority eligibility criteria are currently critical to the local planning and management of SSD operations (Bebbington, Turvey and Janzon, 1996).

PSS data for the year 1994-1995 (Department of Health, 1996) shows the percentage of area population sub groups living in residential care and those supported by the local authority funding (Table 6.18).

East Sussex appears to have relatively low percentages of supported places when compared to its neighbouring counties (op cit, Table O4, p. 14)

**Table 6.19    Estimates from East Sussex Social Services, predicted client numbers, 1994-1995**

| | Average client numbers during the year | | | | | |
| | Residential | | Day care | | Home care | Totals |
| | LA | Other | LA | Other | LA | |
|---|---|---|---|---|---|---|
| Older people | 617 | 3001 | 541 | 306 | 6597 | 11062 |
| Phy disability | | 276 | 27 | 11 | | 314 |
| Learning Diff | 158 | 494 | 752 | 169 | | 1573 |
| Mental Health | | 307 | 98 | 100 | | 505 |
| Totals | 775 | 4078 | 1418 | 586 | 6597 | 13454 |

Notes: Meals on wheels and adaption grants not included. Home care statistics are based on weekly averages in year. Only includes clients whose provision is part supported by the LA.

*Source*: CIPFA (1994) PSS Estimates, copyright CIPFA.


**Table 6.20    Actuals from East Sussex Social Services**

| Data from CIPFA ACTUALS 94-95 | | | Average client numbers during the year | | | | |
| | Residential | | Day care | | Home Care | Totals | £m |
| Provision | LA | Other | LA | Other | All | | |
|---|---|---|---|---|---|---|---|
| Older people | 667 | 1376 | 540 | 69 | 5895 | 8547 | |
| Net expendt'e | | £31.54m | | £2.07m | | | £42.60 |
| Phy disability | 19 | 207 | 30 | 44 | 444 | 744 | |
| Net expendt'e | | £4.83m | | £0.46m | | | £5.29 |
| Learning Diff | 144 | 289 | 722 | 88 | 60 | 1303 | |
| Net expendt'e | | £10.8m | | £4.52m | | | £15.32 |
| Mental Health | | 143 | 80 | 11 | 35 | 269 | |
| Net expendt'e | | £0.95m | | £1.15m | | | £2.10 |
| Others | | | | | 190 | 190 | |
| TOTALS | 830 | 2015 | 1372 | 212 | 6529 | 14053 | |
| £ million | | £48.12 | | £8.20 | £9.02 | | £65.31 |

Notes: Meals on wheels and adaption grants not included. Net expenditure for home care is only available for all client groups. Net expenditures for home care are listed in 'other providers' but include LAs provision. All tables only include clients whose provision is part supported by the LA.

*Source*: CIPFA(1996) PSS Actuals, copyright CIPFA.

but its actual total population of residential homes is likely to be higher, due to an importing of residents from outer London areas where there are few private and independent providers. Once placed in East Sussex these places are usually funded by their home sponsoring authority. An additional factor contributing to East Sussex's low proportions of funded places will be its relatively wealthy older population.

The unit cost per supported resident in East Sussex is £254 per week where the average for shire counties is £255 per week (Department of Health, 1996, Table U1). This is within the range of average weekly costs for residential and nursing care estimated by the government's own market research at £234 and £324. (Secretary of State for Health 1996, p. 56).

Table 6.19 shows that from Department of Health unit cost estimates the total cost of residential care provision as purchased by East Sussex social services department in 1994-95 would be £22.03 million. This assumes that the entire unit cost is paid for each supported resident. Table 6.20 shows the actual expenditure on residential care as computed by CIPFA, 1996 (Chartered Institute of Public and Financial Accountants). The net amount spent by the local authority is £48.12 million, a considerable amount more than the Department of Health data suggests. An aggregated unit cost of the CIPFA data also results in a unit cost for all adult clients in residential care of £387.51 per week.

These discrepancies can be traced to an underestimate of supported residents in the Department of Health data, Table 6.18. The estimates of the number of supported residents calculated by CIPFA are much greater (table 6.19). The statistics in Table 6.18 are not really estimates at all, but tables submitted to the Department of Health for monitoring purposes at the end of year (1994-1995). They are considered less reliable than the CIPFA data (Kelly and Bebbington, 1993). CIPFA actuals for 1994-1995 calculate the yearly cost of each supported older resident in residential care in East Sussex as £16,330. This was the second highest table for all English Shire Counties, exceeded only by Surrey with a calculation of £16,708. The English Shire Counties average cost was £13,820 (CIPFA, 1996, p. 48). The unreliability of the Department of Health PSS expenditure data was reviewed by the Department of Environment's Efficiency Scrutiny in 1997 and influenced the conclusions of the Department of Health Review of PSS Statistics in July 1977. It is hoped in the future to rectify the errors by making more direct links between the collection and calculation of CIPFA data and the returns to the Department of Health (1997b, p. 23).

East Sussex's own summary of its 1994-95 budget and estimates for

1995-96 described a slow decreasing demand for long term residential care, but an associated rise in demand for short term respite residential care, needed to support carers (East Sussex Social Services Department, 1994a).

Table 6.21 adds some basic estimates of cost to the estimates of theoretical demand. The tables are constructed from crude costing estimates for each priority category. The cost for severe need is the unit cost for East Sussex's supported residents (as used in table 6.18). The model assumes that all those in theoretical need are given an allocation of money and this would give the authority an end of year budget of £691 million. This in more than ten times the amount it currently spends on community care provision. Even if an allowance is made for social security benefits paid to the disabled to finance their care, the disjunction between actual need met and theoretical need is likely to be large under the present funding system.

**Table 6.21 Cost of theoretical demand in East Sussex, 1994-1995**

|        | Total   | Low   | Medium | High  |
|--------|---------|-------|--------|-------|
| 16-59  | 28239   | 9104  | 12701  | 6434  |
| 60-74  | 29784   | 11487 | 12469  | 5828  |
| 75+    | 44536   | 9594  | 17832  | 17110 |
| Total  | 102559  | 30186 | 43002  | 29372 |

| Cost per person per week |  | £30 | £120 | £246 |
|--------|--------|--------|--------|--------|

| Total service cost | Totals | Low | Medium | High |
|--------|--------|--------|--------|--------|
| per week | £13,291,332 | £905,580 | £5,160,240 | £7,225,512 |
| Service costs per year | £691,149,264 | £47,090,160 | £268,332,480 | £375,726,624 |

Note:  Total long term ill. 1991 Census. Adjusted for 1994 population.
Priority ratings calculated from OPCS, 1988. Crown copyright.

*Source*: 1991 census and OPCS, 1988, Crown copyright.

# 7 Demand Side Planning and Equity

## The Background and Context of the Standard Spending Assessment

The Standard Spending Assessment (SSA) is used to calculate the payment of block grant from central government to local government and the level at which local council tax is set. Annual SSA calculations are operationalised by the Department of the Environment, Transport and Regions (DETR, 1998a). This calculation also controls the distribution of the uniform business rate. Councils judged to be spending too much above their total SSA level can have their grant 'capped' in the future, the assumption being that they are raising unnecessary extra revenue in local council tax. The SSA, as a control of government expenditure, represents a rigid planning mechanism. It makes councils dependent upon subsidy from the centre for the bulk of their revenue. Local councillors can spend at above the individual service specific SSA (for example above the PSS SSA), but will only avoid capping if they achieve this by small, permitted increases in council tax, or by cutting relative expenditure in another service specific SSA area (for example, from Education). In effect an internal cross subsidy has to be made from another budget.

The SSA planning policy has been criticised for restricting local democracy and economic management, its rationale is that it maintains horizontal and spatial equity and central government control over public expenditure. It is important to understand the political logic behind the SSA. The purpose of its development was to establish an objective indicator that recorded a reasonable and rational level of spending on local authority services which could be generalised across the country. There was, in addition, a need for some regional cost adjustment in London and southern England due to salary levels. Further, in 1994-95, an additional cost adjustment was made to allow for the higher business rates payable in London and the south east (Society of County Treasurers, 1994, p. 4).

The central government rationale for the SSA was that once such a rational-comprehensive assessment was made it could be ascertained which counties and metropolitan boroughs had exceeded their SSAs and had set higher than reasonable local tax charges. These authorities could then be

194

penalised by the imposition of RSG (Revenue Support Grant) capping. Given the deterrent nature of such a policy rationale it is critical that the statistical process is fair, otherwise local authorities are capped for overspending when in reality they are forced to spend more to meet the same levels of need as elsewhere (Owen,1990, p. 63; Goldstein, 1994). The question remains, are the SSAs sufficiently valid? There are doubts about the theoretical underpinning of the SSA calculations given their attempt to model social complexity using OLS (Ordinary Least Squares) regression analysis. The inability of spatial and territorial resource allocation mechanisms to be explicitly related to social theory was a concern expressed about earlier grant mechanisms (Bebbington and Davies, 1980a, 1980b).

*Local management issues with SSAs: the paradox of their 'generality and specificity'*

Given that individual service area SSAs (for example the PSS SSA) are not enforced, and that only the aggregate local SSA is enforced, LAs must manage the inter-relationship of their own service specific SSAs. Despite this 'generality' of the SSA, local authorities are aware of the hundreds of highly specific calculations that make up the service specific SSAs. There is an increasing amount of complex and specific detail computed in the individual service area SSAs. This growth in detail and measurement complexity can be seen by comparing the publication of two Society of County Treasurers publications in 1994 and 1998. When the detail of the data and calculations is examined there is a slight increase in the number of underlying indicators and an attempt to incorporate more measurement complexity into the SSAs. One assumes that the rationale here is to capture growing social complexity in the SSA models so as to make them more valid.

## Measurement Issues with the SSA: What is their Meta-theoretical Purpose?

Such a complex statistical synthesis needs to be linked with a clear meta-theoretical framework about how the component variables of need, cost and efficiency are interacting (Bebbington and Davies, 1980a, 1980b). In the case of the SSA such a theoretical synthesis is lacking. A key concern with measurement validity in the PSS SSAs is the confusion between: efficiency and equity, cost and need, and spatial and individual effects (Goldstein, 1994;

Senior, 1994).

The government's philosophy at the time of launching the RSG indicated that it was more intent politically on achieving horizontal equity than vertical equity; that is equity between similar people in similar areas, rather than equity between rich and poor individuals and rich and poor areas (Boyne and Powell, 1993; Thatcher, 1993, ch. XXII). If spatial equity was being achieved, one would expect the correlation-coefficients between nationally recommended territorial tax levels (for example the old poll tax rates) and local area deprivation scores to be close to zero. Owen (1990) has argued that this was not the case. Rather they were negative, suggesting high taxation in an area correlated with poverty and deprivation. Since Owen's work, the council tax has introduced a new vertical element, by creating an ordinal range of tax bands relating to property values within the local area.

*Horizontal equity and spatial equity*

The attainment of spatial equity is the nearest that the SSA gets to demonstrating a meta-theoretical purpose (Thatcher, 1993, p 660). The fact that manifestations of inequity may be located in spatial proximity leads to the term 'spatial equity'. Truelove (1993, p. 19) has stated that spatial equity 'means treating equals equally irrespective of where they live' and this can be contrast with horizontal equity that aims to: 'treat individuals in like circumstances identically.' Another term for spatial equity is 'territorial justice' (Davies, 1968).

A problem when measuring horizontal equity is defining the 'like' term. What form of social strata will be used to claim that one actor should be like an other? Horizontal equity can be applied to a number of social strata, including age and social class. If it is applied to spatial strata, then it becomes a form of spatial equity.

Spatial equity is often the implicit goal of central government grants to different regions, where geographical regions are the strata applied. Because the hierarchical level of council tax bands are related to the market value of housing, the allocation of council tax can also claim to have a vertical effect, that is, a component of redistribution between rich and poor individuals.

The majority of local government expenditure is financed by the RSG rather than the council tax. One of the spatial features of grant allocation to large geographies, is that vertical inequity will vary considerably within one local authority area. If one local authority receives a larger grant because it has a higher concentration of poor long term ill, it cannot be assumed that this will be spent on those individuals in additional need.

Horizontal and spatial equity are linked  because spatial location is often directly related to other structural inequities. For example in Britain there is a a tendency for the private sector to locate residential care services where wealthy middle class people retire (the south coast and Cheshire for example) and poorer metropolitan areas have less private services (Ford and Smith, 1995; Bebbington and Darton, 1996a). Spatial equity  becomes important to counteracting market distortions, because market distortions have a geographical element. A combined application of horizontal and spatial equity results. Truelove (1993)  states that if planners are to treat like persons identically across the nation, then people must also be treated equally irrespective of where they live.

*Previous research that questions the validity of the SSA*

One key concern is that SSAs fail to take enough account of real local differences caused by social deprivation (Owen, 1990; Broom, 1993; Hale and Travers, 1993). Part of the methodological problem here is finding a theoretical framework for understanding the interaction of individual and spatial causes of deprivation (Macintyre, 1997).

Owen' s argument is that authorities in areas of high social deprivation need an adjustment to allow for more money because the total need for services is greater. But this assumes that the RSG is supposed to achieve an optimum vertical and horizontal equity itself (independent of other fiscal policy), a point that is not clear from the DETR and government planning intentions. A local authority area might have high levels of social need, but also high levels of wealth in other ward/neighbourhoods - the two might partly cancel each other out at the larger geographical level. The relationship between territorial justice and individual social justice (vertical and horizontal equity) is not straightforward and depends to a large extent on the spatial definition of territories. Statisticians have known this for some time, following the discovery of the 'ecological fallacy' (Robinson, 1950) where the relationships of variables computed between territories were shown to be quite volatile when compared to those computed between individuals.

*Spurious associations between historical costs and real needs*

Another criticism is that SSAs are too firmly based in historical cost determinants and therefore are in danger of perpetuating financial inefficiencies rather than efficient ways of meeting need (Audit Commission, 1993b; Senior, 1994). Cost determinants can have an inadequate association with theoretical needs which have not been previously expressed as actual costs. Similarly costs do not indicate the real benefits of output services and the quality of life outcomes gained. The use of cost determinants in the SSA calculations is in danger of confusing efficiency with equity. Senior (1994, p. 28) has stated that SSAs based on previous levels of cost expenditure may be unreliable because of their dependence on a base period. There is a possibility that the previous figures are distorted by non-periodic effects.

## The SSAs and Change Over Time

The SSA structure and process involves constant reviews and re-calculations. Much of this critical review is transparent and well documented by both the DETR and Association of County Treasurers and Association of County Councils (1994). Calculations are often upgraded to reflect more recent data or research findings. An example of this is the upgrading of the PSS SSA potential elderly domiciliary clients calculations (see Society of County Treasurers, 1994, p. 31; Society of County Treasurers, 1998, p. 50). Nevertheless The SSA calculations are based on an updated *historical* analysis, rather than any creative prediction of the future. No explicit statistical attempt is made to predict the future and future needs. Future needs are assumed to equal past needs. This is at its most problematic when future needs are suggested to be equal to past costs. There might be a spurious association between past costs and future needs based on previous inefficiencies in expenditure and unjust targeting of resources.

While much of the data used in the SSA calculations shows only incremental change over time, population age sub groups can change fairly significantly in a short space of time and the patterns here are not necessarily uniform across individual authorities (see Figure 7.1). In effect it may take the overall SSA mechanism some time to catch up with underlying complexity in the data used. An aggregate method like OLS regression will not capture satisfactorily the inclusion of an authority that is going against the trend (see Havering in Figure 7.1). Expenditure and cost data seems to be quite unpredictable data, with variations in the change patterns over time between individual authorities (see Figure 7.2). Here authorities fluctuate between 'boundaries of instability' (Stacey, 1995) and an aggregate cross-sectional linear model cannot capture the detail of what is happening.

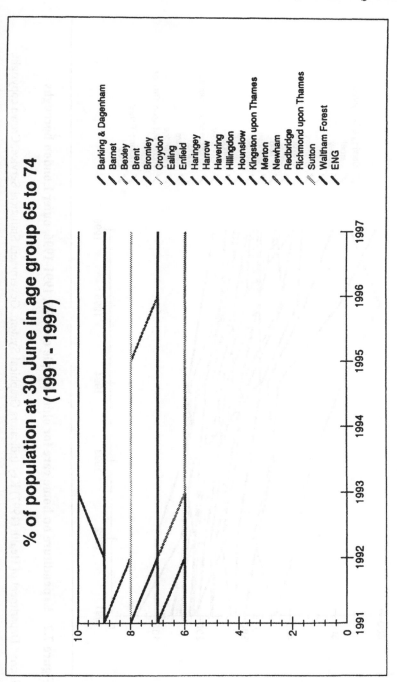

**Figure 7.1** **Population fluctuations: older people, aged 65–74, outer London boroughs**

*Source:* Department of Health (1997) Key Indicators Graphical System, Government Statistical Service, Crown copyright.

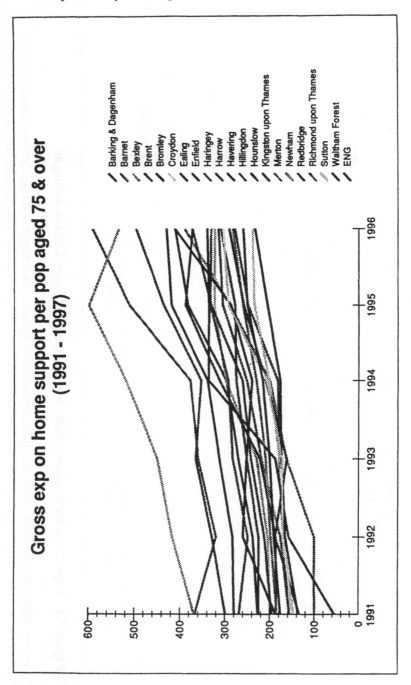

**Figure 7.2  Expenditure on home care for older people over 75, 1991-1996, outer London boroughs**

*Source:* Department of Health (1997) Key Indicators Graphical System, Government Statistical Service, Crown copyright.

Difficult questions arise about whether outliers, or those cases going against the trend, should be left out of the linear model (Kleinbaum, Kupper, Muller, and Nizam, 1998). The overall trend in Figure 7.2 is upwards, but the path taken by different authorities is variable within the boundaries of instability. The incremental linear model cannot capture radical departures from the average incremenal model. When recent changes in details of calculations have lead to authorities receiving less grant, the government was concerned to protect the grant of these authorities in the short term (DETR, 1998b). While in once sense this is to be welcomed if it protects authorities from invalid data, in another sense it is an admission that the calculations are unreliable and do not really measure need in a just manner.

## Examples from the PSS SSA

### *Theoretical issues for the PSS SSA*

The Personal Social Services Standard Spending Assessment presents the SSA methodology with some particular challenges given the complexities of the personal social services welfare system. The contemporary context of PSS is that it is a selective service where much effort goes into means testing and targeting resources that are not universally available. The PSS SSA does not articulate explicitly this targeting, it uses calculation methods that seek to target services at those with the most economic needs (using benefit payment statistics for example) and includes other indicators that do not contain any targeting element (for example population size, total  frequencies of long term illness). There is therefore some meta-theoretical confusion in the aggregate PSS SSA calculations about whether service funding should be strictly targeted at those in economic need, or whether the services should be partially available to all long term ill - regardless of their economic need. This confusion is also evident in political considerations of social care policy. The inability of the PSS SSA methodology to state a clear theoretical approach to this welfare dilemma also confounds attempts to articulate and solve the debate elsewhere. On balance, the underlying range of PSS SSA data implies a high level of local authority intervention and fairly broad definitions of need that LAs SSDs cannot meet in practice once that the need measurements are aggregated to monetary figures.

This theoretical complexity in the PSS SSA can be contrasted with education, where universal per capita population data has more relevance, because education is a universal service targeted at all children. Similarly, education services are still usually provided by local government, while in PSS there has been an increased marketisation of provider services. Some localities have much better market availability of social care services than others, which give marginal costs benefits (Ford and Smith, 1995; Department of Health, 1997a).

*Personal Social Services SSAs*

The Personal Social Services SSA is constituted from three separate sub SSAs: children's services, services for the elderly (residential and domiciliary) and other adult social services. The key variables acting as 'underlying data' and contributing to the prediction of the number of people requiring services and necessary funding are listed in the Society for County Treasures (1998, pp. 48-52), annual publication on the Standard Spending Indicators. The underlying data is then computed with weights to predict client variations between spatial areas. For example, the regression weights for the indicator 'potential elderly domiciliary clients' are reproduced below and they are calculated from unit cost data (Table 7.1).

**Table 7.1    Example of SSA indicator: potential elderly domiciliary clients**

The population aged 65 and over multiplied by the weighted sum :
0.1031* the proportion aged 65+who are aged 75-84
+0.2553*the proportion aged 65+who are aged 85+
+0.0599*the proportion of persons aged 65+ residential accommodation
+0.1062* Elderly on income support
+0.1029*the proportion of residents aged 65 and over with a limiting long term illness -0.0449

Note:    The weights are from a regression analysis of the social, economic and demographic characteristics of a sample of elderly people (GHS) against the costs of domiciliary services they receive (using costs derived form local authority returns)

*Source*:  Society of County Treasurers, 1994, p. 31, note 58.

The final stage is the conversion of these regression indicators into 'actual standard spending assessments per capita'. This involves an algorithm that includes an area cost adjustment factor. The unit costs for the PSS elderly (residential care) indicator reflect national average expenditures per client (Senior, 1994, p. 26) In effect there is an assumption that potential need is related to the costs of services already in existence. This raises questions of internal validity.

This leads to two main errors. First, potential need is measured by actual demands on local authorities, not theoretical need based on social indicators. There can be a mismatch between actual demand and theoretical demand. Second, expenditure reflects local efficiency levels, in addition to actual local demands (Department of Health, 1997a). In effect a local area that has relative low unit costs achieved by efficiency could be penalised by the calculation because it is assumed that it has low levels of need. This assumption might be spurious.

**The Relationship Between Individual Need and Spatial Need**

*Reasons for geographical variation in need*

Adult long term illness accounts for approximately 80% of actual PSS expenditures (Department of Health, 1998). Levels of long term illness vary in the locality because of intervening social variables and physical landscape effects such as poor infrastructure (Macintyre, 1997). This type of variation has been studied in depth by Senior (1995) and Gould and Jones (1995). Senior found that using a geography based on local district council boundaries, Rhondda, in South Wales, had the highest age and gender standardised ratio of long term illness in Britain, with a score of 196.69. Most of the other districts in the top 50 were in the north of England, Wales and Scotland, with the notable exceptions of Hackney (scored 134.11) and Tower Hamlets (scored 125.03). Using a smaller spatial geography based on wards and post-codes, further pockets in England were identified, this demonstrating the importance of examining alternative level geographies to avoid planning conclusions based on ecological invalidity (Robinson, 1950; Jones, 1997, p. 30).

Extensive multi-level, multi-variate analysis of the Great Britain SARs (Sample of Anonymised Records) by Gould and Jones (1995) has concluded that there are increased probabilities of black older people becoming long term ill when compared to whites. Also, that variations in long term illness

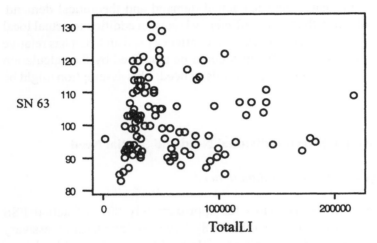

Correlation of SN63 and TotalLI in area = -0.044

**Figure 7.3 Scatterplot of the association between the frequency of total
long term illness (total LI) and standardised
geographical long term illness, 65+ age group (SN63) SSD
areas, England**

*Source*: Department of Health (1997) Key Indicators Graphical System,
Government Statistical Service, Crown copyright.

are strongly linked to measures of older people's socio-economic circumstances such as housing tenure and car ownership. In addition they discovered clear geographical variations in long term illness rates; and that variations between geographical rates remain significant when other individual socio-economic differences are controlled for.

*The relationship between frequencies of long term illness and standardised geographical measures of long term illness*

When comparing large spatial areas, use of a variable that counts the frequency of occurrence will dictate that areas with large populations will automatically have a tendency to receive higher frequency scores. For this reason the research in this paper starts by using the age standardised measures of long term illness for those under 65 and 65 and over. This measure is calculated by the Department of Health (1995c). It shows the amount of long term illness for a specific age range that occurs in relation to that which would be expected, given the age profile of the spatial population. It is a measure designed for comparisons between spatial areas.

Figure 7.3 demonstrates the relationship between the total number of long term ill in local authority SSD areas and the standardised measure of long term illness for those 65 and over. There is no relationship. Some areas have large occurrences of long term illness because they have large sub-populations of retired people and high levels of long term illness are expected. Other areas have small total numbers of long term ill, but still more than would be expected for the age profile of their population. The standardised measure of long term illness uses the same principles as the standardised mortality ratio (SMR). It highlights areas where there are higher than expected rates of long term illness, because of the social and cultural characteristics of the area and its people. There is no clear correlation between these two variables because of the large shire counties that constitute wealthy retirement areas. Such areas have large frequencies of long term illness, but less than expected incidents of illness in relation to the age profile.

*The relationship between social needs indicators and the spatial prevalence of long term illness*

After investigations (Table 7.2) with a number of social needs variables unemployment (1991) was found to have the best association with age standardised rates of long term illness. This analysis is continued with a

**Table 7.2    Correlation matrix. PSS SSA 1994-1995 and social needs indicators, SSD areas, England**

|       | PSSSSA94 | SN50 | SN51 | SN52 | SN54 | SN60 | SN61 | SN63 |
|-------|----------|------|------|------|------|------|------|------|
| SN50  | 0.747    |      |      |      |      |      |      |      |
| SN51  | 0.766    | 0.347 |     |      |      |      |      |      |
| SN52  | 0.825    | 0.679 | 0.504 |    |      |      |      |      |
| SN54  | 0.771    | 0.402 | 0.752 | 0.801 |  |      |      |      |
| SN60  | 0.765    | 0.519 | 0.634 | 0.544 | 0.516 |   |      |      |
| SN61  | 0.815    | 0.758 | 0.430 | 0.635 | 0.413 | 0.771 |  |      |
| SN63  | *0.124*  | 0.581 | *-0.256* | *0.117* | *-0.228* | *0.190* | 0.459 | |
| SN70  | 0.378    | 0.801 | *-0.016* | 0.328 | *-0.037* | 0.337 | 0.584 | 0.907 |

| PSSSSA94 | per capita PSS SSA allocation 1994-1995 |
|----------|------------------------------------------|
| SN61 | % of those of pensionable age in rented accommodation, 1991 census |
| SN52 | % of those in households living in over-crowded accommodation, 1991 census |
| SN50 | % of economically active residents who are unemployed, 1991 census. |
| SN51 | % of those in households living in accommodation that is not self contained, 1991 census |
| SN54 | % of those in households who were born outside the UK, Eire, EC, Old Com and USA, 1991 census |
| SN60 | % of those of pensionable age and over living alone, 1991 census |
| SN63 | age standardised long term illness 65+ |
| SN70 | age standardised long term illness 18-64 |

Notes:   All the above variables have positively skewed distributions, except SN63 and SN70 that have near normal distributions. Figures in italics are not significant at $p=0.05$.

*Source*: Department of Health (1995) , Key Indicators of Local Authority Social Services 1994, pages 10-29, Crown copyright.

regression analysis in Table 7.3.

In Table 7.3, the percentage of those over 65 and living in rented accommodation (SN61) is not statistically significant in the second model (this is after age standardised long term illness 18-64. has been removed as a strong independent variable). Unemployment in 1991 (SN50), is the only social needs variable that makes a statistically significant contribution to the explanation of age standardised long term illness for those over 65.

When the variable of unemployment (1991) is examined in its relationship with the occurrence of long term illness at an earlier age (SN70) the graph over the page results (Figure 7.4). This shows a strong association between the two variables.

The variable of unemployment (1991) explains quite well the geographical occurrence of long term illness amongst the younger 18-64 population. It is concluded that unemployment rates taken from the 1991 recession are a good predictor of areas with a high occurrence of long term illness, because unemployment levels at the bottom the economic circle reflect a number of underlying socio-economic characteristics of a spatial area. Spatial area unemployment rates are likely to explain the occurrence of geographical areas where there were in previous decades large concentrations of traditional working class employment. This will include occupations like mining that have an effect on health (Senior, 1995).

The spatial unemployment rate at the low point of the economic cycle (1991) has been identified as one possible predictor of the geographical occurrence of long term illness. Unemployment has been recently added to the DETR calculation of the other adult PSS SSA. An age standardised rate of long term illness (18-64) is also used in this component part of the PSS SSA (Society of County Treasurers, 1994, p 32).

*The relationship between social needs indicators and government assessment of need (PSS SSA)*

Analysis shows that the total PSS SSA 1994 -1995 can be partly explained by the regression of social needs indicators. In this paper a combined social needs indicator was developed using a correlation matrix, by considering the inter-relationship between some 20 social needs variables available in the Dept of Health PSS KIGS data-set. Six variables were identified as having a strong correlation with the PSS SSA. These can be seen in Table 7.2. Neither SN63 or SN70, the indicators for standardised long term illness, correlated substantially with the PSS SSA and so they were excluded from further analysis.

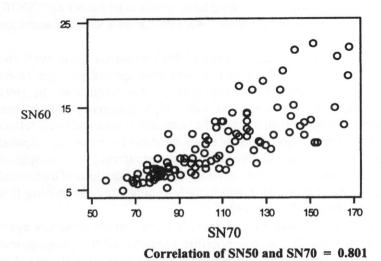

Correlation of SN50 and SN70 = 0.801

**Figure 7.4   Scattergraph of age standardised long term illness (18-64)
(SN70)  by unemployment (1991) (SN60), SSD areas,
England**

*Source*: Department of Health (1997) Key Indicators Graphical System
(KIGS), Government Statistical Service, Crown copyright.

**Table 7.3** **Regression analysis of social needs indicators to explain long term illness, age standardised (65+), SSD areas, England**

The regression equation is
$SN63 = 59.8 + 0.501\ SN70 + 0.0843\ SN61 - 1.37\ SN50$

| Predictor | Coef | Stdev | t-ratio | p |
|---|---|---|---|---|
| Constant | 59.773 | 1.592 | 37.56 | 0.000 |
| SN70 | 0.50144 | 0.02240 | 22.39 | 0.000 |
| SN61 | 0.08433 | 0.03881 | 2.17 | 0.032 |
| SN50 | -1.3690 | 0.1907 | -7.18 | 0.000 |

$s = 3.753$     R-sq = 88.6%     R-sq(adj) = 88.3%

Analysis of Variance

| SOURCE | DF | SS | MS | F | p |
|---|---|---|---|---|---|
| Regression | 3 | 11414.6 | 3804.9 | 270.14 | 0.000 |
| Error | 104 | 1464.8 | 14.1 | | |
| Total | 107 | 12879.4 | | | |

| SOURCE | DF | SEQ SS | |
|---|---|---|---|
| SN70 | 1 | 10591.3 | age standardised LTI 18-64 |
| SN61 | 1 | 97.5 | % of those pension age in rent |
| SN50 | 1 | 725.8 | % econ active, unemployed |

When SN70 is removed from the analysis

The regression equation is
$SN63 = 85.0 + 0.0336\ SN61 + 1.52\ SN50$

| Predictor | Coef | Stdev | t-ratio | p |
|---|---|---|---|---|
| Constant | 85.015 | 2.697 | 31.52 | 0.000 |
| SN61 | 0.03363 | 0.09301 | 0.36 | 0.718 |
| SN50 | 1.5179 | 0.3373 | 4.50 | 0.000 |

$s = 9.010$     R-sq = 33.8%     R-sq(adj) = 32.6%

**Table 7.4    Regression analysis. PSS SSA per capita, 1994-1995, by social needs indicators, SSD areas, England**

The regression equation is
PSSSSA94 = 43.1 + 1.28 SN61 + 4.44 SN52 + 1.88 SN50 + 23.4 SN51 - 0.820 SN60

107 cases used 1 cases contain missing values

| Predictor | Coef | Stdev | t-ratio | p |
|---|---|---|---|---|
| Constant | 43.06 | 17.61 | 2.45 | 0.016 |
| SN61 | 1.2787 | 0.1840 | 6.95 | 0.000 |
| SN52 | 4.4375 | 0.5041 | 8.80 | 0.000 |
| SN50 | 1.8847 | 0.5486 | 3.44 | 0.001 |
| SN51 | 23.415 | 1.768 | 13.24 | 0.000 |
| SN60 | -0.8204 | 0.6279 | -1.31 | 0.194 |

s = 12.73          R-sq = 94.4%          R-sq(adj) = 94.1%

Analysis of Variance

| SOURCE | DF | SS | MS | F | p |
|---|---|---|---|---|---|
| Regression | 5 | 273564 | 54713 | 337.78 | 0.000 |
| Error | 101 | 6360 | 162 | | |
| Total | 106 | 289924 | | | |

| SOURCE | DF | SEQ SS | |
|---|---|---|---|
| SN61 | 1 | 192561 | % pensionable age in rent |
| SN52 | 1 | 43911 | % in households living in over-crow'd acc |
| SN50 | 1 | 378 | % of econactive residents, unemployed |
| SN51 | 1 | 36437 | % in households - not self contained |
| SN60 | 1 | 277 | % pensionable age living alone |

Before regression was computed, variable SN54 was removed from the list of explanatory variables because of its high correlation with two other explanatory variables SN52 and SN51. The remaining social needs indicators were regressed to explain the PSS SSA for 1994-1995 and some 94% of the variance was accounted for (Table 7.4). The largest residuals were London boroughs. These are areas apparently over funded even in proportion to their high needs score. The reality is that unit costs in London are higher due to economic cost factors not modelled in this regression, but allowed for in the PSS SSA calculations (Society of County Treasurers, 1994; Bebbington and Darton, 1996a).

Unemployment 1991 (SN50) and the percentage of those of pensionable age and over living alone, (SN60, 1991 Census) contribute little to the success of the model and the later variable (SN 60) is not statistically significant at $p<0.05$ criteria. When these variables are omitted the analysis still explains 93.4% of the variance.

It is useful to summarise the developing argument. The Government PSS SSA measure is related strongly to a range of geographical social needs variables. However these social needs variables are not strongly associated with the geographical variation in expected rates of long term illness (Table 7.2). Given that approximately 80% of local authority expenditure on social services is known to be directed at adults suffering from a long term illness (Department of Health,1998a), it is a concern to find that government SSA grant calculations for the PSS do not appear to be explicitly related to SSD areas that have a higher than expected prevalence of long term illness.

When examining scatterplots (Figures 7.5 and 7.6) it is possible to identify how the problem might be explained by different types of social service area. Figure 7.5 shows the good linear fit of the combined social needs indicators when explaining the calculation of PSS SSA per capita. London boroughs with their high scores and higher PSS SSA calculations are seen clustered around the top half of the regression line.

When this is compared with the association of PSS SSA with age standardised long term illness (65+) a different pattern emerges (Figure 7.6). It is important to chart the four different types of authority. Inner London boroughs (shown by the letter D) exhibit a near linear pattern at the top of the graph, they receive large PSS SSA assessments when compared to the lower linear patterns of shire counties and metropolitan boroughs, both with similar levels of PSS SSA. Somewhere between these lines is a weak linear relationship for outer London boroughs, suggesting that for some individual outer London boroughs PSS SSA per capita increases quite rapidly with higher than expected rates of long term illness, while for other boroughs it does not.

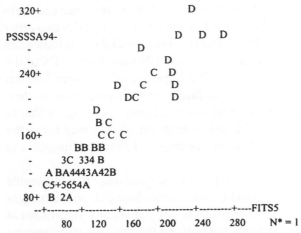

```
320+                    D
  -
PSSSSA94-            D   D   D
  -               D
  -                 D
240+             C  D
  -         D   C    D
  -           DC     D
  -      D
  -        B C
160+        C C C
  -      BB BB
  -    3C  334 B
  -  A BA4443A42B
  -  C5+5654A
80+  B 2A
  --+---------+---------+---------+---------+---------+----FITS5
       80   120   160   200   240   280    N* = 1
```

A=Shire County  B=Metropolitan Borough  C=Outer London Borough  D=Inner London Borough

**Figure 7.5   Regression analysis. PSS SSA per capita, 1994 by social needs indicator fits, SSD areas, England**

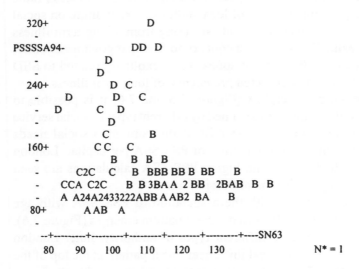

```
320+              D
  -
PSSSSA94-        DD D
  -       D
  -       D
240+        D C
  -   D     D  C
  - D     C  D
  -         D
  -       C    B
160+      C C   C
  -       B  B B B
  -    C2C  C   B BBB BB B BB   B
  -  CCA C2C  B B 3BA A 2 BB  2BAB B B
  -  A A24A2433222ABB A AB2 BA    B
80+    A AB  A
  -
  --+---------+---------+---------+---------+---------+----SN63
     80   90   100   110   120   130         N* = 1
```

**Figure 7.6   Scatterplot. PSS SSA per capita, 1994 by LTI (65+) age standardised (SN63), SSD areas, England**

*Source*: Department of Health (1997) Key Indicators Graphical System (KIGS), Government Statistical Service. Crown copyright.

It is concluded that while in general the PSS SSA rewards London areas with general high social needs, it fails to redistribute adequately to all London areas with higher than expected rates of long term illness. In addition there are question marks over the extent to which the PSS SSA assessment compensates northern SSD areas (symbol Bs in Figure 7.6) that experience higher than expected levels of long term illness, although this second question is beyond the scope of this book which will continue by focusing on outer London boroughs.

The PSS SSA is found to correlate quite well to a range of social needs variables, but it does not reflect adequately the real social needs of the nation's individual long term ill. The danger is that in including current costs and expenditures alongside social needs, the PSS SSA model is capturing actual demand rather than theoretical need. Costs and actual expenditures can become spuriously associated with need. It is known that the majority of PSS output expenditure is spent on adults and by implication on the long term ill, but is not clear to what extent expenditure helps the poorer long term ill access services. This issue is summarised in the charts shown in Figure 7.7 and 7.8. The PSS SSA per capita is associated quite well with the expenditure per person with a long term illness in the area (Figure 7.7), but it does not achieve a strong relationship that can predict those areas with high expenditure related to larger numbers of the long term ill with high social needs (Figure 7.8). In Figure 7.8 the frequency of long term ill with high social needs is calculated from data indicating the numbers in the area of long term ill over 65 who live in rented accommodation (calculated from the 1991 census, SARs). The logic here is that personal social services are at present a selective, often means tested, welfare service where those who are less wealthy should expect to require more expenditure from the local authority. Conversely those who own their own home can expect to make a high contribution towards the cost of their services (Figure 7.11). The PSS SSA does not always reflect these funding realities for individual authorities.

*Are resource allocations to some outer London boroughs unjust?*

To examine this inability of the PSS SSA to focus resource allocation adequately at areas with a high ratio of long term ill over 65 with high social needs it is useful to focus on a small number of local authorities, so that one can see how the calculations affect individual authorities.

In Figure 7.9 it is possible to see how the London Borough of Barking receives a low PSS SSA ranking in comparison with other outer London

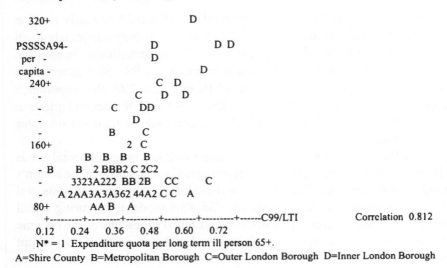

```
   320+                    D
    -
PSSSSA94-              D        D D
  per -                D
capita -                     D
   240+           C  D
    -            C  D  D
    -          C   DD
    -             D
    -         B     C
   160+          2  C
    -       B  B  B   B
    - B     B   2 BBB2 C 2C2
    -       3323A222 BB 2B  CC       C
    -  A 2AA3A3A362 44A2 C C   A
   80+        AA B   A
    +---------+---------+---------+---------+---------+------C99/LTI        Correlation 0.812
   0.12    0.24    0.36    0.48    0.60    0.72
   N* = 1  Expenditure quota per long term ill person 65+.
A=Shire County  B=Metropolitan Borough  C=Outer London Borough  D=Inner London Borough
```

**Figure 7.7   Scatterplot. PSS SSA per capita, 1994-1995 by expenditure per person with long term illness in area (1991)(C99/LTI), SSD areas, England**

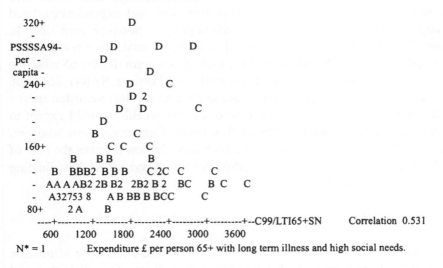

```
   320+              D
    -
PSSSSA94-          D      D     D
  per -          D
capita -              D
   240+          D     C
    -           D 2
    -          D   D         C
    -        D
    -      B       C
   160+       C C   C
    -     B    BB      B
    - B   BBB2 B B B    C 2C  C        C
    - AA A AB2 2B B2  2B2 B 2  BC    B C    C
    - A32753 8   A B BB B BCC      C
   80+    2 A    B
   ----+---------+---------+---------+---------+---------+--C99/LTI65+SN      Correlation 0.531
      600    1200    1800    2400    3000    3600
   N* = 1           Expenditure £ per person 65+ with long term illness and high social needs.
```

**Figure 7.8   Scatterplot. PSS SSA per capita, 1994-1995 by expenditure per person with long term illness and high social needs (1991) (C99/LTI65+), SSD areas, England**

*Source*: Department of Health (1997) Key Indicators Graphical Systems (KIGS), Government Statistical Service. Crown copyright.

boroughs when consideration is given to the numbers of long term ill over 65 with high social needs living there.

The situation for Barking does not improve when the PSS SSA is calculated some five years later (Figure 7.10). The long term ill with high social and economic needs are those who are most likely to require expenditure from local authority social services, but the PSS SSA mechanism does not effectively identify the proportions of long term ill with high social and economic needs from those with long term illness and significant social and economic capital (see chapter 2, Figure 2.3).

## Conclusions

*Is the PSS SSA a useful need based measurement tool?*

The combined two key contributions to local financing, that is local tax and central grant, are now so inter-linked by the SSA that local authorities have minimal flexibility to adjust autonomously local vertical equity by imposing highly levels of local taxation. Local authorities can move money between services, for example increasing PSS at the expense of education, but this is only a limited method of adjustment.

The strength of the PSS SSA is that it represents a balance between an aggregate measure of actual demands and theoretical needs that bears some relationship to previous expenditure and grant received. It is operationalised in a context that still gives some minimal flexibilities for LAs to act independently. As a statistical model the SSA is in danger of falling into disrepute. Whilst it is complex and seeks to include data that allows for efficiency and equity, there are question marks over its appropriateness and ability to achieve these goals. In the numerous SSA calculations, attempts are made to produce a top down aggregation of local needs that reflect the sum of individual needs and its spatial component, but part of the problem is that the overall method is not explicit in its underpinning social theory and value goals and the standard spending amounts that result can seem intricate statistical artifacts rather than truly reflecting spatial needs. Because of this the SSAs has been referred to as the most sophisticated rationing device in the world (Broom, 1993) and they show considerable mathematical complexity in their ability to allocate a fixed sum of money rather than as indicators of real need.

One of the weaknesses of the SSAs is that some individual authorities might suffer unfairly from statistical artifacts that result from the amalgamation

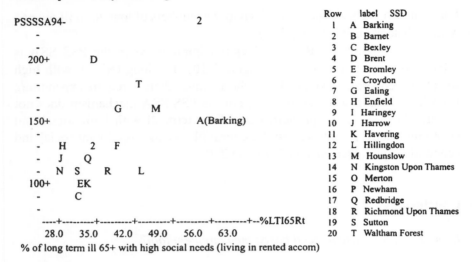

```
PSSSSA94-                              2            Row    label  SSD
   -                                                 1     A  Barking
   -                                                 2     B  Barnet
   -                                                 3     C  Bexley
200+          D                                      4     D  Brent
   -                                                 5     E  Bromley
   -                         T                       6     F  Croydon
   -                                                 7     G  Ealing
   -              G     M                            8     H  Enfield
150+                              A(Barking)         9     I  Haringey
   -                                                10     J  Harrow
   -      H    2    F                               11     K  Havering
   -      J    Q                                    12     L  Hillingdon
   -    N  S     R    L                             13     M  Hounslow
100+        EK                                      14     N  Kingston Upon Thames
   -        C                                       15     O  Merton
   -                                                16     P  Newham
   -                                                17     Q  Redbridge
   ----+---------+---------+---------+---------+---------+--%LTI65Rt   18  R  Richmond Upon Thames
      28.0     35.0     42.0     49.0     56.0     63.0        19     S  Sutton
                                                              20     T  Waltham Forest
```

% of long term ill 65+ with high social needs (living in rented accom)

**Figure 7.9  PSS SSA per capita, 1994-1995, by % of long term ill 65+ with high social and economic needs, outer London boroughs**

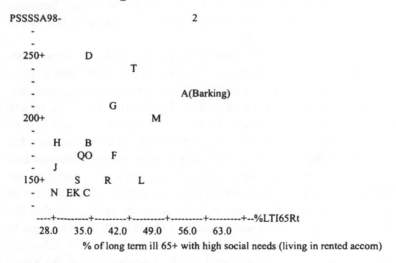

```
PSSSSA98-                              2
   -
   -
250+          D
   -                      T
   -
   -                             A(Barking)
   -                G
200+                        M
   -
   -      H    B
   -        QO    F
   -      J
150+      S    R    L
   -    N  EK C
   -
   ----+---------+---------+---------+---------+---------+--%LTI65Rt
      28.0     35.0     42.0     49.0     56.0     63.0
```

% of long term ill 65+ with high social needs (living in rented accom)

**Figure 7.10  PSS SSA per capita, 1998-1999, by % of long term ill 65+ with high social and economic needs, outer London boroughs**

*Source*: Department of Health (1997) Key Indicators Graphical System (KIGS), Government Statistical Service. Crown copyright.

of measurements. Complexity theory argues that quantitative models can only provide approximation of social reality (Byrne, 1997a; Elliot and Kiel, 1997a; Kiel, 1994) and the problem with the SSA is that that it makes too many assumptions about complexity in its amalgamation of detail. The separate issues of social need and financial cost factors need a better understanding before an adequate synthesis can be constructed. Similarly the interaction of spatial and individual effects is not adequately hypothesised or understood. The calculations do not attempt to explicitly understand difference influences on local need that result from individual compositional, group collective and spatial contextual effects (Macintyre, 1997). The PSS SSAs fail to construct an adequate synthesis of the relationship between theoretical demand and actual expressed demand.

Nevertheless, research in this chapter suggests it would be erroneous to conclude that the PSS SSAs do not reflect social needs at all. The argument is more about the extent to which they achieve this and how appropriately this is applied to resource planning. The danger is that while most authorities benefit as they should, a few suffer inequity from the measurement invalidity. In any event, the horizontal and spatial focus of the SSAs leaves individual service users reliant on a variety of other policy mechanisms like local politics, professional assessment and means testing if they are to negotiate access to money and services.

*Specific grant controls*

One alternative to the SSA methodology of allocation is to move local expenditure towards an even tighter controlled specific grant allocation. At present, for example, there remains a Special Transitional Grant (STG) for subsidising the social care market that was established after the implementation of the 1990 NHS and Community Care Act. This money represents approximately 10% of expenditure on social services in most areas and it is allocated by reference to the adult PSS SSAs. But local authorities have little discretion over the management of this money and must use it to develop specific community care services, as directed by central government (Department of Health, 1998b, p. 7). Griffiths (1988) proposed that this type of fixed grant allocation should be increased in the social care area, so that local authorities could not avoid the care of those with little political voice, choosing instead to make education and other services their priority. In reality since his recommendation local authority social care has taken a higher profile and most authorities now over-spend on their PSS SSA rather than choosing to under-spend.

Given the difficulties with developing a perfect rational method of grant allocation a less flexible grant management system makes the mathematical calculation of grant distribution even more critical than at present and it is difficult to feel confident that a new system could work in a more spatially and vertically equitable manner. A change in methodology from measuring aggregate area need to measuring the sum of individual need, alongside a smaller area weighting, might help. The 1991 census SAR allows the sum of individual need for the long term ill to be sub-divided on the basis of age and tenure in each local authority area. In this chapter it was suggested that tenure is likely to be a good indicator of social need, particularly amongst people over 65 who are long term ill.

*Local discretion over budget management*

An alternative solution to the concern about the measurement validity of the SSAs is to allow local authorities to raise local taxes on individuals and business with much more flexibility. Carter and John (1992) comment that it is misplaced to expect the SSA to be statistically reliable given the huge range of social circumstances and divergent costing criteria that it tries to reflect. They diagnose the real cause of the problem as that the SSA is used to generate too higher a proportion of local government's revenue. It is argued by some that local government needs to be able to, at least in part, calculate its own independent needs and revenue and ideally this should lead to a higher proportion of local government revenue raised at local source via local taxes. (Local Government Information Unit, 1993, p. 52). But in the current political context where government is committed to strict public expenditure targets, it is difficult to imagine central government removing substantial controls over local government expenditure.

*Changing the resource allocation system*

Another alternative is for government to alter fundamentally the demand side of the social care market by setting up a state insurance based system that guarantees all people the universal cost of their social care (Inquiry of the Joseph Rowntree Foundation, 1996). This would create a pool of 'insurance' based money that is targeted at individuals (not areas), giving them a right to access services, via local assessment. Such an alternative insurance system would be based primarily on allocating resources to individuals rather than spatial area.

There would still have to be some local infrastructure monies, based on a reduced RSG/SSA calculation. This type of demand subsidy of the social care market now offers the best chance for overcoming the under-resourcing of social care. It also offers the chance of reaching a correct understanding of the interaction of individual and social/geographical needs. Such a financing scheme also allows for some predictions of demand in future time - rather than reactive funding, based on a year to year incrementalism. Such a method involves, long term compulsory saving via a state/private partnership, thus allowing adequate funding to be targeted at a key policy area over the longer term (Joseph Rowntree Foundation, 1996). Considerable thought will need to be given to the assessment of illness in relation to insurance payouts and service eligibilities. This is likely to require some further professional developments in social work, care management and liaison with General Practitioners. In this respect community care will continue to be: 'more than a funding problem' (Baldock, 1997).

# 8 Conclusion: A Complex Method for Planning

Chaos challenges the practice of social planning because it describes a reality of near continuous disruption to planning activity. Complexity theory takes social planning beyond this and suggests that chaos is time limited and usually related only to specific social and economic systems at any one point in time. Nevertheless chaos is a chain of events that is largely unpredictable, and places considerable restrictions on the ability of social planning to achieve with confidence a single linear vision of the future. The occasional appearance of chaos means that social planning must be speculative, cautious, adaptive and regularly revised. Social planning must comprehend and explore a number of scenarios and future possibilities rather than focusing on one vision of the future. Healey (1993) has referred to this as planning through debate, and Fisher (1998, p. 263) says that strategic thinking must expand 'the options open to the future policy makers.' Social plans must be subject to regular re-analysis and review.

The theory of complexity argues that out of periods of chaos the social world evolves to become ever more complex, spontaneous and capable of adapting and evolving to optimum solutions. There is a paradox within complexity. It is possible both to say that the future looks better, and to observe simultaneously that there is pain in getting there. The concept of 'bifurcation at the point of chaos', warns planners that over simplified, rigid structures and uncompromising ideologies can prevent actors co-evolving to optimal solutions. Planning processes that hope to define themselves through rigid organisational structures are liable to become sub-optimal.

Two key theoretical metaphors were used in this book: 'landscapes' and 'logics'. These are not original and were developed from previous theorists (Kauffman,1995; Kontopoulos, 1993). In both cases these existing concepts were developed so as to suit the empirical task of this book. Kauffman's notion of a 'landscape' is defined in this book as a partly geographical social system; a type of open social system, composed of actors and logics, that also has some associated relationship with areas of physical space. The inevitability of sub-systems inter-linking was emphasised with the book developing a focus on the places, or 'patches' (Kauffman, 1995), where systems join. This is the place where system boundaries break down and the processes and activities of systems overlap. Complexity theory includes new developments in systems theory where open systems are subject to self-regulation, inter-dependency and permeability (Stacey, 1995; Capra, 1996). The public sector faces a growth in multi-agency activity, partnership and projects. The sector can no longer be defined by its previous organisational and structural focus on internal bureaucracy and rigid hierarchy (Medd, 1997). In the late 1990s there is an attention to organisational permeabilities that is of clear importance to planners.

In the past, organisational systems theory tried to explain organisational activity in terms of a rational deterministic process which led to a determination of process through structure (Sibeon, 1991; Pollit, 1990). There are inherent difficulties if social planning tries to implement a social process by coercing it through a strong and permanent structure. Rider (1983, p. 80) says: 'planning in government is a complex business. It is essential to keep the planning process flexible and prevent it from becoming prematurely locked into a rigid design.'

The process of creating CCPs shows one example of this structural strategic planning approach and the dysfunctions that can result. The focus on delivery of an annual plan as the centre point in planning leads to an over adherence on periodic formal structures and may undermine creative analysis and synthesis. Mintzberg (1994, pp. 351-361) has cautioned on the different outputs that organisations achieve in plans when contrasted with planning, in that plans achieve communication and control for organisations rather than analysis and the production of strategy.

During this book it was shown that community care planning is concerned with activity and behaviour that takes place across a number of systems. The movements of actors and planning processes between these systems was shown to be frequent. Three systems were proposed as critical to CCP: politics, state managerialism and markets.

The idea of influential logics being created within, and permeating across, systems was developed from the seminal writing of Kontopoulos (1993). Actors and their cultures combined to generate logics that underpin the structures and order of society. In essence the real social structures that do emerge are relatively fragile and have the qualities of fields (Bourdieu, 1993), or networks, rather than being strong permanent boundaries or hierarchies. This is not a bottom-up process. A paradox of complexity is that hierarchical top-down forces generate an economy of logic, partly to prevent a permanent and ever changing chaos. Occasionally and unpredictably the dominant social logic shifts, as a movement of new, or lower order, logic distorts and rebuilds the mass of fields and totalities. The boundaries between systems need to be understood as open, allowing different sub-cultures and logics to merge and co-evolve.

The culture and logics of each system can become locked into a sub-optimal 'economy of logic'. Managerialism - in particular the 'new managerialism' associated with the logic of marketisation - was shown to be one example of this. Different systems in community care planning have different cultures and value systems that can lead them both to be separate but also to experience communication tensions and new forms of integration when they do have to communicate and reach compromises. Planning and the production of plans were seen as activities that force actors from different systems to communicate.

The book noted the recent dominance of the 'logic of marketisation' (especially in central government ideology) on activities of social care planning. This logic is perpetuated through local government 'new managerialism'. The production of local CCPs can be thought of as a controlling form of structure. This local structure, partly because of its economy of logic, is argued to be limited and only sub-optimal; at best offering some links between users perceived needs and service provision. It has instituted an explicit consumer focus on choice and quality, but these values are constrained from finding optimal expression by an implicit process of rationing, limited public finance, prioritisation and means-testing.

At worst managerial planning prevents the 'political' feedback that is needed, given the limitations of the current planning process. Fundamental public concerns about the needs of the long term ill population and the inability of families to continue to care for themselves can remain unheard, trapped in the local managerial consultation system. Despite the marketisation of care, the real social value of care has not found adequate consideration or expression in society and the national planning process.

A paradox of complexity is that bottom and top are a juxtaposition, because at certain times and in certain places, powers and influences can be reversed, but not permanently, nor by a pre-determined scheme. Kontopoulos talks of 'heterarchy' rather than hierarchy and in this book emphasis was placed on analysing behind the appearance of strong governmental hierarchical structures. In chapter four, examples of such superficial structures are shown as those imposed by local authorities on their consultative and participative social care planning systems. Heterarchy helps to explain a process where actors - despite an imposed hierarchical structure - weakly, but persistently, demand change and improvement. Mulgan's (1994) suggestion that weak power is ultimately more resilient than strong power finds confirmation here.

It is doubtful whether the currently local government structure of CCPs can survive, unless it finds a better method to link with central government and express the real desires and needs of the long term ill and their carers.

A product of chaos is bifurcation. This is the fragmentation of a system into a complex state that enables it to continue improving. Participative planning structures would do better to fragment more into a creative process. This would allow for a better utilisation of the patches that Kauffman (1995) believes to be so important. In reality this means activities such as workshops, working groups, task forces and project management - these being more informal and spontaneous organisations that have a broad and diverse membership and where the blending of culture and ideas moves them from being committed to one system landscape and one logic only. Stacey (1995) describes this transformation from old formal structures as a move towards informal networks, where networks between sub-systems allow the correct blend of order from apparent chaos. These are the new forms of policy management being observed in organisations in the later twentieth century. CCP structures need to fragment into more informal networks that support the building of a creative participative strategy and are able to digest a range of planning analysis.

There are concerns that such a loosely constructed system will fragment government and state managerialism and be dysfunctional, but it is proposed that as such spontaneous systems emerge they will have a clear and natural sense of order when it comes to generating the planning analysis and synthesis required by government and the democratic process (Kiel, 1994).

A key concept emerging from complexity theory that is relevant to the development of strategies in public sector organisations is the idea that tensions between sub-systems can in themselves be a form of order that allows a coherent strategy to be created (Stacey, 1995). Tensions between systems are said to represent chaos 'within boundaries'. Given some network communication between conflicting systems, the apparent chaos and disorder between the systems can become a form of order. Order results from disorder.

It was proposed in chapter four that this theory appears to describe the tensions in the CCP process. Thus it is proposed that the community care planning system has to acknowledge and accept the fundamental tensions it experiences, rather than trying to find a structure that regulates them and minimises them.

The key system tension in the CCP production process is between the political and managerial systems, with management spending too much time managing the consultation politics of user involvement, apparently feeding it into strategy development. This was seen as distracting managers from their analytical role. It is suggested that there is a need to bring local politicians more into this consultative politics. This should not reinforce a traditional government system where political accountabilities and managerial planning roles are structural divided. In effect both managers and users need more informal opportunities to meet with local councillors.

> 'When citizens actively participate in government organisation decision processes, the stability formerly achieved through the dominance of management expertise is supplanted with the instability brought about by citizen input that alters the nature of decision making and thus of government outputs and program outcomes.' (Kiel, 1994, p. 160)

Social planning becomes, as Walker (1984) envisaged a decade ago, composed of small, democratic local groups of people with a high degree of knowledge and commitment to the task. But the sense of a simple, underpinning democratic structure suggested in Walker's structural planning model is missing. Complexity suggests that this order will come from spontaneity and be self-imposed, and that it is rarely instituted by a simple structure. This is the type of order demonstrated in the chaos mathematics of fractuals and attractors. Fractuals are best demonstrated by weather clouds, their appearance and physical construction can be predicted too a large extent, but they are never totally the same and always each cloud is different from another. In short, extremely small units of similar and orderly material will create something unique together. There will be characteristics of similarity in planning networks that give order and short term predictability, but each will also be unique. Local planning cannot be processed through a simple rational structure, but rather there should be sharing of experiments and mistakes - as groups of actors meet to analyse, synthesis, and as a result take decisions. Fisher (1998, p. 251) says: 'the question confronting people interested in public services is not "what is the best way of allocating and delivering public services?" but what , in any particular time and place, is the most broadly acceptable way of allocating and delivering public services?'

It is with considerable disappointment that Barkdoll and Bostin (1997) describe the recent rebirth of a simplified structural planning system in American Government, despite the complex realities that public policy demands. The desire to find an apparent 'holy grail' of planning structure is likely to continue to frustrate those who seek the perfect organisational structure.

The conclusion has discussed the strategic element of social planning, the component that Mintzberg (1994a) describes as 'synthesis'. In this book a public strategy and synthesis is defined as an essentially political activity. But political strategic planning cannot be divorced from the managerial planning analysis that Mintzberg also describes.

In the second half of the book the research moved to consider the uses of analysis in the current national and local community care planning process. Rather than focusing on the supply side of market planning, where the emphasis is now on the regulation of a diversity of supply, the book choose to focus on the demand side of the social care market.

The reasons for this were argued in chapter five. The chapter argued that the logic of marketisation in social care presents government planners with some particular demand side problems. Essentially it was proposed that social care products do not compete particularly well with other consumer goods in the national 'psyche' and that many people try to 'reject' consumption of social care, especially if they are poor. Also there are concerns that the poor who are more likely to become ill are the least able to enter the demand side of a social care market.

A bifurcation of social care on the basis of wealth was previously questioned by Hamnett and Mullings (1992) who suggested that there was an inherent equity in the market system that developed in the 1980s, because of the scale of public intervention on the demand side. The analysis in this book suggests that bifurcation is more likely to be a problem in a market place which deals with low and medium severity social care transactions, where tight controls on public expenditure and the family/kinship expectations of lower socio-economic groups is preventing all social classes from accessing market type transactions. This is partly confirmed by the work of Baldock and Ungerson (1994).

Bifurcation is less of a current problem in circumstances of high priority, according to Hamnett and Mullings (1992) research. In high priority situations even the poor cannot reject the realities of their need for intensive residential social care. At this point the care product has become 'non-rejectable' and state intervention operates a safety net.

The book proposes an analysis of the demand for social care where demand is defined in 'boundaries of instability', rather than by a single economic rationale of consumerism. This element of instability in individual choices about market entry, is related to family, kinship and cultural expectations of care. Such individual expectations of the social care market are argued to be rather unpredictable and quite diverse within society.

The book proposes that demand could be analysed in a number of ways by planners. Theoretical demand is the total possible demand for services that will occur if everyone with long term illness chooses to express their demand in a market place. Actual demand is the actual requests for help that are currently received by PSS and the market place. A third type of demand is that of demand realism, a definition that planners might use to find a balance between the theoretical and actual approaches. The book argues that a diverse market place presents governments with some serious difficulties in planning demand. Essentially this concerns how to use public expenditure, how to redistribute wealth, and how to change cultural attitudes, so as to create more demand. Much of this involves the strategy of national government, in addition to having a correct analysis of the local situation.

In chapter six the research moved to a local analysis of theoretical demand, trying to build on the limited quantitative models observed in the Surrey and Kingston CCPs in chapter four. A model was developed for the old shire county of East Sussex, combining a number of secondary data sources. This model showed that theoretical demand was far in excess of the actual demand that was supplied by local SSD intervention.

In chapter seven the book reviewed the single most important current national government planning activity for distributing resources to the social care market, the PSS SSA. This was shown to be a complex statistical modelling tool, but doubts were cast over its ability to deal with social complexity and in particular the complexity of the needs of the long term ill. A key failure of the model in PSS (1994-1995) was that the model confused a synthesis of actual demand expressed with theoretical demand. This was partly due to some reliance on regression weights based on previous costs, where there were some assumptions that actual demand expressed could be seen as representative of future theoretical demand. Issues of social need and expenditure efficiency also got confused in the synthesis of the PSS SSA.

The research concluded that it is impossible to recreate social complexity in a large scale statistical model of need. Rather in a complex world statistical models become qualitative arguments of what complexity looks like (Byrne, 1997a) and there is a danger with relying on one model or argument (Healey, 1993). While a strength of the SSA system is that it is subject to an annual review with local authorities representatives, and indicators and their weights do change, the analysis is not always related to a clear qualitative or meta-theoretical synthesis. This inability to state explicitly a meta-theoretical basis to a meta-statistical model is due to the belief that political public expenditure strategy and managerial statistical analysis should be separated, when in reality they cannot be.

The statistical research chapters indicate the difficulties that central and local government face when trying to measure demand; enable it, and prioritise it.

The strategic issue of demand management and planning cannot be solved by a statistical realignment of the PSS SSA and formula for distributing the Community Care Grant (STG). The solution is a political-strategic one, involving the redeployment of resources, the socialisation of attitudes, and a fundamental review of public expenditure over the longer term. The recent establishment of a Royal Commission on Long Term Care provides an opportunity to progress these issues.

The separation of central and local government can be observed in the mechanical structures of government, for example the mechanics of voting, but in the process of planning as synthesis and forward analysis (what Mintzberg, 1994c, calls 'strategic programming'), levels of government activity are linked intrinsically and difficult to separate. A national synthesis such as the Joseph Rowntree Review of Long Term Care (1996) is imperative, but it needs to be operationalised alongside consideration of local difference and divergence.

There are numerous places where planning processes are permeable. The same actors potentially vote at both levels of governments. Managers and politicians from each tier of government have to meet on some occasions (for example at the annual SSA reviews) . Budgets and taxes often defy simple explanations, particularly when one tries to analyse their effect on social outputs and outcomes. Much central and local government activity is entangled and has multiple effects.

Part of the conclusion about the nature of social care planning task is that public sector planning is an exceptionally complex task. Planning includes a variety of forms of activity that cover a number of important dimensions and try to create order from disorder (Table 8.1). These dimensions are entangled, they represent a description of possible planning activities rather than offering a conceptual framework through which planning activity must progress in any one time and place.

Planning and the production of plans are defined partly by the measurement of time. Planning activity has to be aware of the different temporal horizons inherent in the structures offered by local and national political elections (Schneider, 1991). Planning and plans are partly defined by the passage of time and relating the future to the past. Consideration of the future is a formidable scientific task. Chaos maths suggest that it may be possible to say with a high degree of confidence that something will happen at some time in the future, but it is impossible to predict exactly when.

The difference between plans and planning as forms of communication illustrates the tension between written records and actual creative thinking about how positive change might be achieved and defining what that positive change might look like. The written plan cannot be dismissed because it commits a synthesis and analysis at any one point in time to future scrutiny, but there is a danger that it will limit forward thinking.

Public planning includes the contrast between the need for a political strategy and a managerialist range of analysis of underlying problems and possible solutions. But the synthesis and vision of planning cannot be divorced from the process of analysis and the routine collection of information.

In addition there is the relationship between planners and strategists within the market. In a policy environment where the market is seen as providing a choice and diversity of supply, government planning becomes linked to facilitating social needs into economic demands and the regulation of supply.

It is not enough that people are consulted about the future of social care. The diversity of arguments and ideas that the public demonstrates need to find expression in the planning process and its strategic decisions. The resulting ownership and responsibility for the outcomes decided upon needs to be as broad as is possible.

Finally there is the spatial dimension of planning, the relationship between planning and the physical landscape. The physical landscape in society is related to a range of logics that give place its meaning. Both the nation, with its power over tax and public expenditure, and the local system in which SSDs are based, can be observed as geographical spaces. The physical landscape is known to reflect a complex relationship with age standardised rates of long term illness and other socio-economic circumstances. Geography is known to influence the setting-up of social care businesses that supply services. Planning has to included an appreciation of spatial factors, and an analysis that can integrate different spatial levels.

In the modern complex world, social care planning cannot be defined by an single organisational or institutional structure. Rather it is a series of activities that involves many different actors. At any one time and place these activities will be constructed and implemented in many different forms. There is no pre-determined perfect form. A complex range of information is needed and there is no single prescriptive method by which this information can be programmed into a policy strategy. The collection of a wide range of information is legitimate and public policy should encourage attempts to analyse and synthesise information in a variety of models and by a variety of social groups. Future research might look in particular to the behaviour of actors in these activities and the ways in which information analysis is related to the politics of policy creation. Some clearer examples of best practice in specific circumstances might then start to emerge.

**Table 8.1    Dimensions of the social care planning process**

| Process type | Dimensions of Process | | |
|---|---|---|---|
| *Temporal* | Past | Present | Future |
| *Communication* | Documentation | Production of ideas | Creativity and vision |
| *Strategic* | Analysis | Programming | Synthesis |
| *Action* | Governance | Supply side | Demand side |
| *Participation* | Consultation | Representation | Ownership |
| *Spatial* | Local | Regional | National |

# Glossary

*Actors*

Individual people, or groups of individuals, whose action contributes to the definition of social life and its processes and systems.

*Bifurcation*

The point in time and space at which a group of actors, or a sub-system, has to change its logical and behavioural characteristics so as to adjust to outside contingencies. Adjustment is necessary if the actors are to retain their optimal social fitness, otherwise the actors may evolve to a sub-optimal outcome (Kauffman, 1995).

*Boundaries of instability*

This is a term used in complexity theory to describe the characteristics of a system that is evolving to an optimal level of performance (Stacey, 1995). Optimal evolution requires sufficient levels of instability (disorder) at any one point in time, so that it can paradoxically maintain a state of order in the future. Hence, over time, a system exists within 'relative boundaries of instability'. Boundaries of instability can be contrast with historical ideas of balance and system equilibrium (Kiel, 1994; Stacey, 1995).

*Cultural capital*

Bourdieu (1993) put forward the proposition that capital could take a number of different forms, in addition to economic capital. For example, he noted the importance of social, cultural and symbolic capital.

*Economy of logic*

In a highly complex society it is impossible for a group of actors, or a single actor, to find a perfect logical system of values and beliefs that explains the world that they experience. In order to survive in a changing world, actors and actor groups therefore accept 'economies of logic', where simplified ideas and value systems are permitted to dominant explanations of social conditions for limited periods of time (Bourdieu, 1977; Kontopoulos, 1993).

*Fitness peak*

Actors, groups and sub-systems are observed to be evolving to evolutionary fitness peaks, where there are substantial and rapid improvements over time in the conditions of their members. However the stability of fitness peaks is unpredictable and can be ultimately undermined by changes in larger systems, or neighbouring environments (Kauffman, 1995).

*Global peak*

A macro point of optimal fitness for society (Kauffman, 1995). See also, fitness peak (above).

*Heterarchy*

Heterarchy is an alternative concept to hierarchy when understanding social structures. The communication of actors and groups across and between systems and sub-systems becomes as important as hierarchical top-down control and domination (Kontopoulos, 1993). There are some similarities with the matrix approach to organisational structure in business studies.

*Landscape*

A sub-system of actors and actor based activities that displays some geographical characteristics (Kauffman, 1995).

*Logic*

A collection of values and ideas that defines the structure and culture of a social system (Kontopoulos, 1993).

*Open system*

Complexity theory places emphasis on the open nature of policy systems given their high level of dependence on outside systems and environments (Capra, 1996).

*Patch*

A place where actors from different systems interact and engage in activities that are in their mutual interest (Kauffman, 1995).

*Process*

The key feature of a social process is that it takes place over time. A 'process' is the linking of individuals (actors), groups and systems into a time series of on-going activities and decisions. Thus the important features of a 'process' can be understood by examining how activities and decisions become constructed (or deconstructed) over time into some higher order category, where the sum of decisions and activities over time has some qualities and features that are greater than the sum of the component parts.

*Social system*

A group of individuals (actors) who are partial linked by their mutual interest in certain activities, tasks and logics. Capra (1997) cites that social systems should be thought of as relatively open, in that individuals will communicate concurrently with a number of social systems. The key systems of interest in this book are the political system, the state management system, and the market system.

*Totalizing logic*

A logic that is influential at both the macro and micro levels of society. Totalizing logics often have considerable dominance on the behaviour of systems for long periods of time and this logic can be disproportionate to their rational justification (Kontopoulos, 1993) - see also the 'economy of logic'.

# Bibliography

Allen, C. and Beecham, J. (1993) 'Costing Services: Ideals and Reality', in Netten, A. and Beecham, J. (eds) *Costing Community Care*, PSSRU/ Ashgate, Aldershot.

Allen, P., Clark,N. and Perez-Trejo,F. (1992) 'Strategic Planning of Complex Economic Systems', *Review of Political Economy*, vol 4, no 3, pp. 275-90.

Ansoff, H. I. (1965) *Corporate Strategy*, McGraw-Hill, New York.

Ansoff, H. I. (1994) 'Comment on Henry Mintzberg's Rethinking Strategic Planning', *Long Range Planning*, vol 27, no 3, pp. 31-32.

Association of County Councils (1994) *Revenue Support Grant*, 1994-1995, England, Association of County Councils on behalf of the English Local Authority Associations, Kent County Council, Maidstone.

Atkinson, P. and Coffey, A. (1997) 'Analysing Documentary Realities', in Silverman, D. (ed) *Qualitative Research: Theory and Practice*, Sage, London.

Audit Commision (1986) *Making a Reality of Community Care*, HMSO, London.

Audit Commission (1992) *The Community Revolution: Personal Social Services and Community Care*, HMSO, London.

Audit Commission (1993a) *Community Care: Managing the Cascade of Change*, HMSO, London.

Audit Commission (1993b) *Passing the Bucks : the impact of standard spending assessments on economy,efficency and effectiveness - vol.1*, HMSO, London.

Audit Commission (1997) *Representing the People: The Role of Councillor,* TSO, London.

Baldock, J. (1997) 'Social care in old age: more than a funding problem', *Social Policy and Administration*, vol 31, no 1, pp. 73-89.

Baldcock, J. and Ungerson, C. (1994) *Becoming Consumers of Community Care: Households within the Mixed Economy of Welfare*, Joseph Rowntree Foundation, York.

233

Baldwin, S. and Lunt, N. (1996) *Charging Ahead: Local Authority Charging Policy for Community Care*, Policy Press/Joseph Rowntree Foundation, York.

Balloch, S. (1994) *Survey of Social Services Charging Policy 1992-1994*, National Institute for Social Work, London.

Barkdoll, G. and Bostin, M.R. (1997) 'Targeted Planning: a Paradigm for the Public Service', *Long Range Planning*, vol 30, no 4, pp. 529-539.

Bebbington, A. (1996) 'Health Expectancy and Long Term Care Costs', *PSSRU Discussion Paper* 1185, University of Kent.

Bebbington, A. and Darton, R. (1996a) *Alternatives to Long-Term Hospital Care for Elderly People in London*, PSSRU Bulletin no 10, University of Kent.

Bebbington, A. and Darton, R. (1996b) 'Healthy Life Expectancy in England and Wales: Recent Evidence', *PSSRU Discussion Paper* 1205, University of Kent.

Bebbington, A. and Davies, D. (1980a) 'Territorial Need Indicators: A New Approach Part I', *Journal of Social Policy*, 9, 2, pp. 145-168.

Bebbington, A. and Davies, D. (1980b) 'Territorial Need Indicators: A New Approach Part II', *Journal of Social Policy*, 9, 4, pp. 433-462.

Bebbington, A., Turvey, K. and Janzon, K. (1996) 'Needs Based Planning for Community Care', *PSSRU Discussion Paper* 1206/2, The University of Canterbury at Kent.

Benwell, M. (1980) 'Public Participation in Planning - A Research Report', *Long Range Planning*, vol 13, pp. 71-77.

Berry, B.J.L. and Kim, H. (1997) 'Long Waves 1790 - 1900: Intermittency, Chaos and Control', in Elliot, E. and Kiel, L.D. (eds) *Chaos Theory in the Social Sciences. Foundations and Applications*, The University of Michigan, Ann Arbor.

Bewley, C. and Glendinning, C. (1994) *Involving Disabled People in Community Care Planning*, Joseph Rowntree Foundation, York.

Bochel, C., Bochel, H. and Page, D. (1995) 'Needs and Numbers in Community Care Planning', *Community Care Management and Planning*, vol 3, issue 2, pp. 39-45.

Bone, M. (1995) *Trends in dependency among older people in England. A Review carried out on behalf of the Department of Health*, OPCS, London.

Bootle, R. (1996) *The Death of Inflation*, Nicolas Brealey Publishing, London.

Bourdieu, P. (1977) *Outline of Theory of Practice*, Cambridge University Press, Cambridge.

Bourdieu, P. (1993) *Sociology in Question*, Sage, London.

Boyarsky, A. and Gora, P. (1996) 'A model of the structure of spacetime', *Chaos, Solitons and Fractals*, vol 7, no 5, pp. 611-630, Pergamon, Oxford.

Boycko, M., Shleifer, A. and Vishny,R.W. (1996) 'A Theory of Privatisation', *The Economic Journal*, March, 106, pp. 309-319.

Boyne, G.A. (1997) 'Comparing the Performance of Local Authorities: An Evaluation of the Audit Commission Indicators', *Local Government Studies*, vol 23, no 4, pp. 17-43.

Boyne, G.A. and Powell, M. (1993) 'Territorial Justice and Thatcherism', *Environment and Planning C: Government and Policy*, vol 11, pp. 35-53.

Bradshaw, J. (1972) 'A taxonomy of social need', in McLachlan, G. (ed) *Problems and Progress in Medical Care*, Oxford University Press, Oxford.

Bradshaw, J. (1994) 'A social policy perspective on need', in Popay, J. and Williams, G. (eds) *Researching the People's Health*, Routledge, London.

Brewer, C. and Lait, J. (1980) *Can Social Work Survive?*, Maurice Temple Smith, London.

Brock, D.M. and Barry, D. (1995) 'What if planning were really strategic? Reframing the strategy-planning relationship', paper submitted to *Department of International Business, Working Paper Series*, November, http://comsp.com.latrobe.edu.au/Paper/brock.html

Brodie, J. (1994) 'The Community Care Plan: A Square Peg in a Round Hole', *Community Care Management and Planning*, vol 2, issue 4, pp. 107-13.

Broom, D. (1993) 'Does the cap fit assessments?', *Search*, 18 pp. 5-7.

Brown, T. A. (1997) 'Measuring Chaos Using the Lyapunov Exponent', in Elliot, E. and Kiel, L. D. (eds) *Chaos Theory in the Social Sciences: Foundations and Applications*, The University of Michigan, Ann Arbor.

Bryson, J.M. and Einsweiler, R.C. (eds) (1988) *Strategic Planning*, Jossey Bass, San Fancisco.

Bryson, J.M. and Roering, W.D. (1988) 'Applying Private Sector Strategic Planning in the Public Sector', in Bryson J.M. and Einsweiler, R.C. (eds) *Strategic Planning*, Jossey Bass, San Fancisco.

Bulmer, M. (1987) *The Social Basis of Community Care*, Macmillan, London.

Byrne, D. (1997a) 'Complexity Theory and Social Research', *Social Research Update 18*, Department of Sociology, University of Surrey, Guildford.

Byrne, D. (1997b) 'Chaotic Places or Complex Places? Cities in a Post-Industrial Era', in Westwood, S. and Williams, J. (eds) *Imagining Cities: scripts, signs, memory*, Routledge, London.

Byrne, D. and Rogers, T. (1996) 'Divided Spaces - Divides School: An Exploration of the Spatial Relations of Social Division', *Sociological Research Online*, vol 1, no 2, <http://www.soresonline.org.uk/soresonline/1/2/3/.htm>

Capra, F. (1996) *The Webb of Life. A New Synthesis of Mind and Matter*, Hutchinson, London.

Carney, T.F. (1973) *Content Analysis*, University of Manitoba Press, Winnipeg.

Carter, C. and John, P. (1992) *A New Accord: Promoting constructive relations between central and local government*, Joesph Rowntree Foundation, York.

Cartwright, T.J. (1991) 'Planning and Chaos Theory', *Journal of the American Planning Association*, vol 57, no 1. pp. 44-56

Caulfield, I. and Schultz, J. (1989) *Planning for Change: Strategic Planning in Local Government*, Longman, London.

Central Statistical Office (1994) *Family Spending, A Report on the 1993 Family Expenditure Survey*, HMSO, London.

Challis, L. (1990) *The Organisation of Social Services*, Longman, London.

Champion, T. (ed) (1993) *Population Matters: The Local Dimension*, Paul Chapman Publishing, London.

Chartered Institute of Public and Financial Accountants (CIPFA) (1994) *Personal Social Service Statistics 1994-1995, Estimates*, CIPFA, London.

Chartered Institute of Public and Financial Accountants (CIPFA) (1996) *Personal Social Service Statistics 1994-1995, Actuals*, CIPFA, London.

Clapham, D. (1984) 'Rational Planning and Politics: the example of local authority corporate planning', *Policy and Politics*, vol 12, no 1, pp. 31-52.

Clark, C. (1996) 'Caring, Costs and Values: A Concluding Comment', in Clark, C. and Lapsley, I. (eds) *Planning and Costing Community Care*, Research Highlights in Social Work 27, Jessica Kingsley, London.

Clarke, J., Cochrane, A. and McLaughlin, E. (eds) (1994) *Managing Social Policy*, Sage, London.

Clarke, J. and Newman, J. (1997) *The Managerial State*, Sage, London.

Clarke, M. and Stewart, J. (1990) *General Management in Local Government: Getting the Balance Right*, Longman, Harlow.

Clarke, R. and McGuinness, T. (eds) (1990) *The Economics of the Firm*, Basil Blackwell, Oxford.

Cohen, J. and Stewart, I. (1994) *The Collapse of Chaos: Discovering Simplicity in a Complex World*, Viking, London.

Common, R. and Flynn, N. (1992) *Contracting for Care*, Joseph Rowntree Foundation, York.

Community Care Support Force (1993) *User Participation in Community Care Services*, NHS Management Executive, Leeds.

Corden, A. and Wright, K. (1993) 'Going into a home: where can an elderly person choose?', in Champion, T. (ed) (1993) *Population Matters: The Local Dimension*, Paul Chapman Publishing, London.

Coulshed, V. (1990) *Management in Social Work*, BASW/Macmillan, London.

Dale, A. and Davies, R.B. (1994) *Analysing Social and Political Change: A Casebook of Methods*, Sage, London.

Dale, A. and Marsh, C. (eds) (1993) *The 1991 Census User's Guide*, HMSO, London.

Davies, B. (1968) *Social Needs and Resources in Local Government*, Michael Joseph, London.

Davies, B. (1993a) *Thinking Long in Community Care*, PSSRU, University of Kent.

Davies, B. (1993b) *British Community Care Reform, Policy Formation and Implementational Level: From Muddle to Model, and Model to?*, PSSRU, University of Kent.

Davies, B. (1994) 'Maintaining the Pressure in Community Care Reform', *Social Policy and Administration*, vol 28, no 3, pp. 197-205.

Davies, B., Bebbington, A., Charnely, H. in collaboration with Baines, B., Ferlie, E., Hughes, M. and Twigg, J. (1990) *Resources, Needs and Outcomes in Community Based Care*, PSSRU, University of Kent/ Avebury, Aldershot.

Davies, B. and Challis, D. (1986) *Matching Resources to Needs in Community Care*, PSSRU/Gower, Aldershot.

Davies, B and Wittenberg, R. (1996) 'Demand, Supply and Finance. Long Term Care Demand, Supply and Finance', *PSSRU Bullentin 10*, pp. 33-36, University of Kent, http://snipe.ukc.ac.uk/PSSRU/bulletin.html.

Department of the Environment, Transport and Regions (1998a) *Modernising Local Government. Improving Local Services through Best Value*, Consultation Paper, http://www.local.doe.gov.uk/cct/improvbv.htm.

Department of the Environment, Transport and Regions (1998b) *Modernising Local Government. Local Democracy and Community Leadership*, Consultation Paper, http://www.local.doe.gov.uk/sponsor/democrac.htm.

Department of the Environment, Transport and Regions (1998c) *Local Government Finance (England) 1998/99*, TSO, London.

Department of the Environment, Transport and Regions (1998d) *Local Government Finance (England) Special Grant Report (No.31)*, TSO, London.

Department of Health and Social Security (1972) *Local Authority Social Services Ten Year Plans 1973-1983*, Circular35/72, Department of Health and Social Security, London.

Department of Health and Social Security (1983) *Care in the Community : A consultative document on moving resources for care in England*, DHSS, London.

Department of Health (1989) *Caring for People. Community Care in the Next Decade and Beyond, Cm 849*, HMSO, London.

Department of Health (1990) *Community Care in the Next Decade and Beyond: Policy Guidance*, HMSO, London.

Department of Health (1992a) *Implementing Caring for People. EL(92) 65/ C1(92) 30*, 25th September, Department of Health, London.

Department of Health (1992b) *Implementing Community Care. Improving Independent Sector Involvement in Community Care Planning*, Department of Health, London.

Department of Health (1993a) *Implementing Community Care: Population Needs Assessment Good Practice Guide*, Department of Health, London.

Department of Health (1993b) *Community Care Plans (Consultation Direction) 1993 LAC(93)4*, Department of Health, London.

Department of Health (1994a) *Community Care Plans (Independent Sector Non Residential Care) Direction 1994. LAC(94)12*, Department of Health, London.

Department of Health (1994b) *Review of Key Indicators for Local Authority Social Services*, Department of Health Statistics Division 3, London.

Department of Health (1994c) *Key Indicators of local authority social services 1991-1991*, Government Statistical Service, London.

Department of Health (1994d) *Residential Accommodation for Elderly and for Younger Disabled People: All Residents in Local Authority, Voluntary and Private Homes Year, ending 31 March 1993. England*, Government Statistical Service.

Department of Health (1995a) *Community Care Plans From 1996/97, LAC(95)19*, Department of Health, London.

Department of Health (1995b) *An Introduction to Joint Commissioning*, Department of Health, London.

Department of Health (1995c) *Key Indicators of local Authority Social Services 1995*, Government Statistical Service, London.

Department of Health (1996) *Key Indicators of Local Authority Social Services 1996*, Government Statistical Service, London.

Department of Health (1997a) *Better Value for Money in Social Services: A Review of Performance Trends in Social Services in England*, Department of Health, London.

Department of Health (1997b) *A Review of Personal Social Services Statistics, July 1997*, Department of Health, London.

Department of Health (1998a) *Personal Social Services current and capital expenditure in England: 1996-1997*, Government Statistical Service, London.

Department of Health (1998b) *Special Grant Report (No.33) Local Government Finance (England)*, TSO, London.

Derricot, N.J. (1983) 'Strategies for Community Care', in Loney, M., Boswell, D. and Clarke, J. (eds) *Social Policy and Welfare*, Open University Press, Buckingham.

Dooley, K., Hamilton, P., Cherri, M., West, B. and Fisher, P. (1997) 'Chaotic Behaviour in Society. Adolescent Childbearing in Texas 1964 - 1990', in Eve, R.A., Horsfall, S. and Lee, M.E. (eds) *Chaos, Complexity, and Sociology: Myths, Models and Theories*, Sage, Thousand Oaks, California.

Dorling, D. (1997) *Death in Britain: How local mortality rates have changed*, Joseph Rowntree Foundation, York.

Doyal, L. and Gough, I. (1991) *A Theory of Human Need*, Macmillan, London.

Drever, F. and Whitehead, M. (eds) (1997) *Health Inequalities*, The Government Statistical Service/The Stationary Office, London.

Dunleavy, P. (1991) *Democracy, Bureaucracy and Public Choice. Economic Explanations in Political Science*, Harvester Wheatsheaf, Hemel Hempstead.

East Sussex County Council (1994) *Community Care Plan. The Population of East Sussex*, East Sussex County Council, County Hall, Lewes.

East Sussex County Council Social Services Department (1994) *Revenue Budget 1995-1996*, Agenda Item 13.2, East Sussex County Council.

Edwards, H. (1978) *Joint Financing between the Health and Social Services - A Study of an Initiation in Social Policy*, M.A. Dissertation, University of York.

Elliot, E. and Kiel, L.D. (1997a) *Chaos Theory in the Social Sciences. Foundations and Applications*, The University of Michigan, Ann Arbor.

Elliot, E. and Kiel, L.D. (1997b) 'Non Linear Dynamics, Complexity and Public Policy. Use, Misuse and Applicability', in Eve, R.A. Horsfall, S. and Lee, M.E. (eds) *Chaos, Complexity, and Sociology. Myths, Models and Theories*, Sage, Thousand Oaks, California.

Ellis, K. (1993) *Squaring the Circle. User and Carer Participation in Needs Asessment*, Joseph Rowntree Foundation, York.

Essex, S. (1996) 'Members and officers in the planning policy process', in Tewdwr-Jones, M. (ed) *British Planning Policy in Transition. Planning in the 1990s*, University College London Press, London.

Etzioni, A. (1967) 'Mixed Scanning: A Third Approach to Decision Making', *Public Administration Review*, vol 27, p.385.

Eve, R.A., Horsfall, S. and Lee, M.E. (eds) *Chaos, Complexity, and Sociology. Myths, Models and Theories*, Sage, Thousand Oaks, California.

Ferlie, E. and Judge, K. (1981) 'Retrenchment and Rationality in the Personal Social Services', *Policy and Politics*, vol 9, no 3, pp. 311-30.

Fimister, G. and Hill, M. (1993) 'Delegating implementation problems: social security, housing and community care in Britain', in Hill, M. (ed) *New Agendas in the Study of the Policy Process*, Harvester Wheatsheaf, Hemel Hempstead.

Fisher, C.M. (1998) *Resource Allocation in the Public Sector. Values, priorities and markets in the management of the public services*, Routledge, London.

Flynn, R., Williams, G. and Pickard, S. (1996) *Markets and Networks: contracting in community health services*, Open University Press, Buckingham.

Ford, R.G. and Smith, G.C. (1995) 'Spatial and structural change in institutional care for the elderly in South East England, 1987-1990', *Environment and Planning A*, vol 27, pp. 225-48.

Forder, A. (1974) *Concepts in Social Administration: A Framework for Analysis*, Routledge and Kegan Paul, London.

Forder, J., Kendall, J. and Knapp, M. (1996) 'Purchasing Domiciliary Care: Provider Characteristics and Competition', *Mixed Economy of Care Bullentin*, no 5, pp. 10-14, London School of Economics.

Forder, J., Knapp, M. and Wistow, G. (1996) 'Competition in the Mixed Economy of Care', *Journal of Social Policy*, vol 25, no 2, pp. 201-21.

George, M. (1995) 'Charged to Survive', *Community Care*, 6th January.

Giddens, A. (1990) *The Consequence of Modernity*, Policy Press, Cambridge.

Gilbert, G. and May, D. (1980) 'The artificial debate between rationalist and incrementalist models of decision making', *Policy and Politics*, vol 8, pp. 147-61.

Glendinning, C. and Bewley, C. (1992) *Involving Disabled People in Community Care Planning - The First Steps*, The Department of Social Policy and Social Work, Manchester University.

Glennerster, H. (1980) 'Prime Cuts: public expenditure and social services planning in a hostile environment', *Policy and Politics*, vol 8, no 4, pp. 367-382.

Glennerster, H. (1981) 'From Containment to Conflict? Social Planning in the Seventies', *Journal of Social Policy*, vol 10, no 1, pp. 31-51

Goldstein, H. (1994) 'The Use of Regression Analysis for Resource Allocation by Central Government', *Environment and Planning C*, Feb, vol 12, no 1, pp. 15-22.

Goss, S. and Miller, C. (1995) *From Margin to Mainstream: Developing user and carer-centred community care*, Joesph Rowntree Foundation, York.

Gould, M. and Jones, K. (1995) 'Analysing Perceived Limiting Long Term Illness using UK Census Microdata', paper presented to *The Insititute of British Geographers, Long Term Limiting Illness Conference, Medical and Population Study Group*, Liverpool University, 17th May.

Greenwood, R. (1979) 'Local Authority Budgetary Process', in Booth, A. (ed) *Planning for Welfare, Social Policy and the Expenditure Process*, Blackwell and Robertson, Oxford.

Gregory, R. (1989) 'Political Rationality or Incrementalism? Charles E Lindblom's enduring contribution to public policy making theory', *Policy and Politics*, vol 17, pp.139-53.

Griffiths, R. (1988) *Community Care: Agenda for Action. A Report to the Secretary of State for Social Servcies*, HMSO, London.

HM Treasury (1991) *Competing for Quality, CM 1730*, HMSO, London.

Hale, R. and Travers, T. (1993) *Standard Spending Assessments*, CIPFA, London.

Hallet, C. (1982) *The Personal Social Services in Local Government*, George Allen and Unwin, London.

Hambleton, R. (1986) *Rethinking Policy Planning. School for Advanced Urban Studies*, University of Bristol.

Hamnett, C. and Mullings, B. (1992) 'A new consumption cleavage? The case of residential care for the elderly', *Enviroment and Planning A*, vol 24, pp. 807-20.

Handy, C. (1991) *Understanding Organisations*, 5th Edition, Penguin, London.

Hardy, B. Wistow, G and Leedham, I. (1993) *Analysis of a sample of English Community Care Plans, 1993/1994*, Department of Health.

Hardy, B., Young, R. and Wistow, G. (1996) 'Purchasing Domiciliary Care: The Provider Perspective', *Mixed Economy of Care Bulletin*, no 5, pp. 5-9, London School of Economics.

Harvey, A. (1995) *Charges for Social Care: Local Government Management Board*, 1993-1995, London.

Hastings, A. (1998) 'Connecting Linguistic Structures and Social Practices: a Discursive Approach to Social Policy Analysis', *Journal of Social Policy*, vol 27, no 2, pp. 191-211.

Haynes, P. (1996) *Community Care Plans: Processes and Logics*, The Health and Social Policy Research Centre, University of Brighton.

Healey, P. (1990) 'Places, People and Policies: Plan Making in the 1990s', *Local Government Policy Making*, vol 17, no 2 pp. 29-39.

Healey, P. (1993) 'Planning Through Debate: The Communicative Turn in Planning Theory', in Fisher, F. and Forester, J. (eds) *The Argumentative Turn in Policy Analysis and Planning*, University College, London.

Henwood, M., Jowell, J. and Wistow, G. (1991) *All things come (to those who wait?) Causes and consequences of the community care delays*, King's Fund Institute, Joseph Rowntree Foundation and The Nuffield Institute.

Hirschman, A.O. (1970) *Exit, Voice and Loyalty: Responses to Decline in Firms, Organisations, and States*, Harvard University Press, London.

Hogwood, B.W. (1992) *Trends in British Public Policy*, Open University Press, Buckingham.

Hogwood, B.W. and Gunn, L.A. (1984) *Policy Analysis for the Real World*, Oxford University Press, Oxford.

Hood, C.C. (1991) 'A public management for all seasons', *Public Management*, vol 69, no 1, pp. 3-19.

House of Commons (1990) *National Health Service and Community Care Act 1990*, HMSO , London.

House of Commons Health Committee(1993a) *Community Care: The Way Forward, vol. 1*, HMSO, London.

House of Commons Health Committee (1993b) *Commuity Care: The Way Forward, vol. 2*, Minutes of Evidence and Appendices. HMSO, London.

House of Commons Health Committee (1995) *Long Term Care: NHS Responsibilities for Meeting Continuing Health Care Needs, volume 2*, Minutes of Evidence, HMSO, London.

House of Commons Health Committee (1996) *Long Term Care: Future Provision and Funding, vol. 1*, TSO, London.

House of Commons Social Services Committee (1981) *Public Expenditure on Social Services, vol. 1*, HMSO, London.

House of Commons Social Services Committee (1982) *1982 White Paper: Public Expenditure on The Social Servcies, vol. 1*, report, HMSO, London.

House of Commons Social Services Committee (1985) *Public Expenditure on the Social Services*, HMSO, London.

Hoyes, L., Jeffers, S., Lart, R., Means, R. and Taylor, M. (1993) *User Empowerment and the reform of Community Care: Studies in Decentralisation and Quasi Markets no 16*, School for Advanced Urban Studies/Joseph Rowntree Foundation, York.

Hoyes, L., Lart, R., Means, R. and Taylor, M. (1994) *Community Care in Transition*, Joseph Rowntree Foundation, York.

Hoyes, L. and Means, R. (1993) 'Markets, Contracts and Social Care Services: Prospects and Problems', in Bornat, J., Pereira, C., Pilgrim, D. and Williams, F. (eds) *Community Care: A Reader*, Macmillan/Open University Press, Basingstoke.

Hudson, B. (1992) 'Community Care Planning: Incrementalism to Rationalism?' *Social Policy and Administration*, vol 26, no 3 pp. 185-200

Hudson, B. (1997) 'Community Care Plans and Children's Services Plans: The Renaissance of State Planning in Welfare?', *Community Care Management and Planning*, vol 5, issue 3, June.

Hunter, D. J. and Wistow, G. (1987) *Community Care in Britain. Variations on a Theme*, King Edwards Hospital Fund for London, London.

Hutton, W. (1991) 'Great Expectations', *Search* 11, Nov.

Jaditz, T. (1997) 'The Prediction Test for Non Linear Determinism', in Kiel, L.D and Elliot, E. (eds) *Chaos Theory in the Social Sciences. Foundations and Applications*, The University of Michigan, Ann Arbor.

Jeffrey, B. (1997) 'Creating Participatory Structures in Local Government', *Local Government Policy Making*, vol 23, no 4, pp. 25-31

Jones, L. (1997) 'Multilevel Approaches to Modelling Contextuality: from Nuisance to Substance in the Analysis of Voting Behaviour', in Dale, A. (ed) *Exploiting National Survey and Census Data: the role of locality and spatial effects*, The Census and Survey Research Centre (CCSR) Occasional Paper 12. University of Manchester.

Jordan, B. (1990) *Value for Caring. Recognising unpaid carers*, King Edward's Hospital Fund for London, project paper 81, London.

Joseph Rowntree Foundation Inquiry (1996) *Meeting the Costs of Continuing Care: Report and Recommendations*, Joseph Rowntree Foundation, York.

Judge, K. and Matthews, J. (1980a) 'Pricing Personal Social Services', in Judge, K. (ed), *Pricing the Social Services*, Macmillan, London.

Judge, K. and Matthews, J. (1980b) *Charging for Social Care: a study of consumer charges and the personal social services*, NISS Library no 38, George Allen and Unwin, London.

Kakabadse, A. (1982) *Culture of the Social Services*, Gower, Aldershot.

Kauffman, S. (1995) *At Home in the Universe, The Search for the Laws of Self Organisation and Complexity*, Viking, London.

Kelly, A. and Bebbington, A. (1993) 'Proceed with Caution: The use of official sources of cost information in soical services departments', in Netten, A. and Beecham, J. (eds) *Costing Community Care*, PSSRU/ Ashgate, Aldershot.

Kempson, E. and Bennett, F. (1997) *Local Living Costs*, Policy Studies Institute, London.

Kendal, J., Forder, J. and Knapp, M. (1996) 'Provider Motivations', *PSSRU Bulletin*, University of Kent, no 10, p. 26.

Kickert, W.J.M., Klijn, E.H. and Koppenjan, J.F.M. (eds) (1997) *Managing Complex Networks: Strategies for the Public Sector*, Sage, London.

Kickert, W.J.M. and Koppenjan, J.F.M. (1997) 'Public Management and Network Management: An Overview', in Kickert, W.J.M., Klijn, E.H. and Koppenjan, J.F.M. (eds) *Managing Complex Networks: Strategies for the Public Sector*, Sage, London.

Kiel, L.D. (1994) *Managing Chaos and Complexity in Government*, Jossey Bass, San Francisco.

Kleinbaum, D.G., Kupper,L.L., Muller, K.E and Nizam, A. (1998) *Applied Regression Analysis and Other Multivariate Methods*, 3rd Edition, Duxbury Press, Pacific Grove, California.

Kimber, D. (1995) 'From "Front Room" day care to co-operatives - the growing independent providers', *Care Plan*, vol 1, no 3.

King, A. (1975) 'Overload: problems of governing in the 1970s', *Political Studies*, vol 23, 284-96.

King, D. (1989) 'The Choice of Population Figures in the New System of Local Govenment Finance', *Local Government Studies*, March/April, pp. 29-44.

King, M. and Llewellyn, S. (1996) 'Costing Care Needs for Disabled People: An Accounting Approach', in Clark, C. and Lapsley, I. (eds) *Planning and Costing Community Care. Research Highlights in Social Work 27*, Jessica Kingsley Publishers, London.

Knapp, M. (1993) 'Background Theory', in Netten, A. and Beecham, J. (eds) *Costing Community Care*, PSSRU/ Ashgate, Aldershot.

Knapp, M., Cambridge, P., Thomason,C., Beecham, J., Allen, C. and Darton, R. (1992) *Care in the Community: Challenge and Demonstration*, Personal Social Services Research Unit, University of Kent/ Gower, Aldershot.

Knapp, M., Wistow. G., Forder, J. and Hardy, B. (1994) 'Markets for Social Care: Opportunities, Barriers and Implications', *PSSRU Discussion Paper* 919, University of Kent.

Kontopoulos, K. (1993) *The Logics of Social Structure*, Cambridge University Press, Cambridge.

Kouzes, J.M and Mico, P.R. (1979) 'Domain Theory - an introduction to organisational behaviour in human services organisations', *Journal of Applied Behavioural Science*, vol. 15, no 4, pp. 449-469.

Kreitzman, L. (1996) 'The affordability of long term care', in Harding, T., Meredith, B. and Wistow, G., *Options for Long Term Care*, HMSO, London.

Krippendorff, K. (1980) *Content Analysis: an introduction to its methdology*, Sage, London.

Laing, W. (1993) *Financing Long-Term Care: The Crucial Debate*, Age Concern, London.

Laing, W. (1998) *A fair price for care? Disparities between market rates and state funding of residential care*, Joseph Rowntree Foundation, York.

Lapsey, I. (1996) 'Costs, Budgets and Community Care', in Clark, C. and Lapsey, I. (eds) *Planning and Costing Community Care*, Research Highlights in Social Work 27, Jessica Kingsley, London.

Law, C.M and Warnes, A.M. (1982) 'The destination decision in retirement migration', in Warnes, A.M. (ed) *Geographical Perspectives on the Elderly*, Wiley, Chichester.

LeGrand, J.L. (1991) *Studies in Decentralisation and Quasi-Markets: Paying For or Providing Welfare?*, School for Advanced Urban Studies.

LeGrand, J.L. and Bartlett, W. (eds, et al) (1993) *Quasi-Markets and Social Policy*, Macmillan, Basingstoke.

Leach, S., Stewart, J. and Walsh, K. (1994) *The Changing Organisation and Management of Local Government*, Macmillan, London.

Lindbolm, C.E. (1959) 'The Science of Muddling Through', *Public Administration Review*, vol 19, no 2, pp. 79-88

Lindow, V. and Morris, J. (1995) *Service User involvement: synthesis of findings and experience in the field of community care*, Joseph Rowntree Foundation, York.

Local Government Information Unit (1993) *Local Government Finance*, Local Government Information Unit, London.

Macintyre, S. (1997) 'What are spatial effects and how can we measure them?', in Dale, A. (ed) *Exploiting National survey and census data: the role of locality and spatial effects*, Centre for Census and Survey Research Occasional Paper 12, The University of Manchester, Manchester.

Marsh, D. and Rhodes, R.A.W. (1992) *Implementing Thacherite Policies: Audit of an Era*, Open University Press, Buckingham.

Martin, J., Meltzer, H. and Elliot, D. (1988) *Surveys of Disability in Great Britain Report 1, The Prevalence of Disability among Adults*, OPCS/ HMSO, London.

Martin, L. and Gaster, L. (1993) 'Community Care Planning in Wolverhampton. Involving the voluntary sector and black and ethnic groups', in Smith, R., Gaster,L., Harrison, L., Martin.L., Means, R. and Thistlewaite, P. (eds) *Working Together for Better Community Care*, School of Applied Urban Studies (SAUS), University of Bristol.

Mather, G. (1989) 'Thatcherism and Local Government: An Evaluation', in Stewart, J. and Stocker, G. (eds) *The Future of Local Government*, Macmillan, London.

McLean, I. (1987) *Public Choice. An Introduction*, Macmillan, London.

Means, R. and Smith, R. (1994) *Community Care: Policy and Practice*, Macmillan, Basingstoke.

Medd, W. (1997) 'Knowing through the structures of welfare policy', paper presented to the UK Social Policy Association, National Annual Conference 1997 at the University of Lincolnshire and Humberside, July 13-15th.

Middleton, L. (1997) 'Census Non-Response: It's effect on values of variables used in calculations of local government standard spending assessments', *SARs (Samples of Anonymised Records) Newsletter*, no 9, Census Microdata Unit, University of Manchester.

Ministry of Health (1963) *Health and Welfare: The Development of Community Care, Plans for the Health and Welfare Services of the Local Authorities in England and Wales*, HMSO, London.

Minogue, M. (1983) 'Theory and practice in public policy and administration', *Policy and Politics*, vol 11, pp 63-85.

Mintzberg, H. (1994a) *The Rise and Fall of Strategic Planning*, Prentice Hall, London.

Mintzberg, H. (1994b) 'Rethinking Strategic Planning Part I: Pitfalls and Fallacies', *Long Range Planning*, vol 27, no 3, pp 12-21.

Mintzberg, H. (1994c) 'Rethinking Strategic Planning Part II: New Roles for Planners', *Long Range Planning*, vol 27, no 3, pp 22-30.

Mulgan, G. (1994) *Politics in an Anti-political Age*, Polity Press, Cambridge.

Netten, A. (1993) 'Costs, Prices and Charges', in Netten, A. and Beecham, J. (eds) *Costing Community Care*, PSSRU/ Ashgate, Aldershot.

Netten, A. (1996) 'The Costs of Informal Care', in Clark, C. and Lapsley, I. (eds) *Planning and Costing Community Care*, Research Highlights in Social Work 27. Jessica Kingsley, London.

Niskanen, W.A. (1973) 'Bureaucracy: servant or master?', *Journal of Economic Affairs*, London.

Office for National Statistics (1997) *The Family Expenditure Survey 1995-1996*, The Stationery Office, London.

Office of Population Censuses and Surveys (1994) *1991 Census:Key Statistics for Local Authorities, Great Britain*, HMSO, London.

Oldman, C. (1991) *Paying for Care*, Joseph Rowntree Foundation, York.

Oliver, M. (1990) *The Politics of Disablement*, Macmillan, London.

Ormerod, P. (1994) *The Death of Economics*, Faber, London.

Osbourne, S.P. (1990) 'Managing Social Services in the Market Place: Issues for the Managers of Community Care Services in the 1990s', *Local Government Policy Making*, vol 17, no 2, pp. 3-6.

Owen, C. (1990) 'The Fairness of the Standard Spending Assessments Underlying the Community Charge', *Local Government Studies*, Nov/Dec. pp. 63-76.

Parker, D. and Stacey, R. (1994) *Chaos, Management and Economics: The Implications of Non Linear Thinking*, IEA, London.

Parker, G. and Clarke, H. (1997) 'Will you still need me, will still feed me? Paying for care in old age', *Social Policy and Administration*, vol 31, no 2, pp. 119-135.

Parton, N. (1994) 'A lost Opportunity', *Community Care*, 21st September, no 1026, p. 18.

Peillon, M. (1998) ' Bourdieu's Field and the Sociology of Welfare', *Journal of Social Policy*, vol 27, part 2, pp. 213-230.

Phelan, S. E. (1995) 'From Chaos to Complexity in Strategic Planning', paper presented at the 55th Annual Meeting of the Academy of Managment, Vancouver, British Columbia, Canada, August 6-9.

Pollit, C. (1984) *Manipulating the Machine. Changing the Pattern of Ministerial Departments, 1960-1983*, George Allen and Unwin, London.

Pollit, C. (1986) 'Democracy and Bureaucracy', in Held, D. and Pollitt, C. (eds) *New Forms of Democracy*, The Open University/Sage, London.

Pollit, C. (1990) *Managerialism and the Public Services: The Anglo American Experience*, Blackwell, Oxford.

Pollit, C. (1993) *Managerialism and the Public Services*, 2nd Edition, Blackwell, Oxford.

Prior, L (1997) 'Following in Foucault's Footsteps: Text and Context in Documentary Analysis', in Silverman, D. (ed) *Qualitative Research: Theory and Practice*, Sage, London.

Richards, E., Wilsdon, T. and Lyons, S. (1996) *Paying for Long Term Care*, Institute for Public Policy, London.

Rhodes, R.A.W. (1997) 'Good Governance', paper presented to the ESRC Social Science Conference, QEII Centre, London, 25th June.

Rider, R.W. (1983) 'Making Strategic Planning Work in Local Government', *Long Range Planning*, vol 16, no 3, pp. 73-81.

Robine, J.M. and Mathers, C. (1993) 'Measuring the compression or expansion of morbidity through changes in health expectancy', in Robine, J.M., Mathers, C.D., Bone, R.D. and Romieu, I. (eds) *Calculation of Health Expectancies: harmonization, consensus achieved and future perspectives*, vol 226, pp. 269-86, Colloque INSERM/John Libbey Eurotext Ltd.

Robinson, W.S. (1950) 'Ecological correlation and the behaviour of individuals', *American Sociological Review*, vol 15, pp. 351-7.

Robson, C. (1993) *Real World Research: A Resource for Social Scientists and Practioner-Researchers*, Blackwell, Oxford.

Sanderson, I. (1996) 'Needs and Public Service', in Percy-Smith, J. (ed) *Needs Assessment in Public Policy*, Open Univeristy Press, Buckingham.

Saltman, R.B and Casten V. O.(1992) *Planned Markets and Public Competition. Strategic Reform in Northern European Health Systems*, Open University Press, Buckingham.

Sartori, G. (1991) 'Market, Capitalism, Planning, Technocracy', in Thompson, G., Frances, J., Levacic, R. and Mitchell, J. (eds) *Markets, Hierarchies and Networks: The Coordination of Social Life*, Open University/Sage, London.

Saunders, P. (1980) *Urban Politics. A Sociological Interpretation*, Penguin, London.

Saunders, P. (1986) *Social Theory and the Urban Question*, 2nd Edition, Hutchinson, London.

Sayer, A. (1992) *Method in social science, a realist approach*, 2nd Edition, Routledge, London.

Schneider, G. (1991) *Time, Planning and Policy Making. An evaluation of a complex relationship*, Peter Lang, Zurich.

Secretary of State for Health (1996) *A New Partnership for Care in Old Age. A Consultation Paper, Cm 3242*, HMSO, London.

Seebohm Committee (1968) *Report of the Committee on the Local Authority and personal social services*, HMSO, London.

Self, P. (1993) *Government by the Market? The Politics of Public Choice*, Macmillan, Basingstoke.

Senior, M. L. (1994) 'The English Standard Spending Assessment system: an assessment of the methodology', *Environment and Planning C*, Feb, vol 12, no 1, pp. 23-52

Senior, M.L. (1995) 'An examination of area variations in limiting long term illness in Britain, 1991', paper presented to the Institute of British Geographers Conference on Long Term Illness, 17th May, University of Liverpool.

Sharkey, S. and Barna, S. (eds) (1990) *Community Care: people leaving long-stay hospitals*, Routledge, London.

Sheppard, E. (1996) 'Site, situation and social theory', *Environment and Planning A*, vol 28, pp. 1339 - 1344.

Sibeon, R. (1991) *Towards a New Sociology of Social Work*, Avebury, Aldershot.

Simon, H. (1957) *Administrative Behaviour*, 2nd Edition, Macmillan, New York.

Smit, J. de and Rade, N.L. (1980) 'Rational and Non-Rational Planning', *Long Range Planning*, vol 13, April.

Smith, G. and May, D. (1980) 'The Artificial Debate Between Rationalist and Incrementalist Models of Decision Making', *Policy and Politics*, vol 8, no 2, pp. 147-61.

Society of County Treasurers (1994) *Standard Spending Indicators 1994-1995*, Society of County Treasurers.

Society of County Treasurers (1998) *Standard Spending Indicators 1998-1999*, Society of County Treasurers.

Social Services Inspectorate (1995) *Children's Services Plans. An analysis of Children's Services Plans 1993/1994*, Department of Health, London.

Social Services Organisation Research Unit (1974) *Social Services Departments: Developing Patterns of Work and Organisation*, Social Services Organisation Research Unit, Brunel Institute of Organisation and Social Studies (BIOS), Heineman, London.

Sokal, A. and Bricmont, J. (1998) *Intellectual Imposters*, Profile Books, London.

Stacey, R.D. (1995) 'The Science of Complexity: An Alternative Perspective for Strategic Change Processes', *Strategic Management Journal*, vol 16, pp. 477-495.

Stacey, R.D. (1996) 'Emerging Strategies for a Chaotic Environment', *Long Range Planning*, vol 29, no 2, pp. 182-189.

Stewart, J. and Clarke, M. (1987) 'The Public service orientation: issues and dilemmas', *Public Administration*, vol 65, no 2, pp. 161-178

Stocker, G. (1991) *The Politics of Local Government*, 2nd Edition, Macmillan, Basingstoke.

Stroup, W. F. (1997) 'Webs of Chaos, implications for research design', in Eve, R.A., Horsfall, S. and Lee, M.E. (eds) *Chaos, Complexity, and Sociology. Myths, Models and Theories*, Sage, Thousand Oaks, California.

Taylor, M. and Hoggett, P. (1994) 'Trusting in networks? The third sector and welfare change', in Perri 6 and Vidal, I. (eds) *Delivering Welfare: repositioning non-profit and co-operative action in Western European Welfare States*, Centre d'iniciatives de l'economia social, Barcelona.

Taylor-Gooby, P. (1998) *Choice and Public Policy: The Limits to Welfare Markets*, Macmillan, London

Thatcher, M. (1993) *The Downing Street Years*, Harper Collins, London.

Truelove, M. (1993) 'Measurement of Spatial Equity', *Enviroment and Planning C: Government and Policy*, vol 11, pp. 19-34

Tullock, G. (1976) *The Vote Motive*, The Institute for Economic Affairs, London.

Tullock, G. and Wagner, R.E. (1978) *Policy Analysis and Deductive Reasoning*, Lexington Books, Toronto.

Waddington, P. (1995) 'Purchasers will need the creative touch', *Care Plan*, vol 1, no 3.

Waldrop, M. (1993) *Complexity: the Emerging Science at the Edge of Order and Chaos*, Viking, London.

Walker, A. (1984) *Social Planning. A Strategy for Socialist Welfare*, Basil Blackwell, Oxford.

Walker, A. (1989) 'Community Care', in McCarthy, M. (ed) (1989) *The New Politics of Welfare. An Agenda for the 1990s?*, Macmillan, Basingstoke.

Walsh, K. (1995) *Public Services and Market Mechanisms. Competition, Contracting and the New Public Management*, Macmillan, London.

Webb, A. and Wistow, G. (1986) *Planning, Need and Scarcity: Essays on the Personal Social Services*, George Allen and Unwin, Hemel Hempstead.

Whitehead, M. (1992) 'The Health Divide', reprinted in, *Inequalities in Health*, Penguin, London.

Wilkinson, R. (1996) *Unhealthy Societies: the Afflictions of Inequality*, Routledge, London.

Williams, A. (1974) 'Need as a demand concept', in Culyer, A. J. (ed) *Economic Policies and Social Goods*, Martin Robertson, Oxford.

Williamson, O.E. (1985) *The Economic Institutions of Capitalism, Firms, Markets, Relational Contracting*, The Free Press, New York.

Wistow, G. (1990) *Community Care Planning: A Review of Past Experience and Future Imperatives*, Department of Health, London.

Wistow, G. (1997) 'Funding Long Term Care', in May, M., Brunsdon, E. and Craig, G. (eds) *Social Policy Review* 9, Social Policy Association, London.

Wistow, G. and Hardy, B. (1994) 'Community Care Planning', in Malin, N. *Implementing Community Care*, Open University Press, Buckingham.

Wistow, G., Knapp, M., Hardy, B. and Allen, C. (1994) *Social Care in a Mixed Economy*, Open University Press, Buckingham.

Wistow, G., Knapp, M., Hardy, B., Forder, J., Kendall, J. and Manning, R. (1996) *Social Care Markets: Progress and Prospects*, Open University Press, Buckingham.

Wistow, G., Leedham, I. and Hardy, B. (1993) *Community Care Plans. A preliminary analysis of a sample of English Community Care Plans*, SSI/Department of Health, London.

Wright, J. and Kerslake, A. (1994) 'Modelling Community Care: Helping to Plan Service Provision', *Community Care Management and Planning*, vol 2, issue 1, pp. 5 -13.

# Index

For Product Safety Concerns and Information please contact our EU
representative GPSR@taylorandfrancis.com Taylor & Francis Verlag GmbH,
Kaufingerstraße 24, 80331 München, Germany

Printed and bound by CPI Group (UK) Ltd, Croydon, CR0 4YY
08/05/2025
01864370-0009